ALSO BY JONATHAN GIL HARRIS

The First Firangis: Remarkable Stories of Heroes, Healers, Charlatans, Courtesans & other Foreigners who Became Indian

Foreign Bodies and the Body Politic: Discourses of Social Pathology in Early Modern England

Sick Economies: Drama, Mercantilism and Disease in Shakespeare's England

Untimely Matter in the Time of Shakespeare

Shakespeare & Literary Theory

Marvellous Repossessions: The Tempest, Globalization and the Waking Dream of Paradise

EDITED

Staged Properties in Early Modern English Drama (with Natasha Korda)

The Shoemaker's Holiday by Thomas Dekker

Indography: Writing the 'Indian' in Early Modern Literature and Culture

How a Firangi Writer Became Indian

JONATHAN GIL HARRIS

ALEPH

ALEPH

ALEPH BOOK COMPANY
An independent publishing firm
promoted by *Rupa Publications India*

First published in India in 2018
by Aleph Book Company
7/16 Ansari Road, Daryaganj
New Delhi 110 002

ISBN: 978-93ͺ92-26-9

1 3 5 7 9 10 ᵗ 2

Printed by Parks ʳaphics Pvt. Ltd., Mumbai

CONTENTS

Act Five: Toofaans

NOTE TO THE READER

Like a Shakespeare play, this book is divided into five acts. Each begins with a Chorus that spells out a point of affinity between Shakespeare and India. But *Masala Shakespeare* is equally a love letter to popular Hindi cinema and other Indian storytelling forms. That is why you will find in these pages, interspersed between chapters on individual plays, interludes—or what I call 'item numbers', to insert something suitably masala and filmi into the otherwise dramatic structure of this book. You can choose to skip the interludes if your business here is to focus primarily on Shakespeare's plays and Indian conversations with them. Or you can dwell on the interludes if you want something more autobiographical or drenched in love for Hindi film, its songs, and other oddities of Indian masala. And if you want a roadmap for the book before starting it, you might concentrate first on the sequence of Choruses, and its ongoing tale of the firangi and the desi. But the masala mix of all these ingredients, as with Shakespeare and as with India, is what ultimately makes for the best flavour.

ACT ONE

khaandaans

CHORUS

This is a tale of two phenomena—one foreign and one local. Let's call them the firangi and the desi. The firangi travels to India. There it is greeted by locals as if it were family. And it turns out that it is family: it has a desi twin, with whom it is often confused. Because the two of them are as similar as do angoor (two grapes) from a bunch.

A tale of twins from different lands: it may sound like what the English term a comedy of errors, and what the Bengalis call a bhranti bilas. How, you may ask, can a firangi have an Indian twin? Yet the twins' tale isn't just a comedy of errors. It's also a highly serious story of rekhta vanshaavaliyan or mishrit khaandaan (mixed lineages). It is, in short, a tale of masala genealogy. The genealogy of masala. But also genealogy as masala.

ACT ONE SCENE ONE

Enter MASALA

I first visited India in the summer of 2001. I'd fallen in love with an Indian; over the course of the next ten years, thanks to annual visits to Delhi and the south, I fell in love with India too, and made the decision to move here permanently. My relationship with the country has been typical of any long-term love affair. India has enchanted me, fed me, afforded me a home, taught me a new language; it has also disagreed with me, infuriated me, made me ill. In loving it, I have had to adapt to its many peccadilloes. But adapting is no easy task in love, especially when the object of your affection is itself constantly changing.

The seventeen years between my first trip to India and now have been bookended by two blockbuster Hindi films produced by the same production house, Aamir Khan Productions: *Lagaan* (2001) and *Dangal* (2016). The two films are in certain superficial ways similar. Each is a well-made, highly enjoyable sports movie. Each depends in large part on the enormous charisma and bankability of the actor–producer Aamir Khan. And each tells a powerful story about India. Yet the two films are also radically different because India has changed so much since *Lagaan* was made, with the result that the story about India that each tells is very different from the other.

Lagaan was the first Hindi film I saw in India. I had seen others in the US and the UK, but only on video or in small art cinemas. Nothing had prepared me for the thrill of being part of a large Indian movie audience. I watched *Lagaan* in July 2001, at the grand but somewhat dilapidated Chanakya Theatre in Delhi. The Chanakya seated 1,080 people, though I suspect there were many more in the auditorium that day, crammed willy-nilly into its aisles, landings, and nooks. Tickets for the densely packed front stalls sold for a mere 30 rupees, but my partner and I opted for the sanctuary of the 80-rupee balcony seats. Even up there, the atmosphere felt reminiscent (as was only appropriate, given the film's cricketing theme) of a sports game. Unlike more restrained cinema audiences in the West, people talked loudly and incessantly throughout the film—to each other and to the characters on the screen. They applauded when the heroic villager Bhuvan (Aamir Khan), showing off his well-sculpted pectorals, made his first appearance. They hissed at the splendidly villainous, wax-mustachioed Captain Russell (Paul Blackthorne) when he challenged Bhuvan and his fellow villagers to a devil's wager on a cricket game that, if lost, would result in triple lagaan (taxation). They clucked when Captain Russell's sister (Rachel Shelley), appalled by her brother's cruelty, offered to coach the witless villagers in the art of cricket. They cheered and booed during the game between the ragtag Indian team and the local British officers' side. And even though the game's result was never in doubt, pandemonium erupted in the 30-rupee stalls when Aamir Khan struck the winning six. I will never forget the sight of people in the Chanakya Theatre stalls stamping and dancing and flinging coins at the screen out of pure joy as the dastardly Captain Russell lost both the game and his wager.

Lagaan impressed on me how the venue in which a film is screened is a crucial part of its story. The Chanakya Theatre may have been located in well-off South Delhi. But its size and ticket prices were designed to accommodate a mixed audience, one consisting of people from many classes and communities. *Lagaan* was made to be screened in venues just like the Chanakya Theatre. Aamir Khan's victorious cricket team—made up of Hindu, Muslim, Sikh and Dalit, supported by men and women, young and old, maharajahs and commoners alike—symbolically mirrored its diverse audience.

It was a distorted mirror, of course. Who in the audience could match Aamir Khan's sublime physique or his irresistibility to all the film's female characters, both desi (Gracy Singh) and firangi (Rachel Shelley)? And for all the lip service it paid to India's diversity, *Lagaan* presented its non-Hindu characters as isolated individuals: its Muslim, Sikh, and Dalit cricketers were not shown as part of larger communities. The only fleshed-out community in *Lagaan* was Hindu: the mandir was Champaner's spiritual centre, and an entire song and dance routine was devoted to Lord Krishna and Radha. But *Lagaan*'s story of India was, for all its omissions and biases, a fundamentally inclusive one. When Aamir Khan told us in the song 'Mitwa' that 'yeh dharti apni hai (this land is our own)', his 'apni' seemed to embrace every one of us in the auditorium—even a culture-shocked firangi like me.

My culture shock was leavened that day by an epiphany of sorts. As a teacher, scholar, and occasional actor–director of Shakespeare, I suddenly realized that what I'd experienced at the Chanakya Theatre was in some way profoundly Shakespearean. Not the Shakespeare of ruffs, doublets and hose. Nor the Shakespeare of actors declaiming pompously in Queen's English. Rather, my experience of *Lagaan* in the Chanakya Theatre pointed to something more fundamentally Shakespearean: an ethos of inclusive mixture. Echoing Hamlet's insistence that 'art hold up the mirror', if not to nature, then to its audience, the Chanakya's socially, religiously, and linguistically diverse filmgoers found themselves reflected in the aesthetic and political pluralism of the movie they were watching.

This reflection is the essence of what is called the masala movie—a film that, like *Lagaan*, is grounded in a mixture of genres and languages that caters to an equally mixed audience. A masala is a concoction that is tasty and spicy, but it is also literally a mixture. The masala movie's stories mix tragedy with comedy as well as scenes of dialogue with song-and-dance routines. Its lovers, too, are mixtures, often coming from different communities. And its sources are equally mixed: there is usually no 'original' story in a masala movie, as its narrative is a khichdi of other, earlier stories or formulas. *Lagaan*, for example, combined elements of the spaghetti western and the underdog sports-team film with the tried-and-tested Bollywood love triangle. All these mixtures were a reflection of an India that is itself a mixture of many cultural ingredients.

Some might counter that there's very little about the masala movie that reflects the more brutal realities of India. The phrase was devised in the 1980s to describe a certain type of formula film that was supposedly a world away from the socially conscious Hindi movies of earlier decades. This new formula film, associated with directors such as Manmohan Desai, was avowedly escapist. As Desai has said, he wanted to take his audiences 'into a dream world where there is no poverty, where there are no beggars, where fate is kind'. The 1980s masala movie that Desai helped create presented its audiences with charismatic heroes, pantomime villains, and badly choreographed musical item numbers. And the genre, it must be conceded, has included many truly ghastly films. They are rife with mindless sexism, vacuous dialoguebaazi and random song-and-dance routines. All depart from the explicit social engagement of a classic 1950s film like *Mother India* (1957) or a 1970s film like *Namak Haraam* (1973).

Yet, in a sense, the masala movie doesn't really represent a radical break with the Hindi 'socials' that preceded it. The distinctively mixed style of the masala movie is, rather, a consummation of an ethos that has been part of onscreen Indian entertainment for decades—an ethos of everything-and-the-kitchen-sink. High seriousness, low screwball comedy, theatrical dialogue, song-and-dance, poetry, slang, characters from many communities speaking a mix of languages: all these ingredients distinguish a sensibility that has defined Hindi films for decades. Any film that features both dialogue and musical numbers, in a language that isn't pure because it includes the trace of other tongues, is already infused with a masala sensibility. And no matter how sentimental or escapist or convoluted or chaotic it might seem to be, this sensibility is in one way profoundly realist: in its unabashed commitment to mixture, it recognizes that India, too, is mixed.

The masala mixture is also, as I will argue throughout this book, a defining feature of Shakespearean theatre. But it is hard to acknowledge this because we have been conditioned, in India as much as in the West, to regard Shakespeare and Hindi cinema as fundamentally different.

Just take *Shakespeare Wallah* (1965), the Merchant Ivory film that pays homage to the famed actor–impresario Geoffrey Kendal and his attempts to bring Shakespeare to Indian audiences in the 1940s and 50s. Kendal plays a version of himself in *Shakespeare Wallah*; he leads a troupe of Shakespeare actors embarked on a noble but quixotic pursuit of performing Shakespeare throughout India. But they are hopelessly out of step with the new fashion for Hindi cinema. In the film, the English proprietor of an old, regal British hotel laments the loss of her customers, saying they now prefer the 'new hotel opposite, all cheap flash'; the remark serves as an implied metaphor for the eclipse of Shakespeare by Bollywood. Sanju (Shashi Kapoor), the young Indian who has to choose between a cheap flashy film star (Madhur Jaffrey) and Kendal's ingénue stage actress–daughter (Felicity Kendal), notes that 'Shakespeare… is very philosophical' and acted by 'real artist[s]', but laments that 'people don't care so much for the theatre these days. Only for films.' Shakespeare, like the grand old British hotel, has no place in a new India that is 'all cheap flash'.

Many of my Anglophone Indian friends, even if they grew up on a steady diet of masala movies, have imbibed the attitude of *Shakespeare Wallah*. They involuntarily cringe when I talk about how I find the cheap flash of Hindi film Shakespearean. 'Gilji,' they say, 'random item numbers, idiotic dances by lovers around trees, unoriginal stories: surely all this is a world away from the lofty accomplishment of Shakespeare! You of all people should know that!' These friends are nonplussed when I tell them that Shakespeare's plays—at least as performed 400 years ago to mixed audiences of literate and illiterate, noble and poor—also routinely featured naach-gaana (song-and-dance numbers), often celebrated sanams (lovers) in the presence of trees (just ask Rosalind and Orsino in *As You Like It*), and plundered their kahaaniyan (stories) from everywhere. Watching *Lagaan* was, for me, a moment of awakening to masala possibilities in Shakespeare and his drama that I had until then largely overlooked. Conversely, it was an awakening to how there is something Shakespearean about the masala movie even if it is not an adaptation of Shakespeare.

But as I fell in love with the masala movie—in particular, its twin embrace of stylistic mixture and a mixed audience—I soon sensed that my love was star-crossed. Because I'd fallen in love, like a Romeo or a Venus or a Pyramus or a Cleopatra or even a Geoffrey Kendal, with a lover whose days were numbered. For the masala movie is in many ways a relic of an increasingly outdated idea of India that enjoyed its heyday in the age of Nehruvian socialism, an India that is a mix of many rather than a rajya (state) of one.

Fast forward sixteen years. In the intervening time, the Chanakya cinema has closed and been demolished. Bollywood now makes its profits increasingly in air-conditioned pockets of exclusivity that we call multiplexes. There the tickets are 300 rupees or more; the cost of a movie mushrooms further when one factors in the vastly overpriced popcorn and soda available from the concession stands. There are no cheap front stalls for the poorer sort. As a result, multiplex audiences are more homogenous: overwhelmingly upper middle-class, often young and fashion-conscious, largely Anglophone. They are as noisy as the Chanakya Theatre audience, but not because they are talking back to the characters or erupting in joyous dance. It's because they are chattering loudly on their mobiles about today's clothes purchase, tonight's dinner reservation, or tomorrow's business meeting. Importantly, multiplexes are located in huge shopping malls. To reach your movie, you have to walk through a gauntlet of luxury stores selling expensive stuff you don't really need. The siren call to retail therapy is hard to resist. So is the fantasy that India has somehow become entirely rich and clean: in the mall-multiplex, one never has to set eyes on a beggar or even a chaiwallah, walk up urine-stained gallis, or deal—God forbid!—with the heat. This is the climate-controlled environment in and for which Bollywood tells its new stories of India. And it is in one such AC-chilled mall-multiplex that I saw *Dangal* in January of 2017.

Let me clarify: I saw the film in a mall-multiplex in Toronto, not Delhi. Yet the packed Canadian hall in which I watched *Dangal* was in virtually all respects identical to its counterparts in Delhi or Bombay. It consisted almost entirely of NRIs—non-resident Indians—eating the same popcorn and sipping the same soda that are sold at the cinemas I am now used to frequenting at the Select Citywalk Mall in Saket. The ticket prices were exorbitant. And, as a result, the audience was demographically similar to those who frequent the Saket multiplexes: wealthy and mostly Punjabi, carrying bags laden with goods acquired from their shopping experience en route to the cinema. In short, a completely different constituency from the Chanakya Theatre audience with whom I had watched *Lagaan* sixteen years earlier. And, in subtle ways, *Dangal* reflected that difference.

At first *Dangal* seemed to represent a return to the 'dharti' of *Lagaan*. It is an Aamir Khan-starrer where an underdog triumphs against the odds. It again features characters of the poorer sort, this time from a village in Haryana. And its climax involves 'India' winning a sports competition against a foreign adversary. But so much of what made *Lagaan* a masala movie is missing from *Dangal*. For one, the lively group song-and-dance numbers of *Lagaan* have been eclipsed by a musical soundtrack that, Hollywood-style, simply provides a backing score to the story. And *Dangal*'s story embraces an individual pursuit, wrestling, rather than a team sport such as cricket. Indeed, the film celebrates less the triumph of sportspeople than the unique man whose will is responsible for their success: the barrel-chested Mahavir Singh (Aamir Khan). A former champion wrestler whose heart has been broken by not having a son to carry on his sporting legacy, Singh single-mindedly trains his two daughters—against their meek objections—to win gold in wrestling at the Commonwealth Games.

This is not *Lagaan*'s inclusive vision of diverse peoples coming together to fight a common oppressor. Instead it is a cinematic counterpart to a more recent dream of India, in which a charismatic strongman with a chhappan-inch (56-inch) chest demands and wins the unquestioning compliance of those he rules. And here the significant pronoun is not the inclusive 'apni'. It is instead the coercive 'hum', the royal 'we' that transforms the aspirational will of a patriarchal individual into the will of his subjects. When Mahavir Singh tells his daughters and other family members that 'kal hum Rohtak jaa rahe hain (tomorrow we are going to Rohtak)', that 'hum' marks not the coming together of diverse peoples or perspectives but, rather, the imposition of an imperial edict that will brook no dissent. The 'hum' of the father expands to embrace his children and then, through the gold medal, all of India.

The Indian audience presumed by *Dangal* in the international multiplex hall as much as in the village single-screen theatre is part of this imperial 'hum'. Aligning with a patriarchal authority made synonymous with India, it rises as one to the sound of the national anthem just as Mahavir Singh's daughters rise each morning to the alarm bell set by their father for their training. Indeed, a scene at the film's end generated widespread discussion in the wake of the then-recent ruling by the Supreme Court of India that all cinemagoers must stand for the national anthem. The anthem sounds in *Dangal* when the elder daughter of Mahavir Singh wins gold. Many Indian audience members felt under a legal as well as emotional obligation to stand at this point. During the screening I saw in Toronto, even some of the Canadian Indians stood up with their hands on their hearts. The 'a' brand insignia of Aamir Khan Productions, it was clear, had come to stand not for 'apni', but for 'anthemic'. The former embraces the plural and the masala, the latter the singular and the uniform.

If *Lagaan* tells us something about Shakespeare, then what does *Dangal* tell us? Like *Dangal*, Shakespeare's plays are more often than not performed nowadays at elite theatrical venues for well-off, cosmopolitan Anglophone audiences. And like *Dangal*, the performance of Shakespeare's plays tends to command loyalty around the world to a man who uniformly overpowers us with the force of his will. A popular poster carrying the familiar image of Shakespeare from the First Folio edition of his works bears the caption 'Will Power'. It is not new masala entertainment that people want when they opt to see a Shakespeare production, after all, but a known product associated with a powerful male brand.

All this is a far cry from the conditions of the plays' performance during Shakespeare's lifetime. The original Globe Theatre in Southwark, London, was, like the Chanakya Theatre, a venue that catered to an audience from all social ranks. Patrons who wanted to see a new play would pay two pennies—the price of two loaves of bread—to sit in the lower balconies and a penny extra to sit on a cushion; the very richest paid several pounds to sit on stage with the actors and flaunt their expensive clothes. But the poorest sort—apprentices, day-jobbers, artisans—could stand in the pit for a mere penny. Paisa vasool, na (Value for money, no)?' By contrast, the new Shakespeare's Globe Theatre, located in the same spot as the original playhouse and offering a loving reconstruction of its physical structure, is more Select Citywalk than Chanakya Theatre. Those who stand in the pit now have to cough up at least 10 pounds, beyond the capability of London's poor and certainly much more than one loaf of bread. And all who enter the playhouse have to pass through an air-conditioned complex that contains numerous Shakespeare brand-related shopping opportunities for those with disposable incomes far larger than those of the beggars who stand outside.

Yet in India, something of the Chanakya Theatre survives. Not just in *Lagaan*, but also in a wide variety of popular masala traditions that enter into creative conversation with Shakespeare. These masala traditions are by no means a monolith: they vary greatly over the subcontinent, and they have changed with time. But they all debunk *Shakespeare Wallah*'s distinction between 'regal' Shakespeare and 'cheap flashy' popular entertainment. They also represent very different forms of cosmopolitanism from that of the brand-conscious multiplex consumer: they long not for global desi homogeneity, with wealthy Indians across the world rising as one in air-conditioned bubbles to the national anthem, but for local heterogeneity. They find space for everyone. And as such they are deeply resistant to the idea of 'us' versus 'them', and of the borders that accompany that idea. In sum, these masala traditions recognize that, in the village as much as the city, mixture—the more-than-one—is the irreducible foundation of society and culture.

This book is an attempt to lend historical flesh to the epiphany I had that day in the Chanakya Theatre. Like the Chanakya, some of what I celebrate in these pages has died. A new India increasingly craves singular purity rather than masala mixture in its cultural as well as its political tastes. This craving for purity isn't a new phenomenon: toxic versions of it have existed for centuries all over the subcontinent, enshrined (for example) in strict silos of purity enforced by the caste system. Indeed, mixture in some quarters is now seen as the foreign adulteration of a supposedly original purity, and hence as 'dirt' that needs to be expunged through a cultural version of Swachh Bharat. Syncretism is becoming a dirty word. Yet the old masala forms still retain an unexpected afterlife throughout India in a flood of popular reimaginings of Shakespeare. These reimaginings—popular because they are well-liked but also because they have a profound affinity with the mixed cultural traditions of the subcontinent—are what I call masala Shakespeare.

For a Shakespearean like me, the encounter with masala Shakespeare, whether in the form of a Bollywood film, a jatra performance, a nautanki musical, or a kathakali presentation, does two very different things simultaneously. It presents me with an entertainment that is linguistically and culturally unfamiliar. Yet it also evokes in me something deeply and resonantly recognizable: it gives Shakespeare back to me in a form that re-illuminates his own masala craft in all its inclusive brilliance. For Shakespeare *is* masala, in his stories, his language, his genres, his performance techniques, and his audiences. And that masala craft, *Lagaan* has taught me, is not just a form of entertainment. It is also a utopian political vision. Indian masala embodies an idea of India, and an idea of the world, that has acquired an unexpected dissident power in the current political moment.

In the chapters that follow, I focus on eleven plays—*The Comedy of Errors, A Midsummer Night's Dream, Romeo and Juliet, The Taming of the Shrew, Twelfth Night, Macbeth, Othello, Hamlet, King Lear, The Tempest* and *Pericles*—that have acquired Indian lives independent of the familiar English texts of the plays. You can call this my masala Shakespeare Cricketing XI (with Shakespeare's early play *Titus Andronicus* making a late non-masala appearance, at tea, as twelfth man). Like the team of *Lagaan*, this masala Shakespeare Cricketing XI is a diverse mixture whose Indian avatars are very different from each other. Yet they all, in their own ways, chafe against an oppressive power by refusing the current vogue for shuddhta (purity) and singularity. Other Shakespeare plays have been translated into Indian languages on screen or in the theatre. But Indian reimaginings of these eleven plays, primarily in Hindi but also across a variety of languages, have especially resonated with Indian audiences and readers. In the process, conversations with Shakespeare have played a role—no matter how small—in shaping subcontinental masala sensibilities with respect to a wide variety of ideas: genealogy, language, love, stories-within-stories, gender, time, caste, ghosts, and storms. The sensibilities we see in these conversations don't derive straightforwardly from Shakespeare. They have emerged also from social, political, economic, cultural, and linguistic realities specific to India. But they can also help us reread Shakespeare's work and recognize elements in his craft that might otherwise elude us.

Let me stress that I'm not seeking to provide here an exhaustive summary of Indian conversations with Shakespeare. Two plays that have been enduringly popular in the subcontinent but which remain mostly ignored by Hindi cinema—*The Merchant of Venice* and *Julius Caesar*—have not found a place in *Masala Shakespeare*. This book is, rather, an idiosyncratic critical memoir, a story of how an immigrant learned how to recognize Shakespeare in India, through India, as India. But India is not static. India is changing, as are India's conversations with Shakespeare.

The story I tell plots my evolution as a reader of Shakespeare in relation to India and Indian films in a time of growing authoritarianism and majoritarian hatred, here and globally. As a result, *Masala Shakespeare* might initially strike some as an Indian counterpart to Azar Nafisi's fascinating book, *Reading Lolita in Tehran* (2003). Nafisi's personal memoir of reading banned Western literature in the years after the Iranian Revolution is a saga of individual resilience—her own, her friends' who secretly read Austen, Fitzgerald, James and Nabokov alongside her—in the face of tyranny. This book, however, is rather different from Nafisi's. It, too, marks an attempt to resist authoritarianism. But resistance, in this book, comes not from the heroic will of individuals. Because *Masala Shakespeare* is not, ultimately, a story about individuals—Shakespeare or me or anyone else. It is a story about the more-than-oneness that is at the heart of masala, a more-than-oneness that I believe is crucial to resisting authoritarianism in all its forms. I have tried to outline here what that more-than-oneness tells us about India as much as Shakespeare.

Understanding India's more-than-oneness has meant suppressing the impulse—an impulse that I see at work in Nafisi's book—to adopt a largely Western vocabulary of individual liberty so that we can better resist authoritarianism. That vocabulary privileges the 'one' of the individual as the foundation of freedom. Instead I have endeavoured to find in popular Indian forms of entertainment and storytelling the materials with which to think against the grain of reductive singularity. And these materials have led me to rather different readings of the Shakespeare texts I was trained to teach in the West. Over and over again, these texts value not the 'one' but the more-than-one, the mixing and mingling of supposedly separate entities. This embrace of the more-than-one has led me also to rather different understandings of the proper noun of my book's title. As I will try to show, Shakespeare, like India, is not an individual but, rather, something fundamentally plural.

And that means Shakespeare, in this book, is not the chhappan-inch-chested father of *Dangal* imposing his will on Indian writers and audiences. He is not the expensive but fading British regal hotel of *Shakespeare Wallah*. Nor is he even the well-meaning English cricket coach of *Lagaan*, benevolently teaching Indians how to find themselves in all their diversity. The Shakespeare who emerges in these pages is not an exclusive or unique individual in any shape or form: he is neither master nor genius nor progenitor nor hero. He is, rather, a collaborative and irreducibly plural partner. In this book, he is the *twin* of traditional Indian storytellers: a colourful, well-travelled awaara (vagabond) who has found, in desi masala entertainment, a long-lost sibling. And Shakespeare has been transformed in the process. He, like so many foreign migrants before him, has been welcomed into an India whose 'dharti apni hai'. He has become apna Shakespeare. Apna masala Shakespeare.

ACT ONE SCENE TWO

Masala Genealogies (*The Comedy of Errors*)

Shakespeare, English-accented, first sailed to the subcontinent with the British more than 400 years ago. *Hamlet* was supposedly acted on board an East India Company ship in 1607; but onshore performances came only much later. We don't know which Shakespeare play was first performed in India, nor when or where. By 1775 he was a staple of the Raj playhouses of Calcutta, where British actors performed his plays to largely British colonial audiences. And by 1822, Hindu College in Calcutta had made Shakespeare a part of its English curriculum—the first time in the world that he was included in a university syllabus. Other Indian universities followed suit. Because Shakespeare's language was often difficult for Indian students, Charles and Mary Lamb's *Tales from Shakespeare* (1807), which strip down twenty of his thirty-seven plays to highly readable prose stories, were also prescribed at many colleges, as well as made compulsory reading for the Civil Service Examination. Reciting Shakespeare speeches from memory also became a common teaching tool. At Elphinstone College in Bombay in the 1850s, young Parsi students were made to memorize select passages; this was a prelude to the rote-learning that still remains a feature of Indian education, a pedagogy designed to encourage docile submission to authority.

Arundhati Roy brilliantly parodies the rote-learned Shakespeare of Indian education in a memorable scene from her novel, *The God of Small Things* (1996). Comrade Pillai shows off to local villagers by getting his young son, Lenin, to recite Mark Antony's 'Friends, Romans, countrymen' speech from *Julius Caesar:*

> *Lend me yawYERS;*
> *I cometoberry Caesar, not to praise him.*
> *Theevil that mendoo lives after them,*
> *The goodisoft interred with their bones...*

'He shouted it fluently,' writes Roy, 'without faltering once. Remarkable, considering he was only six and didn't understand a word of what he was saying.' Many who have been taught Shakespeare in Indian high schools and colleges might feel the same way about the Shakespeare

14

they have been made to mechanically learn.

As Lenin's strange version of Shakespeare shows, though, the project of indoctrinating Indians in Shakespeare has also helped spawn strange Anglo-Indian offspring. One can see, or hear, this offspring everywhere. There he is in a street in Kolkata, Shakespeare Sarani (pronounced Shekspeeyair Sharoni). He can be found in Raisina Hill too: former Indian President Pranab Mukherjee, then the finance minister in the Congress-led UPA government, channelled *Hamlet* when he said of his budget 'I must be cruel only to be kind'; Smriti Irani, then the HRD minister in the ruling BJP, accused her opponents of believing, like *Macbeth*'s witches, that 'fair is foul and foul is fair'; Sitaram Yechury, the Communist Party of India leader, also tweaked the Scottish play when criticizing the government's record on sanitation, averring that 'All the perfumes of Arabia will not sweeten this little hand.' And Shakespeare has been repeatedly Indianized in Anglophone novels, from Vikram Seth's staging of *Twelfth Night* in *A Suitable Boy* (1993) and Salman Rushdie's riff on Othello in *The Moor's Last Sigh* (1995) to Anjum Hasan's *Hamlet*-quoting Mr Das in *Neti, Neti* (2009), Saikat Majumdar's grand guignol production of *A Midsummer Night's Dream* in *The Firebird* (2015), and Preti Taneja's devastating reimagining of *King Lear* in *We That Are Young* (2017).

The Indianization of Shakespeare isn't just an English-language phenomenon. His plays have been translated into countless Indian languages and adapted within native performance traditions from the nautanki of north India and the jatra of Bengal to the bhangwadi of Gujarat and the kathakali of Kerala. Shakespeare's influence is apparent even in the vocabularies of Indian languages. In Hindi, Punjabi, Bengali, and Marathi, as well as several southern Indian languages, 'Romeo' has become a term for a swaggering street Casanova—as we have been reminded by Uttar Pradesh's recent 'anti-Romeo' squads, supposedly designed to stop women from being harassed. But nowhere is Shakespeare's influence more profound than in the cinema. His plays have been adapted for diverse regional-language cinemas, from Malayalam and Tamil and Kannada to Punjabi and Marathi and Bengali; indeed, Shakespeare is arguably Bollywood's most successful screenplay writer, with many Hindi-language versions of his plays—and countless more influenced by them—attracting large audiences. Even his words seep into Hindi films: the theme song of the smash hit *Three Idiots* (2009), which certainly ends well, is the Indian-accented Shakespeare homage,

'Aal Izz Well.'

It is easy to see Indian Shakespeare, like the railways or Horlicks or even the English language itself, as simply one of the legacies of British colonialism in India. According to this genealogy, Indian Shakespeare would be the bastard child of the English playwright. But Shakespeare's presence throughout India is not just the culmination of Thomas Macaulay's *Minute on Education* in 1835, in which the colonial official infamously declared that 'a single shelf of a good European library [is] worth the whole native literature of India and Arabia'. It also has a lot to do with profound resonances between Shakespeare's craft and Indian forms of entertainment. Shakespeare has not so much colonized India as he has found a twin in desi storytelling and performance traditions that have reimagined him.

And what joins these twins can be boiled down to one ingredient. One ingredient that is more-than-one: masala.

◆

'Masala' is a word that means many things and conjures up many associations. For Westerners, it most immediately suggests exotic eastern spices and flavours. That sense is apparent also in the word's most widespread metaphorical use in India—to add masala to a story is to give it, through embellishment or exaggeration, an extra spicy flavour. The association with food has a long history: 'masala' derives, through Persian, from the Arabic *masalih*, meaning ingredients. There are other meanings lurking in the term. The spiciness of masala often hints at the heat of desire, as suggested by the title of the film *Mississippi Masala* (1991). But 'masala' more precisely means a mixture—originally a mixture of different ground spices, as in the case of masala chai, but more metaphorically any kind of diverse mixture: we might talk, for example, of an Indian growing up in Britain with a masala of cultural influences. The masala mixture is not simply a collation of discrete individual elements in the manner of a mosaic. It is, rather, a blend, where different ingredients communicate with each other in dynamic ways.

All three senses—of spicy narrative flavour, the heat of desire, and dynamic mixture—combine in the masala movie, that genre of Indian film which, like *Lagaan*, involves outlandish exaggeration, intense passion, and a hodgepodge of styles. A common complaint about masala movies is that they stretch the bounds of credibility; they are *too much*. That too-muchness extends from the lengthy duration of the masala movie

JONATHAN GIL HARRIS

(it is often three or more hours, double that of a Hollywood film) to its melodramatic depiction of love (at the supposed expense of 'real' concerns) and its sheer generic excess (high seriousness accompanied by screwball comedy, sentimental romance accompanied by dhishoom punch-ups, beautiful shayari or Urdu poetry accompanied by rows and rows of Michael Jackson-type dancers). In the masala movie, there is no space for purity. Elements that are supposedly separate and even incompatible bed down under the same roof: tragedy consorts with comedy, poetic language with coarse slang, prim morality with unbounded desire, congested Indian gallis with rolling Swiss mountains, conversational dialogues with song and dance, desi cowboys with desi Indians, Hindi with Urdu, Hindustani with English, Punjabi with Bhojpuri.

These kinds of mixture are arguably what the great early twentieth-century Indian writer Premchand was alluding to when he said that the indispensable ingredients of a novel include, in addition to plot and character, masala. He was recommending more than just the addition of narrative spice. In advocating for masala he was advocating for mixture. Premchand is often described as a Hindi writer, but he originally wrote in the Nastaliq script of Urdu and was more accurately an exemplar of that blended language called Hindustani. His embrace of masala was an embrace of a recognizably Indian experience as well as concept, an experience of cultural mixing at the level of thought as much as language.

Indeed, I would argue that masala—and in particular, the masala movie—is not just a style or genre. More accurately, it embodies a certain idea of India that celebrates the plural, the syncretic, the polyglot, the all-over-the-place. Interestingly, adaptations of Shakespeare have provided the pretext for some of the most committed expressions of this idea of India. A recent bhangwadi Gujarati-Hindi stage version of *All's Well That Ends Well*, for example—its Hindi title is *Mere Piya Gaye Rangoon* (My Love Went to Rangoon)—interrupts its Shakespearean narrative for a lively song-and-dance routine that celebrates Bombay as a city in which Parsi, Maratha, Madrasi, and Angrez (English) live side by side, not in a tidy vision of rainbow harmony but rather in a jostling, messy super-abundance.

However, Premchand's and *Mere Piya Gaye Rangoon*'s masala visions of a plural India are arguably ceding ground to another that, by contrast, fetishizes purity, singular origins, and cultural homogeneity. This latter vision has been articulated most vehemently by the acolytes of what is known as Hindutva or Hindu fundamentalism. For proponents of

Hindutva, India's pluralism is an adulteration of a once pure 'Hindustan', so called because it was and should always be a nation of Hindus. This false etymology conveniently forgets that the 'Hindu' in 'Hindustan' derives not from the religion but from a river that flows through what is now Pakistan, the Indus (or Sindhu). It forgets too that 'Hindustan' was a term coined by Muslims who ruled over a mixed polity.

Akbar and Dara Shikoh attempted to craft syncretic blends of diverse Hindustani spiritual traditions in their visions of Din-i-Ilahi or Majma-ul-Bahrain: what we might call Mughlai masala. Hinduism, too, has been for the longest time engaged in transformative dialogues with the religions of neigbouring peoples. There is something fundamentally masala about Hinduism, with its pantheons of gods derived from numerous religious traditions and cultures. As the eleventh-century philosopher king Bhoja of Dhar enjoined his 'Hindu' subjects: 'Learn Buddhism, behave like a Jain,…meditate on Shiva.' Even today, one of the most popular saints among Hindus is Shirdi Sai Baba, a satguru and fakir who lived in a masjid and customarily said, 'Allah malik (Allah is lord)'. Despite the prevailing political winds of the moment, India's syncretic pluralism remains an inescapable lived reality.

Masala, then, is a deeply Indian concept, even if it is one that is arguably under attack. But it also describes to a tee what makes Shakespeare's plays—their styles, their idioms, their audiences—so distinctive. For Shakespeare's writing is not the father of Indian masala. It is its twin.

◆

What is the word most frequently found in the titles of Shakespeare's works? Barring 'King' or 'Henry', it is 'and'. That simple word, so easy to skip over, does a huge amount of work. It always conjoins lovers: *Romeo and Juliet*, *Antony and Cleopatra*, *Troilus and Cressida*, *Venus and Adonis*. We also shouldn't forget *A Midsummer Night's Dream*'s play-within-a-play, 'Pyramus and Thisbe'. What could be more fundamental to the logic of masala than the conjunctive 'and'? All of these titles represent a mixture, a potentially subversive coming together of people otherwise divided by social convention (clan rivalry), culture (Rome and Egypt, Troy and Greece), species status (god and mortal), or just a plain wall.

This kind of mixing in love is familiar to aficionados of masala movies. The titles of films like *Veer-Zaara* (2004), *Jodhaa Akbar* (2008), and *Bajirao Mastani* (2015) may not contain the word 'aur (and)', but each brings together a Hindu and a Muslim lover. Tellingly, the credit sequences of these movies about mixed jodis (couples) feature their titles in Devanagari and Nastaliq as well as Roman scripts—a once standard convention that has mostly vanished in the Hindi cinema of the past two decades. As a result, something of Shakespeare's vision of mixed lovers is mirrored by the language in these film's credit sequences: each entails a mixture across the boundaries of community, a more-than-oneness.

Shakespeare's love mixtures are symptomatic of other, more profound mixtures that again recall the masala movie. Above all, he mixes genres. We may laugh at the pedantic Polonius in *Hamlet*, who talks up a troupe of travelling actors as the best performers of 'tragical-comical-historical-pastoral' (2.2.381). What a nonsensical hyphenated creature of the imagination, defying logic as well as good taste! It is almost as fantastical as, say, a story of three brothers from three completely different religious communities. *Amar Akbar Anthony* (1977), anyone?

Yet Polonius's demented term is a perfect description of Shakespeare's dramas and how they refuse generic singularity. His great tragedies are full of clowns. His comedies are dark. And Shakespeare's characters often belong to multiple genres at once. Romeo is tragic, yet when he spouts clichéd love poetry at the beginning of the play, he is one of Shakespeare's great comic characters. *Twelfth Night*'s Malvolio is in a comedy, yet his character leaves the stage with a distinct whiff of tragedy about him. Hamlet may be a character who, in his habit of thinking rather than doing, embodies the depth of a tragic modern psyche, yet for one brief instance in Act 4, he morphs offstage into a comic two-dimensional action hero—a swashbuckling Errol Flynn-type character who fights pirates single-handed. Clearly Shahid Kapoor (himself the son of a mixed marriage) was born to play him.

Everywhere one looks in Shakespeare, one finds this deep masala investment in the more-than-one. His plays return over and over to the idea of double identity, and in ways that can seem pure Bollywood. *The Comedy of Errors* and *Twelfth Night* feature twins mistaken for each other, as do a long tradition of Hindi films from *Afsana* (1951) to *Dhoom 3* (2013). *Twelfth Night, As You Like It, The Merchant of Venice* and *The Two Gentlemen of Verona* all include cross-dressed women acting as men, as do movies from *Victoria No. 203* (1972) to *Dil Bole Hadippa!* (2009). *Hamlet, A Midsummer Night's Dream*, and *The Taming of the Shrew* feature characters as actors in a play-within-a-play, just as characters appearing in a film-within-a-film are found in movies from *Bhumika* (1977) to

Luck by Chance (2009). And *Henry IV Part 1*, *The Taming of the Shrew*, and *Cymbeline* all include characters who are doubles of other characters, as do films from *Don* (1978) to *Fan* (2016).

Identities double in Shakespeare. So do meanings, because Shakespeare also adores the more-than-oneness of the pun. Samuel Johnson famously wrote that the quibble, or punning wordplay, was the 'fatal Cleopatra' to which Shakespeare was most attracted. It is a fatal attraction that he shares with Hindi cinema, which is likewise riddled with playful puns. From the character Peter K. Murray in *Saazish* (1975), whose name puns on 'peeke mare' (drank and died), to the song 'Bhaag Bhaag DK Bose' in *Delhi Belly* (2011), which turns a Bengali name into the profane 'bhosdi ke (of the vagina)', screenplay writers and lyricists have revelled in double entendres. Shakespeare, too, loves innuendo: Gratiano in *The Merchant of Venice*, convinced that he has been cuckolded by a clerk (who is in fact his cross-dressed wife), vows to 'mar the young clerk's pen' (5.1.236). But his investment in the slipperiness of meaning isn't just for the sake of bawdy jokes. An entire play, *Macbeth*, revolves around the doubleness of meaning, or what it terms 'equivocation'—the art of saying something that can be interpreted in more than one way. Equivocation in *Macbeth* may be the demonic practice of wayward witches, evil tyrants and treasonous Jesuit priests. But it is also the hallmark of Shakespeare's punning craft: it is not just witches, as Macbeth complains, who 'palter with us in a double sense' (5.10.20), but Shakespeare's masala language as well.

On top of double identities and double meanings, Shakespeare also gives us double locations. The simple 'Wooden O' in which his plays were staged could contain, as the Prologue to *King Henry the Fifth* observes, many countries: in that play alone, the one stage is simultaneously England and France. What could be more Bollywood, which likewise hurtles from location to location? It isn't just that, post-economic liberalization, films moved from India to Switzerland or New Zealand in lockstep with the travelling aspirations of Hindi film viewers. Even when set in a small village, the masala movie has always sought to be expansive in its vision of place, and in a way that returns us to the conjunctive lovers of Shakespeare: one of the songs in the retro-masala film *Chennai Express* (2013), sung by the lead romantic couple, tells us that 'Kashmir main, tu Kanyakumari'. Likewise, the island of Shakespeare's *The Tempest* is simultaneously located in the Mediterranean and the Caribbean and is populated by elements that come from the Roman writer Ovid's depiction of Asia and early European travel narratives' accounts of South America.

Starting with *King Henry V* in 1599, Shakespeare's plays were performed in the aptly named Globe Theatre. It is rumoured that, at the entrance of the Globe, playgoers would walk through a door over which was written the Latin caption, 'Totus Mundus Agit Histrionem (All the World Acts a Play)', a loose translation of his famous line from *As You Like It*, 'all the world's a stage' (2.7.138). Inside the Globe, as *The Tempest* makes clear, the stage expanded to become the world. And that world, in Shakespeare as much as in Bollywood, was a world of mixed lovers, genres, meanings and places. Romeo and Juliet and Pyramus and Thisbe. Tragic and Comic and Pastoral and Historical. Sacred and Profane and Equivocal and Direct. Caribbean and Mediterranean and Asian and South American. A world of masala.

◆

Why all these mixtures? And what is the genealogy of Shakespeare's masala?

The sixteenth-century English poet, Sir Philip Sidney, complained that contemporary 'plays be neither right tragedies nor comedies, mingling kings and clowns'. This mingling didn't sit well with those of Shakespeare's contemporaries versed in classical poetics. The Greek philosopher Aristotle had declared that a play should observe the unities of genre, place and time, meaning it should follow one generic convention, it should be set in one location, and its duration on stage should be as long as the time that elapses in the play itself. In short: absolutely no mingling. These strictures became popular in the years after Shakespeare's death. It is through an Aristotelian lens that the critic Thomas Rymer, writing in 1693, pronounced the plot of *Othello* completely absurd, and the playwright Edward Ravenscroft in 1686 called *Titus Andronicus* 'a heap of rubbish'.

One man's rubbish, though, is another's masala. Because rubbish is not just rubble, a toppled structure. It is also a lively grab bag of disparate materials that have been discarded by their past users. Shakespeare's plays are rubbish in precisely this sense. In terms of invention, he is a kabaadi walla (scrap dealer), collecting his stories from everywhere. Each of his surviving thirty-seven plays borrows its story from somewhere else or, more accurately, from a variety of sources. Take *The Merchant of Venice*. The tale of Shylock the Jew is lifted from one of a fourteenth-century collection of comic Italian stories by Ser Giovanni Fiorentino called *Il*

Pecorone, meaning 'The Sheep' or 'Simpleton'. *The Merchant of Venice*'s subplot, involving the princess Portia and her suitors from around the world, is teased out of Fiorentino's story too. But Shakespeare's treatment also bears the influence of a medieval collection of English fairy tales, the *Gesta Romanorum*. And Portia's first suitor, the Prince of Morocco, delivers a speech that is cut and pasted directly from a tragedy, *Soliman and Perseda*, performed on the London stage some years before *The Merchant of Venice*.

The promiscuity of influence here—Italian comic story, English fairy tale, oriental tragedy—recalls the mixed inspirations for masala movies. *Ghajini* (2008), the Aamir Khan blockbuster, was a remake of a 2005 Tamil film, which stole large sections of Christopher Nolan's cult classic Hollywood film *Memento* (2000): like the latter, *Ghajini* presented us with an amnesiac hero whose wife has been killed, and who has tattooed his memories onto his flesh. Yet *Ghajini* interspersed this disturbing scenario with comic romantic scenes taken diversely from the British musical *Happy Go Lovely* (1951) and the French comedy *Amélie* (2001).

To accuse *The Merchant of Venice* or *Ghajini* of a lack of originality is to miss the point. The assumption that a new entertainment must have an 'original' story derives from a capitalist understanding of creativity as individual intellectual property, produced by the artist from his or her lofty imagination alone. Yet the craft of Shakespeare and Bollywood might suggest the analogy not of property but cooking. A good chef does not devise a brand new recipe every time she cooks. Rather, she cooks with old familiar recipes, but flavours them in new ways, adding fresh ingredients to the mix. Shakespeare and Bollywood scriptwriters are chefs in exactly this manner. They work with a mixture of elements from a variety of sources—a masala—to prepare tasty new versions of old dishes for diverse diners.

Shakespeare arguably refused the Aristotelian ideal of unity because of the diversity of his audiences. Clearly they found in his plays a pleasing khichdi of possibilities that reflected their own mixture. For one, they spanned all social classes, from royalty and gentry to artisans and apprentices. And this prompted a pervasive diversity of language styles in the entertainments Shakespeare served them. He stuffed his plays with ornate poetry in line with the expectations of higher-class, educated audience members. But he also was a champion writer of earthy prose, particularly in those of his scenes where clowns speak directly to the poorer audience members in the pit. Something similar happens in masala films, whose language alternates between high and low in ways that again presume a mixed audience. The film *Dedh Ishqiya* (2014) perfectly illustrates this: Naseeruddin Shah's character poses as a nawab who spouts exquisite Urdu shayari, but he is in real life a swearing conman who speaks the most colourful Hindi gaalis (cuss words).

Shakespeare wrote at a time of radical, perhaps even unprecedented, social upheaval. The country had experienced a bewildering series of changes in its state religion: King Henry VIII took England out of the Roman Catholic fold, his daughter Mary took it back in again, and her sister Elizabeth then declared England a Protestant nation once more. It also witnessed a massive social and economic transformation that resulted in tens of thousands of people being displaced from their villages and migrating to London to sell their labour—a situation not unlike what is happening currently in India, where cities such as Delhi and Bombay are swollen by an influx of migrant workers from poor rural areas. Shakespeare's audiences, like Bombay cinemagoers now, consisted of a huge number of people who had shifted from other parts of the country. Most still had one foot planted in an old rural feudal order and the other in a new urban commercial world. As a result, Shakespeare had to accommodate a huge spectrum of taste, dialect, religious belief, and ways of thinking. Mixture was the currency not only of Shakespeare's entertainment business but also of a time in which any dream of a singular England was troubled by the inescapable reality of its plurality.

It is in this context that Shakespeare wrote what many take to be his first play, *The Comedy of Errors*.

◆

The Comedy of Errors's earliest recorded performance was in 1594. But it was most likely written up to five years earlier. Shakespeare had arrived in London in the late 1580s, a migrant from the provinces looking for work in the rapidly growing city's booming theatre business. It is safe to presume that, to someone who had grown up in the sleepy western English town of Stratford, the teeming city of London was both exciting and frightening. So it is probably no coincidence that *The Comedy of Errors* vividly depicts the experience of migrants in a new city. This city is full of marvellous sights. But, as London must have been for young Shakespeare, it is also a space of danger in which a migrant can lose his sense of self.

Shakespeare's main source was a classical Roman play by Plautus, the

Menaechmi—a farcical comedy of mistaken identity involving a separated pair of twins. Like Plautus's play, *The Comedy of Errors* is set in one place, Ephesus, and its duration is about as long as the duration of events in the play, i.e. one afternoon. So far so Aristotelian. But look at how Shakespeare mixed up the seemingly singular place and time of his source. The Ephesian setting features a main street populated by hotels and artisans' shops straight from Shakespeare's London. The play jokes about the irregular flow of time: one of the characters notes that although it was previously two o'clock, 'now the clock strikes one' (4.2.54). In the topsy-turvy world of this play, where migrants are disoriented in a new city, time as much as place refuses unity.

Shakespeare mixed up the *Menaechmi* in even more profound ways. First, he added another set of twins to Plautus's story. This second set are, unlike the upper-class pair, the children of a 'mean-born woman' (1.1.54) and raised as servants to the other twins. But none of the twins know their lost identical brothers, having been separated from them as babies in a shipwreck. One master/servant pair has migrated to Ephesus; the other has stayed in Syracuse. As the play begins, the Syracuse pair visit Ephesus and, mistaken for their lost brothers, the comedy of errors of the title ensues. Yet the extra pair of twins also injects a darker tone into the play, with four characters haunted by lack and loss. As one of them says: 'I to the world am like a drop of water/ That in the ocean seeks another drop' (1.2.35–6). The sheer enormity of this twin's quest, together with the utter lack of distinction of the drop, does not suggest the mistaken identity of farce. Rather it insists, tragically, that singular identity itself is a mistake, doomed to failure: 'I…unhappy, lose myself' (1.2.39–40).

The generic more-than-oneness unleashed by the extra pair of twins is augmented by a further addition. Shakespeare has let the story of the four divided twins simmer in an added frame narrative. The story of the merchant Egeon of Syracuse, which opens the play, was inspired by the old tale of Apollonius of Tyre, as rendered by the medieval English poet John Gower in his *Confessio Amantis*. This tale is far removed from the farcical world of Plautus's comedy. Apollonius loses his wife and child in a shipwreck, is convinced that they are dead, and then loses himself as he wanders from place to place. He is eventually reunited with them. Yet his happy ending cannot banish the traumatic memory of separation and despair. The theme of loss and repossession was the basis of an entire genre, the romance. This genre is a perfect illustration of

Polonius's 'tragical-comical-historical-pastoral'. But loss and repossession also describe the traumatic reality and utopian hope of many migrants, including Shakespeare and much of his audience in the London playhouse.

By adding the story of Egeon, Shakespeare gave two of his twins not only a father but also a mother: Egeon's lost wife Emilia, an abbess (or Mother Superior nun) who has been living in Ephesus unknown to her sons, miraculously appears at the play's end to reunite the previously divided family. The servant twins are not so lucky, as their 'mean-born' mother never returns. But by adding these parents, Shakespeare also gave *The Comedy of Errors* mixed literary parents. Plautus's farcical comedy hooks up with Gower's sentimental romance: from Aristotle's point of view, this is the generic equivalent of a Montague meeting a Capulet, a forbidden mingling. The illicit mingling of farce and romance teaches us something about the mixed genealogy of masala as a genre. No masala entertainment can have one lineage. It must have many.

The Comedy of Errors also reminds us of an inescapable truth about genealogy. On the one hand, we often trace our identity back through a singular line, usually that of our father and his name. On the other, we are all the products of genealogical masala: no person has one biological parent, as every one of us is the outcome of genetic mixture. In this respect, the two sets of twins of *The Comedy of Errors* are a metaphor for how all of us, through our genealogies, simultaneously multiply and divide in our identities. Go back one generation, and our oneness splits into two; go back two, and one becomes dispersed across four. The abiding conceit of *The Comedy of Errors*'s two sets of twins is that identity is never singular and unique. It is always haunted by something else, a shadow self.

For modern Western readers, this shadow self might recall Sigmund Freud's insistence that we are all strangers to ourselves, driven by unconscious impulses from which we have been divided through the repressive power of social conditioning. And a Freudian understanding of psychology might seem to answer a question posed to one of the twins: 'how comes it/ That thou art then estranged from thyself?' (2.2.119–20). But I see the shadow selves of *The Comedy of Errors* as stemming less from the inner workings of individual psychology and more from a recognition of a social reality in Shakespeare's time: that all of us are potentially related, whether as siblings or as children, to people who pray to different gods and belong to different communities. In Shakespeare's case, this recognition may have been born of his family circumstances.

His father, John Shakespeare, was a committed Roman Catholic at a time when Protestantism was the official state religion; he was fined for failing to attend services in the local church. And his mother, Mary Arden, had many Catholic relatives in her wider family. Whether Shakespeare was a believer in the old faith we cannot be sure. But he and his brother Gilbert, both of whom were actors, probably had to act in real life as much as on stage, crossing boundaries of religious identity and passing as good Protestants.

The twins of *The Comedy of Errors* have been divided by accident across borders of geography and culture. And the play insists that these borders are maintained through violence: straying across them leads to possible death. Egeon, in the first scene, has been ordered to die because it is a capital offense for citizens of Syracuse to visit Ephesus, and vice versa. But the play also asks us to recognize unexpected affinities—twinships—across the seemingly sacrosanct borders of identity. Despite the culture of paranoid fear prevailing in the play, *The Comedy of Errors*'s conclusion has loving, trans-cultural brotherhood prevail over myopic, aggressive nationalism. As one character tells his twin in the play's closing couplet: 'we came into the world like brother and brother,/ And now let's go hand in hand, not one before another' (5.1.426–7).

Brother and brother, hand in hand. I believe that it is this masala impulse to solidarity across supposed difference, far more than any Indian zeal in implementing or internalizing Macaulay's Minute, which has allowed Shakespeare's plays—including *The Comedy of Errors*—to flourish in a vast country whose innumerable, mingled cultural lineages embody what it means to be a masala mixture. It is less that the English introduced Indians to Shakespeare and his mixtures. It is more that India, with its mixed genealogies, has always been Shakespearean. Indian masala and masala Shakespeare are twins. With similarly mixed parentages.

◆

The first intimation I had of Shakespeare's and Hindi cinema's comparably mixed lineages was when I saw the film *Angoor* (1982), the poet/lyricist/director Gulzar's adaptation of *The Comedy of Errors*. The film, as we will see, has a mixed genealogy to rival those of Shakespeare's plays. But *Angoor* also explicitly dramatizes the problem of lineage as part of its own story, and in a way that provides a brilliantly self-conscious meditation on the mixed genealogy of the Hindi masala movie.

To characterize *Angoor* as an adaptation of Shakespeare is to assume that it has a single patriarchal lineage. In its opening sequence, *Angoor* encourages that assumption. The film starts with a homage of sorts to Shakespeare. We see the black-and-white face of a man in a beard who stares at us sternly while a voiceover hails him, 'aap hain (this is) William Shakespeare', adding that 'aaj tak duniya ke sabse bade naatakkaar maane jaate hain (to this day considered to be the greatest playwright in the world)'. The face obligingly cracks a sly smile. As the scene cuts to a shot of a father riding in a rickshaw with his twin babies, the voiceover continues. We are informed that the story is based on Shakespeare's *The Comedy of Errors*. The homage continues with the father, Raj Tilak, saying of his babies, 'yeh toh *Comedy of Errors* ke bacche hain (these are *Comedy of Errors*'s children)'. And at the film's end, after one of the twins has asked who could have possibly thought of such a crazy scenario, the image of Shakespeare returns with his sly smile, raising his hand to claim responsibility.

Yet not all is as it may first seem. The face that stares at us at the beginning of *Angoor* looks nothing like the standard First Folio image of Shakespeare: it seems to belong more to the early twentieth than the seventeenth century, and is more Indian than English. Indeed, it looks strikingly like the face of Rabindranath Tagore. Perhaps that faint smile is not one of Shakespeare accepting praise but of a shared inside joke with an Indian viewership. And those viewers in on the joke might even remember that Tagore had himself published a novel in 1906, *Noukadubi*, about a case of mistaken identity following a shipwreck—the exact scenario with which *Angoor* also begins. The face, then, gives us a fleeting glimpse of *Angoor*'s mixed lineage. Shakespeare himself becomes a case of mistaken identity, haunted by an Indian twin who can also lay claim to creative parentage of the film.

Indeed, there is much about *Angoor* that, even as it seems to faithfully follow Shakespeare's lead, is born of Indian cultural and artistic traditions. Like *The Comedy of Errors*, *Angoor* offers its viewers two pairs of twins: the upper-class Ashok Raj Tilak brothers, played by Sanjeev Kumar, and the lower-class Bahadur twins, played by Deven Verma. But *Angoor* crams all sorts of Indian masala into this Shakespearean recipe. Like his counterpart in *The Comedy of Errors*, the migrant Ashok is paranoid about his new city. *Angoor* explains Ashok's paranoia by making him an aficionado of popular Hindi crime fiction, whose hyperbolic tales of dastardly murders, stratagems, and evil-doers infect his thinking about the world around him. We first see him on board a train reading a pulp novel called *Agyaat Apraadhi*. This becomes a spur to his response to the city, where in his mind everyone is an agyaat apraadhi (unknown criminal) belonging to a sinister gang.

Also born of Indian cultural and artistic traditions are *Angoor*'s three song sequences, with lyrics by Gulzar and music by R. D. Burman. Chief among these is a scene in which Tanu (Deepti Naval), the sister of the local Ashok's wife, performs a song to a large audience that includes the visiting Ashok and Bahadur. Its lyrics, a blend of Hindi and Urdu, tell of a bee, who 'roz roz (every day)' writes on a branch about its past sufferings.

This song introduces a very different tone into the film. Gulzar has removed the dark romance frame narrative of Shakespeare's play: unlike *The Comedy of Errors*, the Ashoks' father is not sentenced to death, nor are they reunited with him. *Angoor* concentrates more on the farcical material that Shakespeare inherited from Plautus. But Tanu's song, with its remembering of 'dard puraana (old pain)' reintroduces the mixture of loss and longing that is a feature of the missing frame narrative. In other words, the masala mixing of genres in *The Comedy of Errors* is enabled in *Angoor* through this song—just as its lyrics, blending Hindi and Urdu, represent a masala mix at the level of language.

It is tempting to see in the song's reference to the 'beete hue mausam (past weather)' an evocation of the ghost of Tagore and *Noukadubi*, whose plot, like *The Comedy of Errors*, is haunted by a long-ago storm. But there is arguably another ghost evoked by the song. In 1968, a very young Gulzar had scripted an earlier Hindi film adaptation of *The Comedy of Errors*—*Do Dooni Char* (1968). This film was a musical about a banker and his assistant who, while visiting a town, are mistaken for a local merchant and servant. *Do Dooni Char* was a box-office flop. Although produced by Bimal Roy, who was famed for social realist movies such as *Sujata* (1959), the film adopted the full-blown masala musical style that was popular at the time; but it did so ineffectually. Gulzar was bitterly disappointed by how his script had been mangled in production, sliced and diced according to the demands of the film's commercial backers. In writing *Angoor*, he was himself a 'bhanwra (bee)' remembering the 'nishaani (trace)' of his own past weather and pain. His new film was an attempt to reconstitute a story that had been lost, a story that had more literary aspirations than *Do Dooni Char*'s final form (as *Angoor*'s opening references to Shakespeare and Tagore suggest).

Yet in *Angoor*, Gulzar retained one important aspect from *Do Dooni*

Char: the musical item number. On this score, the film's parentage is not literary but, rather, theatrical as much as cinematic. It is often pointed out that musical Hindi cinema has its roots in the Parsi theatre of Bombay, also known in Marathi as sangeet naatak (musical drama). The sangeet naatak began in the late nineteenth century as a commercial entertainment for highly mixed audiences in Bombay. Its signature melodramatic style was as diverse as its audiences, drawing on both indigenous and western dramatic traditions. Reworkings of Sanskrit plays featured heavily in the repertoire of the sangeet naatak; but thanks to the training of Parsi students at Elphinstone College who wrote for the sangeet naatak, the leading source material was Shakespeare.

Between 1860 and 1910, the Parsi theatre produced up to seventy-five adaptations of Shakespeare's plays, as well as countless more distantly influenced by them. These adaptations were written in a variety of local languages: initially scripted in Gujarati and Marathi, they increasingly employed the more widely spoken Urdu—itself a mixture or rekhta (as Urdu is often called). *The Comedy of Errors* was a perennial favourite of the sangeet naatak adaptors. There were at least two Gujarati productions, in 1865 and 1903, and three in Urdu, *Bhool-Bhulaiyan* (Labyrinths) in 1896 and 1913, and *Gorakhandananda* (A Labyrinth) in 1912. These productions were as hybrid in their stagecraft as they were in their language and audience, combining elements of British Victorian pictorial theatre, indigenous Indian folk theatre, and—always—naach-gaana.

The first Bombay talkies were often filmed versions of Parsi sangeet nataaks—including adaptations of Shakespeare. For instance, the Parsi theatre director Sohrab Modi adapted his stage reworking of *Hamlet* into the film *Khoon Ka Khoon* (1935); a year later, he adapted Shakespeare's *King John* into a film called *Saed-e-Havas*. As the Parsi theatre morphed into the Bombay talkies, it retained in its DNA not only the song-and-dance routines, but also many other elements that arguably trace back to Shakespeare and the sangeet naatak adaptations of *The Comedy of Errors*—mixed audiences and genres, master-servant conflict, and separated brothers. In short, the sangeet naatak helped produce the masala not just of *Do Dooni Char*, but also other musical blockbusters featuring long-lost brothers such as *Amar Akbar Anthony* (1977) and *Gol Maal* (1979). These two masala musical films are just as much a part of *Angoor*'s sangeet naatak lineage as well; without their commercial success in the years just before *Angoor* was filmed, it is inconceivable that Gulzar's redo of *Do Dooni Char* would have been green-lighted.

This quick genealogy of *Angoor's* masala is insufficient, however, because it presumes a straight, singular line of descent from Parsi theatre to Hindi cinema. But a masala sensibility—particularly one that recognizes the features of Tagore in the face of Shakespeare—will know that there can never be one singular ancestral line. There are other tributaries beyond the sangeet naatak that flow into Bollywood masala movies in general and *Angoor's* masala sensibility in particular.

For instance, there has been a long tradition of reading and performing Shakespeare in Bengal. As I have already noted, his plays were staged in Calcutta theatres during the British Raj in an attempt to preserve English-accented Shakespeare for colonial audiences. But by the mid-nineteenth century, his plays were also being translated into and performed in Bengali. These productions were far more faithful to Shakespeare's playtexts than those of the Parsi theatre. This was not just because of a slavish adherence to the colonizers' tastes; the Bengali Renaissance promoted Shakespeare as a duniyakobi (world poet), who could also speak to specifically Bengali concerns in their native tongue. Unlike the sangeet naatak adaptations, Bengali productions had a strong sense of Shakespeare as high literature rather than simple commercial entertainment. Which is to say, Shakespeare was seen as an authority to be respected rather than as a producer of raw material that could be freely adapted. Yet somehow, this more reverent tradition spawned another distinctive masala sensibility.

The crucial figure in this Bengali genealogy is Utpal Dutt. A gifted actor-director, he had performed Shakespeare in the late 1940s and early 1950s with English actors, including Geoffrey Kendal, and had admired Sir Laurence Olivier's performances of Shakespeare. He even wrote a book about Shakespeare. But he was also a lifelong Marxist with a strong commitment to democratizing theatre. Influenced by radical German playwright Bertolt Brecht, he helped set up the Indian People's Theatre Association (IPTA). From the 1960s onwards, he translated and performed Shakespeare in Bengali; increasingly he put Shakespeare in dialogue with jatra, the operatic village theatrical style performed in the open air. Utpal Dutt exemplifies a bhadralok communist sensibility that is typical of Bengal. His is a very different kind of masala, one driven less by commercial than by socialist concerns. We see its offshoot in a Bengali tradition of cinema, including the work of Satyajit Ray, which is both more 'arty' and socially engaged.

Angoor is arguably an adaptation less of Shakespeare than it is of a

Bengali film reimagining of *The Comedy of Errors, Bhranti Bilas* (1963), directed by Manu Sen. *Bhranti Bilas* belongs to a very different idiom from *Do Dooni Char*; it is a typical Bengali film of the period—slightly cerebral, artistic, a counterpart to Satyajit Ray's films. It draws on the kind of masala that characterizes Utpal Dutt's theatre: a mixture of Shakespeare and local Bengali forms. Importantly, *Bhranti Bilas* is itself based not directly on Shakespeare but on an earlier translation of *The Comedy of Errors* into Bengali, Ishwar Chandra Vidyasagar's *Bhrantibilas* (The Play of Errors). Despite the title, Vidysagar's version was not a play at all but, rather, a novella. And its source was not just Shakespeare's text but also Charles and Mary Lamb's prose version of *The Comedy of Errors*. By following the Lambs, Vidyasagar sought to extend to Bengali writing the prestige of Shakespeare but also, more specifically, of the nineteenth-century prose novel. *Angoor* has roots in the Bombay of sangeet naatak, but its lineage can be traced back to the Calcutta of Vidyasagar's novella too. If its songs come from the former, then its literary aspirations come from the latter.

In *Angoor*, this second lineage is evident in Gulzar's casting choice for Raj Tilak, the film's counterpart to Egeon. By casting Utpal Dutt, Gulzar acknowledged the mixed genealogy of his Hindi masala twins, giving them a father associated with Bengali Shakespeare and, in particular, a political and populist radical Shakespeare theatre that draws on indigenous forms. *Angoor*, in its self-conscious deviation from the more commercially oriented *Do Dooni Char*, rides on the back of Utpal Dutt's experiments with a masala Shakespeare that respected the playwright's literary authority while seeking to refract it through local Bengali forms. So when Utpal Dutt says 'yeh toh *Comedy of Errors* ke bacche hain,' he doesn't simply pay homage to Shakespeare. The children of *The Comedy of Errors* have been spawned by a wide array of masala lineages across India too.

These aren't just artistic but also lived masala lineages. We can glimpse them in *Angoor*. We have already seen the blend of Hindi and Urdu in Tanu's song. But the film keeps asking us to recognize how its language is mixed. When confronted by the jeweller Mansoor Miyan, the visiting Ashok says, in typically paranoid fashion, that he can't understand him because he speaks Urdu. But they proceed to have a conversation that veers between Urdu and Hindi. And when hailing a taxi, the visiting Ashok greets the driver with a 'salaam'. If the lineages of the film's form are a mix of Parsi and Bengali, the lineages of its language equally acknowledge the masala genealogy of India, a mix of cultures and languages that we all exemplify in our everyday speech. Gulzar himself, born into a Sikh family (his birth name is Sampooran Singh Kalra) and a poet in Urdu and Hindi and Punjabi and Saraiki, is a shining illustration of this mix.

Both at the level of its plot and in its self-conscious references to multiple influences, then, *Angoor* keeps posing questions about lineage. It starts by acknowledging Shakespeare's paternity. But his subliminal twinning with Tagore at the beginning of the film is only the beginning of a mad proliferation of lineages that trouble Shakespeare's claim to single parentage. *Angoor*'s many parents also include Plautus, Gower, Charles and Mary Lamb, Vidyasagar, Utpal Dutt, sangeet naatak, Hindi fiction, Urdu poetry, Bengali novels, Bollywood movies and, of course, Gulzar himself. And it is worth noting that *Angoor* has spawned many children too, across many different regional traditions: its story has been remade again and again in Indian cinema, from the Kannada *Ulta Palta* (1997), remade in Telugu the following year, and the Hindi *Bade Miyan Chote Miyan* (1998) to the Tulu *Aamait Asal Eemait Kusal* (2012) and the brilliantly titled Punjabi *Double Di Trouble* (2014). This mixed lineage is highly Shakespearean. But in its cross-regional masala, it is also unmistakably Indian.

ACT ONE SCENE THREE

'Mera Yaar Mila De'

The year after I first visited India, I saw the film *Saathiya* (2002). This Rani Mukerji-Vivek Oberoi starrer about lovers who elope, separate, and reunite is in many ways a predictably sentimental potboiler. There are tears galore, as well as scenes of Rani dancing around trees with dupatta held aloft. But what affected me most about this masala film were its songs. These were composed by A. R. Rahman, with lyrics by Gulzar. The lovers, Aditya and Suhani, are from Hindu families in Bombay. But the song that plays during their period of separation, 'Mera Yaar Mila De (Unite Me With My Beloved)', is a Sufi ghazal sung in Urdu and Punjabi by the Pakistani qawwali singer Rahat Fateh Ali Khan. And the longing it describes is not just that of the agitated Aditya, desperately seeking Suhani. It is the longing also of a Sufi devotee searching for khuda or God.

The song is a remarkable masala concoction: the spiritual compass points of one religious tradition chart a map of the heart for characters from a supposedly different tradition. The tale of two Indian lovers becomes, in masala fashion, a Hindu–Muslim conversation. But the song is more than that. It expresses its longing in a voice that comes from across the border with Pakistan, recalling a painful experience of separation specific to recent subcontinental history. The cultural mix of Hindu and Muslim is complemented by an emotional mix of longing and trauma. Even though *Saathiya* is set in Bombay, and its soundtrack composed by a Tamilian, Gulzar's lyrics help create a golgappa that belongs specifically to North India.

One thing we must always remember about masala: it cannot ever be one. It is not a uniform, one-size-fits-all category of mixture. A masala dish is more-than-one in its internal composition; it is more-than-one also in its many possible permutations. After all, the subcontinental cuisine boasts a billion and one versions of masala. The masalas of the north are different from the masalas of the south; both are different again from the masalas of the east and the west. And the masala of any cook differs from the masala of another. Even one cook makes different masalas at different times, depending on from where he sources his ingredients and which ingredients he wants to highlight. Each masala mixture tastes slightly different as a result.

And a second thing: a masala concoction isn't always uniformly pleasant to taste. It often contains ingredients that are unpalatable. Think of the golgappa. One first tastes the crispness of the little puri and the chaat masala inside it, before the fierce heat of the mirchi (chilli) kicks in, followed by the slightly unsavoury odour of the pudina paani (mint water) and the sweetness of the tamarind. It took me quite a while to learn how to enjoy a golgappa. The first time I ate one, I gagged. My palate simply couldn't reconcile the pleasure of tamarind with the recoil induced by the double whammy of sour mint and hot chilli. My tastebuds had been too conditioned by the single-tasting snacks of western cuisine. But over time I began to enjoy how a golgappa is a mixed-taste experience that unfolds over time. The joy of the golgappa is that the pudina paani tastes so much better because it cools the heat of the mirchi, and the tamarind tastes so much better because it softens the sourness of the pudina. But the tamarind's sweetness is not too cloying because it is in turn qualified by the lingering heat of the chilli. This goes to show how a good masala dish isn't one in which anything goes. Simply mixing random items would create a chaotic broth. The golgappa is, rather, an artful combination of ingredients that cause both pleasure and pain. And the pain of the hot mirchi or the sour pudina paani is not entirely superseded by the pleasure of the other ingredients: what is unpalatable remains as a foundation, a memory that sharpens the impact of the snack.

This is as true of masala entertainment as of masala cuisine. It is true of *Saathiya*. And it is particularly true of the different masala entertainments we associate with the story of divided twins—including the story of Shakespearean and Indian masalas I have told in the previous chapter. Not only are the mixed literary and dramatic lineages of *The Comedy of Errors* and *Angoor* different. The lived experiences of their creators and audiences, which surely have contributed something to the distinctive masala flavour of each, are different too. The experiences of pain vary as do the flavours of pleasure. I have mentioned how, in *The Comedy of Errors*, we might sense something of the traumatic dislocation of a young playwright who had left his hometown for a scary new city. But surely there is another, even more powerful painful experience that haunts Gulzar's conversations with *The Comedy of Errors*, an experience that also animates his lyrics for 'Mera Yaar Mila De'—an experience, like Shakespeare's own, that entailed being uprooted from the village of his birth. And that is the trauma of Partition.

Born around 1934 in the village of Dina in what is now Pakistani Punjab, the young Sampooran Singh Kalra witnessed first-hand the cataclysmic events of 1947. The trauma he experienced—which included separation from many members of his Sikh family—has never left him. A compilation of Gulzar's writings on Partition, *Footprints on Zero Line*, makes clear how the events of 1947 have profoundly affected his understandings of language, culture, politics, and desire. It is striking how much the themes of his writings on Partition haunt *Angoor* too. As Gulzar writes in the poem that provides the compilation with its title,

I am back at the Zero Line
My shadow whispers from behind me
When you give up this body
Come back to your home
Your birthplace, your motherland.

The poem's agonized sense of self-division across a border, its recognition of a shadow that lives in another land to which the narrator is intimately connected, evokes the darkness that haunts the otherwise sunny world of *Angoor*. Despite the film's comic pratfalls and hilarious misunderstandings, it also expresses a profound longing for reconciliation between what has been painfully separated. But the reconciliation we witness at the film's end is not a total union: the two Ashok Tilaks cannot become one Ashok. They remain more-than-one as they embrace, as do Hindu and Muslim, Hindi and Urdu.

I recently went to see Gulzar talk about his latest novel, tellingly titled *Two*. A profound meditation on the events of 1947, Gulzar wrote it first in an Urdu peppered with Punjabi and Saraiki, and then translated it into English himself. The cover blurb says: 'We were one people. One parted. Now we are two.' For all its epigrammatic simplicity, this blurb could also be a synopsis of *The Comedy of Errors* and *Angoor*. In one of *Two*'s most memorable episodes, Gulzar writes about two teacher friends from the same village, Karam Singhji and Fazlji, who suddenly and accidentally find themselves—much to their bewilderment and pain—on separate sides of the new border. They are told that they belong to separate countries, even as they protest in vain that they are the same. We might call their story 'A Tragedy of Errors'. We might also call it 'Do Angoor'. Or even 'Mera Yaar Mila De'. This tale, like so much of what Gulzar has written in his films, lyrics and poems without referring explicitly to Partition, recounts the experience of being uprooted, of negotiating a strange new location, of longing for a loved one from whom one has been divided but who remains integral to the more-than-oneness that is the self.

At the end of his talk, I asked Gulzar in my halting Hindi whether *Angoor* was, in its own way, a prequel *and* a sequel to his belated stories of Partition. Gulzar's reply, after a long pause: Haan (Yes). Ekdum (Absolutely). I am very happy you got that message from the film.

But of course yes. The winds of Partition blow like the Loo through Hindi cinema: so many films post-Independence—like *Angoor*—tell masala versions of Gulzar's story of *Two*, Two who are separated but remain emotionally tethered to each other, Two who are one but also always more-than-one in their languages, their loves, their inexhaustible longings. Shakespeare's plays express related longings in other keys, in other contexts. The trauma of Partition may belong to a different time and place from Shakespeare's. Yet his many plays about separation and the desires that cross social and geographical divisions uncannily anticipate the emotional topography of post-Partition northern India. Successfully working through trauma often entails not looking directly at its blinding source but, rather, tracing its shadows on the wall. Shakespeare's own versions of the tale of *Two* have offered north Indians, particularly Punjabis like Gulzar, some post-traumatic succour.

We might do well to remember that Partition is not a one-off event from 1947. It is happening still. The vivisection of India, as Gandhi put it, continues apace. At a time when Indian Muslims are told by Hindutva rabble-rousers that they are anti-nationals who should move to Pakistan; when Muslims and Dalits suspected of trading in and eating beef are lynched without comment or condemnation from the government; when dreams of a Ram Rajya prompt programmes of 'ghar wapsi' on the presumption that all non-Hindus—Muslims, Christians, Dalit converts to other religions—should come 'back' to a supposedly original and pure Hinduism; when the rapists of a little Muslim girl are supported by Hindu fundamentalist politicians waving Indian flags—we can see how Gulzar's childhood experiences of Partition continue to have a ghastly afterlife in this culturally composite subcontinent.

Yet the masala movie has repeatedly provided Indians—and their neighbours—with a language for busting Partition in all its forms, past and present. And so has Shakespeare. Let me tell one last story of a desi

Comedy of Errors. In 2012, I saw an extraordinary performance of the play in a small Delhi theatre by the Rah-e-Sabz company from Kabul. The script had been translated entirely into Dari, and its story adapted to an Afghan scenario (twins separated by a sandstorm, reunited in the bustling back streets of Kabul). The performance was extraordinary, less for its language (which I couldn't understand) or the staging (which was rudimentary) than for its mixed audience. This consisted almost equally of Anglophone Dilliwalas who were familiar with Shakespeare, and Afghan immigrants, both Dari and Pashto-speaking, who were not. What happened that evening can only be described as a hilarious clash, and then blend, of cultures. As the lights dimmed, many of the Anglophone theatregoers, including me, settled back in our seats for what we thought would be a night of theatre where we would sit quietly and anonymously in the dark. Yet what we got instead was an evening of raucously convivial interruption, courtesy of the Afghans in the audience. They wandered in and out of the performance, talking noisily with each other—and with us. One good-natured older man did the rounds of the rows while the actors performed, shaking the hands of confused and slightly irritated audience members, thanking us for coming, and asking us—in a heavily-accented mixture of broken Hindi and English—whether we were having a good time. Clearly many of us weren't. As one wag wryly cracked: 'Please, this isn't a shaadi, uncle.'

And of course it wasn't. Western conventions of theatre audience etiquette demand codes of restraint and polite anonymity that respect other audience members' personal space. Yet I think the welcoming uncle got something fundamentally right about the play. Because, in a sense, the occasion *was* a shaadi. After all, a shaadi is never just about two individuals. It is about the joyous coming together of a mixed group who forge new connections across what has been previously separate. And for these exiles from a shattered country, talking to the other members of the audience expressed a series of longed-for family connections: with the home from which they have been separated, with other Afghans from whom they have been divided by reason of ethnicity and language and politics, with Indians to whom they are 'foreign' yet with whom they share a Mughal cultural genealogy. Those connections across divisions—so uncannily close to the theme of *The Comedy of Errors*—differed sharply from the Western audience etiquette of polite individuals segregated from each other in the dark. The noisy Afghans helped create that night an audience who were no longer a collection of individuals but, rather, a masala association. Associating across divisions. Associating across partitions. Mera yaar mila de.

And associating across partitions is exactly what Shakespeare's plays have occasioned, in the golgappas of their mixed emotions, mixed styles, mixed themes, mixed lineages, and mixed audiences. No wonder Gulzar has been a lifelong student of Shakespeare. No wonder he has been able to write uncannily moving lyrics for masala Shakespeare films long after *Angoor,* as we will see in Act Four of this book. And no wonder Shakespeare continues to provide the makers of Hindi films and their audiences with new ways of lending voice to specifically subcontinental longings. Even now, in an age of increasing segregation inside and outside the mall–multiplex, masala Shakespeare gives voice to powerful longings for a different world. Trauma, personal and collective, is a crucial part of the masala genealogy of both Shakespeare and Hindi cinema. But what beautiful jugalbandis—what beautiful songs of Two—each sings as a result.

ACT TWO

jugalbandis

CHORUS

The firangi and the desi twins share a love for an old tale. Versions of it are known by different names in Europe and Asia. A classical Roman poet called it Pyramus et Thisbe; a Renaissance Italian composer called it Giulietta e Romeo; a medieval Persian poet called it Leili o Majnun; a medieval Punjabi poet called it Heer Ranjha. But what's in a name? The basic scenario remains the same in each instance. Two houses, alike in dignity but ancient in enmity, produce children who refuse their parents' strictures and the walls that divide them. They fall in love. They are star-crossed, so they must die. In some versions of the story, the lovers' deaths force the parents to recognize the folly of their enmity. It even leads to the recognition that those who believe themselves to be opposed—because they speak different languages or pray to different gods—can actually have a lot in common.

The firangi and the desi tell versions of this story over and over again. They tell it to their fellow country people; they tell it also to each other, often resorting to more than one language to do so. For both know that language as much as love cannot be contained by walls, at least not in a masala story. Masala walls are walls that don't hermetically seal what is inside them. Like the jaali of a jharoka, they mark a divide between inside and outside but also act like a membrane through which taazi hawa (fresh air) can blow. Taazi hawa, yet also mirchi hawa, the spiced air of masala mixture.

ACT TWO SCENE ONE

'Todenge Deewaar Hum'

One of my earliest memories of Shakespeare is a production of *A Midsummer Night's Dream* at the Mercury Theatre in Auckland in the 1970s. My recollection of the performance is fuzzy, probably because I understood little of what I was seeing and hearing. But I have a vivid memory of the actors resorting to the plummy, emotionless version of English that New Zealand television newsreaders had used at a time when 'Home News' was still news from Britain. The actor who played the country bumpkin-turned-ass Nick Bottom, David Weatherley, was a brilliant comic actor with a booming voice and a fine sense of timing; London-born and raised, his Home Counties accent represented an aspirational ideal for his fellow cast members. (It later landed him a bit part in the kid's TV series *Power Rangers: Operation Overdrive* as Spencer the Butler.) I learned to think of this accent, rather different from my own, as 'Shakespearean'.

In 1977, I was cast as Demetrius in a high-school production of *A Midsummer Night's Dream*, and I dutifully channelled my inner Prince Charles. Little did it matter that, by contorting my Kiwi mouth and larynx into outlandish shapes, I understood nothing of what I was saying and completely mutilated what Shakespeare had written. I wasn't alone. The poor actor playing the trickster fairy Puck, for example, repeatedly stumbled over her Queen Elizabeth-inspired accent and transmuted the play's last lines, 'Give me your hands if we be friends' (Epilogue, 15) into the threatening command, 'Give me your friends if we be hands.' I don't recall the audience obliging our hand-y Puck: the production certainly didn't gain us any friends. Still, we thought we were presenting Great Art as it should be presented.

Of course, we were also bored witless by the experience. Studying Shakespeare had already become for us the secular equivalent of Sunday school. Which is to say, it was a dreary requirement designed to instill in us neither love nor understanding but, rather, docile subjection.

Against the odds, I became a scholar of Shakespeare. I owe this development, again, to *A Midsummer Night's Dream*. In 1985, I was cast once more—this time in the bit role of Egeus—in a university production

41

of the play, directed by someone widely regarded at that point as the doyen of Auckland theatre. He had a brilliant eye for an onstage tableau, but he was something of a tyrant and had no compunction about being mean to his actors. He was all the more unanswerable because, despite coming from a small New Zealand city, he upbraided us in a carefully cultivated upper-class English accent—referring to himself royally as 'one'—which we were encouraged to emulate in our delivery of Shakespeare's lines.

Lurking beneath the director's would-be Englishness, however, was a typically 1970s Age-of-Aquarius-type Orientalism. Like many of Auckland's actors at that time, our director was a practitioner of an obscure Indonesian form of Islam led by a teacher who had renamed him, not Ali or Mohammed, but the arrestingly English 'Raymond'. Something of this Anglicized Orientalism also shaped Raymond's interpretation of *A Midsummer Night's Dream*. Taking his cue from a scene in which the fairy queen Titania reminisces about cavorting with her female attendant in the 'spiced Indian air' (2.1.124), he asked us, much to our dismay, to do the fairy world in pan-'Asian' style—casting a very talented actor of Indian origin as Puck, and dressing the fairies in Japanese kabuki robes—even as he insisted that we speak Shakespeare's lines in upper-class English accents.

On the basis of this experience, I was press-ganged—against my protests—into tutoring the undergraduate course on Shakespeare and Renaissance Tragedy at the University of Auckland. I hadn't thought of studying Shakespeare at all. But it was an assignment that stuck. And not because I came into my classes with any great love for Shakespeare. My theatrical experience of *A Midsummer Night's Dream* had, if anything, made me a doubter. My partnership with Shakespeare was, rather, an arranged marriage that slowly led first to an appreciation, and then to love.

In 1987, I moved to the United Kingdom to do my doctoral studies, in which Shakespeare figured prominently. At the time I thought I was returning to the wellspring not only of Shakespeare's creative intelligence but also my own: when growing up in New Zealand, the vast majority of my cultural reference points—the novels I read, the plays I saw, the television shows I loved, the music I listened to—were English. In retrospect, my desire to connect with English culture was the legacy not just of growing up in a former British colony. It was also a way of plastering over cracks in my sense of self. I am the child of a mixed marriage—my father is a New Zealander with Norman–Irish and

Huguenot Quaker roots, and my mother, born in Poland to Austrian Jewish parents, grew up in Russia, Uzbekistan and Israel. I had always felt slightly foreign in all the communities that I could lay claim to: I wasn't Kiwi enough in the schoolyard, and I wasn't Jewish enough for the Ichud Habonim youth group I belonged to. Englishness became my aspirational horizon. And so, as my plane descended into Heathrow and I saw the green farmlands below me, I muttered to myself, quoting the title of the D. H. Lawrence book: *England, My England*.

That fantasy didn't last long. During my three years in the UK, I felt deeply alienated. Too often I found my supposed difference, and my Kiwi accent in particular, remarked upon by English people keen to put me in my place. I felt even more foreign than I had in my native New Zealand. Unsurprisingly, perhaps, my research ended up being about ideas of the foreign in Shakespeare's culture: not just foreign migrants like myself, or my parents, but also foreign words, foreign ideas, foreign bodies. And I began to see that Shakespeare's plays were riddled with foreign elements. *A Midsummer Night's Dream*, the play that had modelled Englishness for me, suddenly became very alien indeed: Shakespeare had patched his play from various sources, including a French romance about fairies who travel to India, a Greek novel based on a Persian tale about a man transformed into an ass, and a Latin poem about star-crossed lovers from Babylon.

This Shakespeare was not a promulgator of the pure but of the impure, the plural, the mixed. *A Midsummer Night's Dream* showcased this for me. The comic scenes in the woods bear the trace of tragedy. The tragic narrative of 'Pyramus and Thisbe' is the play's comic set piece. Lysander describes this play-within-a-play as 'tragical mirth' (5.1.57), and asks: 'hot ice and wondrous strange snow./ How shall we find the concord of this discord?' (5.1.59–60). But his question applies equally well to the play as a whole. *A Midsummer Night's Dream*'s committed blending of opposite genres seems to find embodiment most fully in Theseus himself. He is an action hero who spends the play waiting idly for his own marriage, a rationalist character from antique legend who does not believe in 'antique fables' (5.1.3), a protagonist of Athenian epic who presides over a comic plot that culminates with the performance of a tragedy turned into a lamentable farce.

The play's deep commitment to mixture has resonated with my sense of myself. But, since my first visit to India in 2001, it has also related to something else that I have come to find distinctively Indian about

A Midsummer Night's Dream—something more conducive to masala than any orientalist fantasy of fairies cavorting in the 'spiced Indian air'. And that is the play's treatment of walls. Walls in much of India, whether in the city or in the village, are not always the impermeable dividers that they are in the dreams of Donald Trump or the Wagah Border authorities. They are often thin membranes separating neighbouring families and communities by a matter of centimetres. As such they are easily breached. Sounds carry through them, leaks spill through them, even the smell of cooking can waft through them. Entities supposed to remain divided from each other—languages, stories, communities, lovers—mingle across walls in an overcrowded nation where many people live cheek by jowl.

'Wall' is also a character in the play-within-a-play of 'Pyramus and Thisbe'. This theatrical Wall, played by the feckless Tom Snout, has a 'chink' through which the lovers can communicate:

> ... I, one Snout by name, present a wall;
> And such a wall, as I would have you think,
> That had in it a crannied hole or chink,
> Through which the lovers, Pyramus and Thisby
> Did whisper often very secretly.
> This loam, this rough-cast and this stone doth show
> That I am that same wall; the truth is so:
> And this the cranny is, right and sinister,
> Through which the fearful lovers are to whisper. (5.1.155–63)

Wall may divide Pyramus and Thisbe, but in Indian fashion, Wall also allows a titillating contact between them through his 'chink'. Shakespeare draws a great deal of attention to the material properties of the chink. It isn't just the means by which the lovers can communicate; creating the chink onstage is clearly also an important piece of theatrical business.

How should the chink be staged? In all the productions of *A Midsummer Night's Dream* that I have seen, the actor playing Snout playing Wall has followed the stage direction we find in most editions of the play: '[WALL *holds up his fingers*]'. But this direction was added to the text only in the eighteenth century, more than 120 years after the play was first performed. Teaching *A Midsummer Night's Dream* in the United States during the 1990s, I became increasingly convinced that Snout isn't meant to perform the chink in the Wall with his fingers. Rather, he does so by forming a cranny with his parted legs, 'right and sinister' (5.1.162); 'sinister', after all, is Latin for 'left'. In other words, the chink or 'crannied hole' forms an inverted V between right and left leg, finding its apex in the actor's groin and backside. Staging the chink this way can make sense of Thisbe's remark that 'My cherry lips have often kiss'd thy stones,/ Thy stones with lime and hair knit up in thee' (5.1.188–9). It can also make sense of Theseus's response to Bottom's cursing (and presumably physical pounding) of Wall's 'stones' (5.1.179, 188)—'the wall, being sensible, methinks should curse again' (5.1.180–1). These are clearly bawdy double entendres.

When Bottom and Thisbe, crouched on either side of Snout, kiss his anal 'hole' (5.1.198) and punch his testicular 'stones', something extraordinary—something irreducibly masala—happens. It's not just that, in the play-within-a-play, we can simultaneously see *both* the antique upper-class Babylonian characters Pyramus and Thisbe speaking words of tragic love through a Wall *and* the contemporary English rustic actors Bottom and Flute comically mussing Snout's private parts. It's also that Wall, ostensibly a solid marker of division, has now been transformed into something different. Wall has now become an opportunity for congress between people from rival communities who cannot stay divided, despite the will of their patriarchs: 'the wall is down that parted their fathers', says Bottom (5.1.337–8). These words might remind Bollywood music fans of the rousing anthem from the Amitabh Bachchan/Sanjay Dutt/Akshaye Khanna-starrer *Deewaar* (2004), 'Todenge Deewaar Hum (We Will Break Down the Wall)'. That film is in many ways a bland patriotic thriller about rescuing Indian prisoners from Pakistan. But as its title song suggests, it is also about tearing down the wall between the two countries. South Asian audiences might hear in Bottom's 'the wall is down that parted their fathers' a reminder of that other wall, willed into existence by British colonial architects and desi political 'fathers'. And when Demetrius sarcastically calls Wall 'the wittiest partition that ever I heard discourse' (5.1.165–6), it might remind us even more bracingly of the historical trauma that divided India and Pakistan. In *A Midsummer Night's Dream*, partition may be part of the scenery—but it also cannot hold.

Even before I moved to India I had begun to recognize in *A Midsummer Night's Dream* what I hadn't seen while approaching it through a fog of Queen's English: its refusal of set genres, its relentless mixture of different poetic and prose styles, its committed yoking of opposites, its willingness to locate English country bumpkins in a classical Athens whose fairies, a combination of ancient Roman and French and Celtic folk spirits, also gallivant in the 'spiced air' of India. But after moving here I began to recognize too how *A Midsummer Night's Dream* both refuses *every* kind of partition, metaphorical as much as physical, and paradoxically needs all these partitions to exist in order to be able to break them down. I began to see how *A Midsummer Night's Dream* sings 'Todenge Deewaar Hum'.

I began, in short, to recognize Shakespeare's masala.

ACT TWO SCENE TWO

Masala Languages (*A Midsummer Night's Dream*)

In 2015, the Vishva Hindu Parishad (VHP) objected to the title of an about-to-be released masala movie, *Bajrangi Bhaijaan* (2015). The film, which went on to become a huge box-office smash, starred Salman Khan as a Hanuman bhakt from Haryana who crosses the border with Pakistan in order to return a mute girl, accidentally separated from her mother, to her home in Pakistan-occupied Kashmir. The film's title combined a Sanskrit-derived name for the Hindu monkey god Hanuman—'Bajrangi' comes from 'vajra', thunderbolt—with an Urdu term of endearment for a brother. According to the VHP, 'Bajrangi Bhaijaan' wasn't just a religiously offensive phrase. It was also a linguistic affront. Sanskrit and Urdu: how can they even be conjoined?

Yet *Bajrangi Bhaijaan*'s title reflects lived realities for the film's director, Kabir Khan. Born of a mixed marriage between a North Indian Muslim and a Telugu Hindu, Khan has spoken about acting the part of Hanuman as a child in a Ramleela performance. The Ramleela, or the play of Ram, comes in many folk variants. But its story is the same in each instance: based on the Ramayana, it presents the life of the god Ram, the abduction of his wife Sita by Ravan, and Ram's travels with Hanuman in search of her. Though a 'Hindu' story, the Ramleela play has traditionally been performed by Muslims as well as Hindus. Khan's personal memory of this tradition—a reminder of the long-standing syncretism of the subcontinent's religious observances—no doubt contributed to *Bajrangi Bhaijaan*'s Hanuman-goes-to-Pakistan tale and title. It equally serves as a reminder of how a folk drama can provide, in masala fashion, a meeting place for different communities. In this respect, the Ramleela play finds powerful counterparts in what Shakespeare wrote during the watershed year of 1595.

In 1595, Shakespeare's company staged a pair of new plays that represented a significant step forward in his evolution as a playwright: *A Midsummer Night's Dream* and *Romeo and Juliet*. What prompted this breakthrough? A contributing factor was an ancient Middle Eastern tale, retold by the poet Ovid in his epic Latin poem, the *Metamorphoses*. In Book 4 of his poem, Ovid briefly relates the tragic story of two young lovers, Pyramus and Thisbe, who come from rival clans. The tale clearly grabbed Shakespeare: it haunts both *A Midsummer Night's Dream* and *Romeo and Juliet*. Not only is a version of it staged in the last act of *A Midsummer Night's Dream*; it is also a cousin of the Romeo and Juliet story. But Ovid's tale of lovers from opposed communities also seems to have inspired Shakespeare to bring together several other, seemingly disparate, phenomena. In particular, he attempted a bold experiment in linguistic syncretism reminiscent of *Bajrangi Bhaijaan's* title. Both plays mix different forms of language in ways Shakespeare had not attempted before.

In the case of *A Midsummer Night's Dream*, this mixture comprises diverse forms of distinctively patterned rhythmic speech. Shakespeare used these forms to mark differences of class, community and even species. In this, *A Midsummer Night's Dream* echoes something about the Ramleela play or, more precisely, Kabir Khan's childhood performance of Hanuman. The two plays are already similar at the level of plot: they both tell stories of an otherworldly lord, the wife he doubts, a trickster non-human, and a forest populated by different kinds of beings. But it is in their use of rhythmic sound that the plays share something particularly profound. Both employ music extensively—or rather, both render the dialogues of their characters into diverse forms of music. And in performance, both also show how different forms of speech, which is to say diverse dialects and tongues, can collaborate to tell a masala tale of conjoined communities.

A masala tale requires masala language. But masala language also requires ears that can listen to its masala. It requires ears that can listen to the music of many notes sounding simultaneously and not feel horrified—as the VHP did at the sound of *Bajrangi Bhaijaan*—by that multiplicity. It requires ears that can hear, in the words of a musical metaphor from *A Midsummer Night's Dream*, 'the concord of this discord' (5.1.60), the music in what, to ears of a purer bent, might otherwise sound jarring.

◆

But nowadays we have forgotten how to listen to Shakespeare. And that is for two principal reasons.

First, we largely encounter Shakespeare's plays in print, and so we read them quietly, as if they were novels. This is as true in the West as it is in India. When I was teaching Shakespeare in the United States,

I used to joke that, if I were to receive $10 for every time I received a student paper that referred to 'Shakespeare's novel *Hamlet*', I would be a very rich man. But Shakespeare's plays were, of course, written primarily to be performed rather than read in silence. And as such, they were written to be heard. That is why we speak of an 'audience' for a play; and it is telling that in Shakespeare's day, people customarily said they went not to *see*, but to *hear* a play. Listening to the sound of its language was paramount.

Second, we modern English speakers tend to flatten out the rhythms of Shakespeare's language. When asked to read his lines out loud, we usually try to bend their strange terms and syntax into something that makes sense to us, focusing on their meaning rather than listening to their sounds. In the process, we forget that the music of Shakespeare's lines—in particular, their rhythm—also contributes greatly to their meanings. I am not referring here to those songs in his plays that have been set to music. *A Midsummer Night's Dream* features a song sung by fairies, and Nick Bottom sings to himself. But the play's musical flavour extends well beyond these sung interludes. Throughout *A Midsummer Night's Dream*, Shakespeare uses different types of musical rhythm to represent different sets of characters.

The upper-class characters of Athens—Theseus, Hermia, Lysander, Demetrius and Helena—speak in iambic pentameter. This is a term we all associate with Shakespeare, usually without knowing what it means. Indian high-school students routinely trot out 'iambic pentameter' as a mugged-up keyword for the Shakespeare question in their Board Exams. I always hear this last phrase as 'Bored Exams', and there can be few things more boring than rote memorization of meaningless keywords. But iambic pentameter is meaningless only if we disconnect it from the music of Shakespeare's language. An iambic pentameter is a line of verse that consists of five rhythmic 'feet', each made up of an unstressed followed by a stressed syllable. But perhaps 'feet' is not the most appropriate term. If iambic pentameter corresponds to a part of the body, then it is the heart, whose rhythm—'da-DHAK'—it mimics five times in each line. That is why, despite its seeming artificiality on the page, iambic pentameter can *sound* natural when spoken: its steady 'da-DHAK' beat keeps time with our hearts.

And the heart is also, conventionally, the seat of love. In *A Midsummer Night's Dream*, iambic pentameter is the musical rhythm of lovers. These lovers often say things that make them seem faintly ridiculous; but their pronouncements of love *sound* passionate and sincere, largely because of the energetic heartbeat of their iambic lines. Take, for instance, the four lines with which Theseus begins the play. I have capitalized the stressed syllables according to the disyllabic rhythm of 'da-DHAK':

NOW, FAIR/ Hip-POL/y-TA/, our NUP/tial HOUR
Draws ON/ a-PACE./ FOUR HAP/py DAYS/ bring IN
a- NO/ther MOON/—but O,/ me-THINKS,/ how SLOW
This OLD/ moon WANES!/ She LIN/gers MY/ deSIRES...
(1.1.1–4)

Apart from those first two stressed syllables ('NOW, FAIR') and two more in the next line ('FOUR HAP'), all of Theseus's speech is in consistent iambic pentameter. The repeated upswing of the rhythm makes him sound authoritative, as befits his status as Duke of Athens. It also makes him sound literally upbeat as he talks of his upcoming wedding to the Amazon princess Hippolyta. But the regular alternation of unstressed and stressed syllables additionally unleashes a pulsating throb of longing, a throb that we can hear in the obviously aroused Theseus's impatient remark about four days being too long a time to wait.

In the fairy world of the forest, by contrast, the trickster sprite Puck—the name evokes a Celtic word for the devil—speaks in a starkly different musical rhythm. Listen to his words as he complains about not being able to do the bidding of his master, Oberon the Fairy King, who has asked him to put magic potion in the eyes of Demetrius, one of the Athenian lovers:

THROUGH the/ FO-rest/ HAVE i/ GONE,
BUT a-/THEN-ian/ FOUND i/ NONE
ON whose/ EYES i/ MIGHT ap/PROVE
This /FLOW-er's/ FORCE in/ STIR-ring/ LOVE. (2.2.72–5)

The lines here are shorter—seven rather than ten syllables—and their feet reverse the pattern of the iambic da-DHAK, each starting (except for that last line) with a stressed syllable followed by an unstressed syllable. The effect of this reversal is a little eerie—Puck's lines sound like an incantation. The technical term for his unusual rhythm is trochaic tetrameter. Shakespeare uses it for supernatural characters: the Witches in *Macbeth* also speak in trochaic tetrameter, most famously in the line 'FAIR is/ FOUL and/ FOUL is/ FAIR' (1.1.12). This is the music of an otherworldly space outside of human civilization, such as a blasted heath in Scotland or an enchanted forest in Greece. Indeed, 'FO-rest' is itself a trochaic unit.

And finally, the lowly English-named artisans who perform 'Pyramus and Thisbe' tend to speak in disorganized prose. When prose tumbles out of the mouth of the clownish Nick Bottom, we can hear just how disorganized his thoughts are. Here he is trying to explain his strange experience in the forest, where he was given an ass's head and made the temporary paramour of Oberon's wife Titania, Queen of the Fairies:

> I have HAD a MOST RARE VIS-ion. I have HAD a DREAM,
> PAST the WIT of MAN to SAY what DREAM it WAS: MAN is
> BUT an ASS, if HE GO a-BOUT to ex-POUND this DREAM.
> Me-THOUGHT I WAS—there IS NO MAN can TELL WHAT.
> Me-THOUGHT I WAS—and me-THOUGHT I HAD—but
> MAN is but a PATCHED FOOL, if HE will OF-fer to SAY
> WHAT me-THOUGHT I HAD. The EYE of MAN hath not
> HEARD, the EAR of MAN hath not SEEN, man's HAND is not
> A-ble to TASTE, his TONGUE to con-CEIVE, nor his HEART
> to re-PORT, WHAT MY DREAM WAS. (4.1.199–207)

This speech, coming after scenes full of the love-stricken da-DHAK of iambic pentameter and the hypnotic trochaic tetrameter of the FO-rest, cannot help sounding chaotic. Bottom jumbles his senses—'the eye of man hath not heard, the ear of man hath not seen'—but we can also *hear* his cognitive chaos in the erratic rhythm of his language, which follows no discernible pattern. The closest we get to a pattern is the repeated consonant 'm' (five instances of 'man' and four of 'me-thought'), which hints at the bray of an ass.

Yet the noise of Bottom's prose does not simply provide an urban audience with an excuse to laugh at a foolish country bumpkin. It also provides a soundtrack to the confusion of the audience itself, confronted with inexplicable magical happenings that, as Bottom's stuttering dashes suggest, are impossible to represent according to normal structures of syntax and poetry. Indeed, the most profound remark of the play comes a few lines later: Bottom—again in prose—announces his plan to turn his inexplicable experience into a play that he will paradoxically call "'Bottom's Dream", because it hath no bottom' (4.1.208–9). Here prose is the language not just of clownish foolery but also of a power to think outside the box. This power is denied to upper-class Athenians whose hearts sound the da-DHAK of iambic pentameter or to fairies speaking incantations in the trochaic rhythms of the FO-rest. Prose is no less musical for its lack of regular rhythm. It can acquire the force of free jazz, drawing its audiences out of the predictable beats to which they are accustomed.

A Midsummer Night's Dream does more than contrast these different forms of music. The worlds they represent are not hermetically sealed; they mix as surely as Bottom's senses do. Bottom has congress with fairies; the fairies transform the lovers; the lovers watch Bottom and his fellows perform. And in the final scene's enactment of 'Pyramus and Thisbe'—the tale that unites lovers from opposed communities—we also hear the play's linguistic worlds mingle. At first the mingling seems farcical, as Bottom and his fellows botch the rhythms of poetry. Francis Flute, playing Thisbe, asks the corpse of Pyramus, acted by Bottom: 'a-SLEEP, my LOVE?/ What, DEAD, my DOVE?' (5.1.311–12). This couplet reduces the iambic heartbeat of love poetry to the rimshot of a comic pratfall. But as the scene unfolds, and the lovers watching the performance start to find themselves emotionally transported by it, we hear what might be described as a 'translation' in the literal Latin sense of that word—a movement across boundaries. So even as Bottom and Flute haltingly transition from prose to verse, the lovers switch from verse to prose to profess their amused appreciation for the village actors' play. This is not a synthesis, where opposing voices join as one. It is, rather, a multi-rhythmic jugalbandi that answers Theseus's musical question: 'How shall we find the concord of this discord?' (5.1.60). Musical concord does not do away with difference: it rather allows different notes and beats to resound together.

Between these different musical forms and their supposedly discordant lifeworlds, then, Shakespeare finds concord. Though *A Midsummer Night's Dream* is nominally set in classical Athens, what we see—or hear—is a masala mix of different dialects associated with diverse English communities: village and city, artisan and courtier, low and high. It is difficult to know what exactly prompted Shakespeare to attempt this khichdi of different dialects. Reading Ovid's tale of Pyramus and Thisbe certainly focused his attention on the possibility of people from different communities coming together. But his playhouse itself already represented that possibility. Those sitting in the balconies were mostly well-to-do types, many of whom read poetry and spoke a Latinate and French-filled dialect. And those in the pit included poor artisans and day-jobbers, some of them migrants to London who spoke a variety of regional village dialects more inflected by Anglo-Saxon and Scandinavian terms. It isn't that Theseus's iambic pentameter was identical to the language of Shakespeare's well-heeled audience members, or that Bottom's disorganized prose reproduced what a displaced Stratford prentice might speak. But, in its masala mix, the musical soundscape of *A Midsummer Night's Dream* held up an auditory mirror—though a distorted one—to the multiple, mingled dialects spoken by playgoers in Shakespeare's London.

◆

Indian reimaginings of *A Midsummer Night's Dream* have been consistently more attentive than their monolingual English counterparts to the social dimensions of Shakespeare's mingled musics. After all, Indian writers, directors and actors—like Shakespeare's audiences—have all grown up in ambient soundscapes that have bombarded them with many different languages and dialects. These soundscapes broadcast the noise of diverse lifeworlds that resemble those of *A Midsummer Night's Dream* and its first audiences: gaon and sheher (village and city), basti and haveli (slum and palace), jangal and khet (jungle and field), uttar and dakshin (north and south), paschim and purab (west and east). Yet, for all their differences, India's lifeworlds are repeatedly put into conversation with each other in our homes, streets, workplaces, dhabas, scooter-rickshaws, government offices, sports stadiums, schools, bazaars—and theatres. Out of such conversations emerges a politics of the more-than-one, a politics that requires constant movement and negotiation across linguistic difference.

Perhaps this is why *A Midsummer Night's Dream*'s Indian life has been primarily theatrical rather than cinematic. Post-Independence, Indian theatre has straddled the fault lines between indigenous and foreign, rural and urban forms of drama. It has placed folk performance traditions in proximity to dramatic forms imported from the West, as well as local bhasha dialects in proximity to English and 'official' Indian languages such as Hindi and Bengali. Indian adaptations of *A Midsummer Night's Dream* have likewise drawn on the diverse performance traditions of the subcontinent as well as the multilingual worlds of their audiences. The result has been more Ramleela than *Bajrangi Bhaijaan*—which is to say, more 'folk' than 'masala' entertainment. Yet, as we have seen with the career of Kabir Khan, the masala movie often contains echoes of desi theatrical traditions, just as these traditions embody versions of masala.

An arresting portrait of a now-lost masala theatre tradition is offered in Saikat Majumdar's 2015 novel *The Firebird*. And in Majumdar's telling, this tradition finds its most compelling expression in a production of *A Midsummer Night's Dream*. Set in Calcutta in the 1980s when the Bengali popular theatre had entered a phase of terminal decline, the novel's main character, Ori Basu, is a young boy whose mother, Garima, is an actress. Seeking theatrical work wherever she can find it, Garima performs in productions not just of foreign plays in Calcutta but also open-air folk jatra dramas in Bengali villages. This novel about a dying theatrical tradition comes to a climax with a literally deadly production of *A Midsummer Night's Dream*. The production is staged in a run-down Bengali-language playhouse whose ambience is cheap and seedy. The actors who play Bottom and the fairies smoke cigarettes backstage. They perform on a cantilevered stage, raised by hydraulic pistons, that is normally used by dancing girls. Its set is made of 'gaudy streamers and shining creepers'. And the seediness of the production is only deepened after the murder of Ori's cousin Shruti, mid-performance, by the psychotic scion of the family who owns the playhouse.

Majumdar's seedy *A Midsummer Night's Dream* murders not just a character but also languages. It kills Shakespeare's English by rendering the play in Bengali, but then kills the Bengali in which the play is performed by translating it back into English. Likewise, the novel describes a billboard advertising a production of a Bengali play called 'The Wishcar'—an English mistranslation of the play's Bengali title, which in turn mistranslates Tennessee Williams's *A Streetcar Named Desire*. Even the title of Majumdar's novel, *The Firebird*, is a mistranslation of the title of a Bengali play that mistranslates the French *L'Alouette* (The Lark), the title of Jean Anouilh's 1951 play about Joan of Arc. Each mistranslation murders its source language. Yet each also gives that source language an afterlife in a host tongue transformed by what it murderously mistranslates.

What all these multiple mistranslations suggest is not a one-way process of 'indigenizing' Western plays by replacing their English (or French) with Bengali. Rather, we witness a two-way conversation—often more fraught than friendly—that results in a masala of colonial and indigenous languages. *The Firebird* revels in the linguistic as well as generic impurity of Bengali popular theatre, which like Shakespeare's play is a meeting ground for many tongues. But Majumdar also recognizes something deadly about this impurity; it is a volatile mix, the product of colonial and class violence. Born of violence, it ends in violence too, when opportunist Communist party-workers burn down the playhouse in which *A Midsummer Night's Dream* has been performed.

Majumdar has told me that, when writing *The Firebird*, he was influenced by a production of a Bengali translation of *A Midsummer Night's Dream* that he saw in 1989, *Chaitali Raater Swapno*. The translation, by Utpal Dutt, had been commissioned in 1964 as part of the quater-centenary celebrations of Shakespeare's birth. That year Dutt's theatre company, the Little Theatre Group, mounted four productions of Shakespeare, including *Othello* in English, and three in Bengali— Jyotirindranath Tagore's translation of *Julius Caesar*, and Dutt's own translations of *Romeo and Juliet* and *A Midsummer Night's Dream*. At the time of its first performance, *Chaitali Raater Swapno* was roundly panned. What seems to have most provoked the ire of the reviewers was the production's set. The fairy scenes were performed behind a transparent cellophane wall, which struck many reviewers as cheap and tacky. Dutt imagined the fairies' world as a shadow dream world—a 'swapno'—to the world of Athens. But his 'cobwebs of cellophane', as one reviewer put it, also suggested the acoustic permeability of walls that supposedly divide different lifeworlds and languages.

In his 1972 book, *Shakespearer Samaj Chetana* (Shakespeare's Social Consciousness), Dutt insisted that Shakespeare's plays repeatedly dramatize the conflict between the old idyllic world of the forest and a new European capitalist world associated with the Mediterranean. And he saw this conflict as applying equally to Bengal. This is why *Chaitali Raater Swapno* didn't offer just one 'pure' form of Bengali. Even as it converted the iambic rhymed poetry of Shakespeare's Athenian lovers into Bengali free verse, it retained those characters' links to a specifically European history associated with cities: Thessaly and Sparta are referenced in Dutt's script as they are in Shakespeare's play. We might call this dialect Banglo-Saxon. By contrast, the forest world tongue is recognizably that of rural Bengal; instead of Shakespeare's wild thyme and violets, Dutt's fairy world is populated by swadesi shamas and koels.

Other Indian theatrical productions have used *A Midsummer Night's Dream* to give voice to the many languages of the subcontinent. The best-known example is the English director Tim Supple's *A Midsummer Night's Dream* (2007). Conceived by Supple in Pondicherry with a large team of collaborators, this was a daring multilingual production, weaving together English, Hindi, Bengali, Marathi, Malayalam, Tamil and Sinhalese. It also drew, with great effectiveness, on diverse Indian folk performance styles:

the acrobatic Marathi street-theatre of Bombay, the gestural techniques of Malayali kathakali, the nautanki of Hindi, the jatra of Bengal, the therukkuttu of Tamil Nadu. Supple's express aim, however, was less to think about India's linguistic and cultural pluralism or the legacy of colonialism than to retrieve the ritualistic dimension of drama. For him, modern English productions, in thrall to psychological realism, have lost sight of the archaic, magical ritualistic elements of *A Midsummer Night's Dream*. Indian folk performance conventions, in his view, are similarly immersed in ritual. The masala language of his production was therefore designed to defamiliarize what a modern English-speaking audience member, habituated to the mindset of realism, might make of the play's story and characters.

The Bombay actor-director Atul Kumar's recent 2016 adaptation, *Khwaab-Sa* (Dreamlike), was another imaginatively hybrid production in terms of its performance techniques and its language. *Khwaab-Sa* featured contemporary dance and dubstep trance music in the scenes involving the Athenian lovers, Hindustani classical music and thumris in the fairy scenes, and gibberish Hindi in the scenes featuring the village actors—a technique developed in Kumar's earlier collaborations with the actor–director Rajat Kapoor in a series of clown interpretations of Shakespeare. *Khwaab-Sa*—like Supple's production—was an exercise in masala aesthetics rather than the pointedly political masala of Dutt's *Chaitali Raater Swapno* or Majumdar's *The Firebird*. It was less interested in what its masala has to say about the social, linguistic and political dynamics of India than in offering an ingeniously curated playlist of different styles of music, sound, and movement. This is not surprising, perhaps, given that it was first commissioned to be performed in Taiwan. As a result, *Khwaab-Sa* tasted less like a thali for a mixed Indian audience than a desi-flavoured entrée into the growing market for 'global Shakespeare'.

By contrast, two notable productions have used indigenous performance forms and languages to think about mixtures and conflicts specific to India. Habib Tanvir's highly acclaimed 1993 production, *Kamdev ka Apna Basant Ritu ka Sapna* (The Love-God's Own Springtime Dream), was the culmination of his Naya Theatre company's decades-long engagement with folk performance styles and practitioners. Born in Raipur in what is now Chhattisgarh, Tanvir had worked in Bhopal from the late 1950s with performers from tribal village backgrounds. Though he initially trained them according to the cosmopolitan acting styles he had been taught in Delhi and Europe, he increasingly incorporated their native languages and performance traditions into his theatre. His best known work, *Charandas Chor* (1975), dramatized an old Rajasthani folk tale using the conventions of Chhattisgarhi nacha, a heavily stylized folk form rich in music and comedy. Yet Tanvir didn't seek simply to revive old folk forms. He also created a unique masala idiom by placing nacha and other rural performance styles in dialogue with the conventions of western theatre, including the epic drama of the Marxist German playwright Bertolt Brecht.

Kamdev ka Apna Basant Ritu ka Sapna was a brilliant exercise in this idiom. Tanvir had originally commissioned British actors to play the lovers and nobles. When he ran out of money, he replaced them with urbane Delhi actors who spoke official Hindi. By contrast, he cast tribal performers from Bastar as the troupe of village actors; they spoke in the Bastar Chhattisgarhi dialect. Indeed, Tanvir's production, both in conception and execution, was very much focused on the tribal performers. He created their roles through improvisations in which they employed their own language and conventions of dance and song. Performing on a bare stage, and with a minimum of props, their movements as much as their language marked an interruption of the world of the elite characters. Their use of Bastar Chhattisgarhi dialect underlined Tanvir's keen sensitivity to the different lifeworlds audible in the musics of different languages. He wrote in 1994 that 'a particular language is always encushioned in a particular culture. Metres differ from language to language; the music and rhythm inherent in metres differ accordingly.' Translating Shakespeare's verse into chaste Hindi verse and his prose into colloquial Bastar Chhattisgarhi prose, Tanvir recognized how the musical rhythms of each form of language correspond to different ways of being in the world. The tribal performers, like the 'pure' Bengali-speaking sprites of Dutt's forest, communicated in a language appreciative of nature. But this time the language of the forest was an 'impure' variant on a Hindi norm, critiquing it from the margins.

Chetan Datar's extraordinary 2004 Marathi adaptation of *A Midsummer Night's Dream, Jangal mein Mangal* (Fun in the Jungle), was also set in the forest. And like *Kamdev ka Apna Basant Ritu ka Sapna* it too derived from a folk performance tradition—in this case lavani, a Marathi form of theatre. Lavani is a dance-drama performed primarily by women wearing traditional nine-yard saris, accompanied by male backing dancers moving to quick-tempo music. Cross-dressing features often in its performances. These are often highly erotic and satirical in their content. And a lavani performance's language tends to be a coarse version of Marathi, using sexually provocative terms to mock authority.

Drawing on these conventions, *Jangal mein Mangal* involved an unusual twist on Shakespeare. It presented *A Midsummer Night's Dream* as a play-within-a-play performed by a travelling lavani company from which all the men have magically disappeared, apart from its cross-dressing performers. There is nobody to play the male roles until a troupe of women cross-dressers turn up to play the roles of Bottom, the village actors, and the male lovers. Together the two troupes mount a totally cross-gendered lavani performance, in which the forest becomes the space of crude Marathi-speaking 'fairies' who turn conventional understandings of sexuality and language upside down. The male actor playing Titania, primped up in jewellery and make-up as well as a nine-yard sari, redefined the expression 'fairy queen'. And the female actor playing Bottom acted—as a head-spinning play-within-the-play-within-the-play—all the lead parts from the legendary film *Mughal-e-Azam* (1960), a Hindustani story of love forbidden by parents and thwarted, with deadly consequences, by a wall.

As this suggests, Datar ingeniously referenced desi folk theatre and masala cinema history to reimagine *A Midsummer Night's Dream*. But he also found justification for his Indian-themed reimagining in Shakespeare's text. The female Bottom's renderings of *Mughal-e-Azam*'s lovers, the Mughal prince Salim and the naach girl Anarkali, responded to the original Bottom's wish to play both Pyramus and Thisbe. And the lavani-style cross-gendering of the actors found justification in Oberon's insistence that his battle with Titania has turned everything topsy-turvy. That topsy-turviness not only extended to the cross-gendering of the actors. It also reproduced some of the masala linguistic force of Habib Tanvir's adaptation, using the colloquial vernacular of a traditional folk form as a counterpoint to the chaste Sanskritized observances, in typical lavani style, that began the performance. In the process, like *Kamdev ka Apna Basant Ritu ka Sapna*, *Jangal mein Mangal* demonstrated how folk drama can be an unorthodox medium of masala language.

Or, as the old saying goes: there's nowt as queer as folk.

◆

Bollywood's treatment of language differs somewhat from the volatile masala tongues of these theatrical adaptations. It tends not to see language as a medium shot through with conflicts between different classes or communities. It isn't inclined to reflect on the impact of colonialism on local bhashas, inasmuch as its target audience is much broader than that of 'regional' cinemas in (say) Bengal, Punjab, Maharashtra, Karnataka, Kerala or Tamil Nadu. It rarely gives voice to anti-authoritarian critiques of official language. For although it receives international distribution and is increasingly bankrolled by foreign production companies, its objective is primarily one of nation-building—even as it projects as 'national' a largely northern language that is not spoken by a significant portion of India's population.

Yet masala language has been one of Bollywood's traditional hallmarks, and in a way that underscores a deep commitment to cross-community conversation. This is evident from the decades-long—though now largely vanished—practice of presenting a film's title in Devanagari, Nastaliq, and Roman scripts. As we have already seen in *Angoor*'s songs and dialogues, 'Hindi' cinema's language has traditionally been a blend of Hindi and Urdu, or what is often termed Hindustani. A masala film like *Jodhaa Akbar* even offers a mythic history of how this blend came into existence by having its title characters initially speak in distinct languages—a shuddh Hindi in the case of Jodhaa, and a heavily Persianized Urdu in the case of Akbar—that, as the romance between the pair blossoms, combine into a mixed Hindustani that the audience is encouraged to recognize as 'apni' language.

This happy yet singular conjunction is not the only form of masala language that can be found in Hindi cinema. Other films, driven less by the goal of mythic nation-building than by the commercial imperative to hold up an acoustic mirror to the many linguistic worlds of its mixed audiences, have produced rather different soundscapes. Given that theatre has been the primary medium for Indian attempts to think through the complexities of masala language, it is notable that a recent Bollywood adaptation of *A Midsummer Night's Dream* is immersed in a folk dramatic tradition—the Ramleela play with which I began this chapter. And its treatment of this play provides a foundation for a fascinating cinematic exploration of masala language that speaks, not one mixed Hindustani tongue, but many.

10ml Love (2010) is a Bombay-based reworking of *A Midsummer Night's Dream* written and directed by Sharat Katariya. In the absence of a forest, the film makes the streets of Bombay the stomping ground of its Oberon and Titania; this Oberon—a Muslim street apothecary named Ghalib who sells aphrodisiacs—is pathologically jealous of his wife Roshni, a mehndi-artist, and compulsively stalks her as she goes about her work. Meanwhile, the Athenian lovers have been transformed into Bombay yuppies. The spoilt Hermia character, Shweta, loves her meek Lysander, Peter; she wants to elope with him to avoid her arranged marriage with the film's shopaholic Demetrius, Neel, who is in turn best friends with, and secretly in love with, the Helena character, Mini. And the preparations for Shweta and Neel's shaadi—at which Roshni will apply mehndi under the paranoid gaze of the jealous Ghalib—also introduce us to a group of Bombay street actors, who in between rehearsing a Ramleela production are employed as waiters and attendants at the wedding.

10ml Love could not reproduce the iambs, trochees and prose of Shakespeare's play. But it foregrounded the sonic masala of *A Midsummer Night's Dream* in a way that no English-language stage or film production that I have seen has. One reviewer gushed that the film retains the play's 'mix of romance, mischief, lust and fantasy'. But this is arguably not the main mix of *10ml Love*—or of *A Midsummer Night's Dream*. Indeed, the most successful masala dimension of the film is precisely what has sounded most 'wrong' in the ears of its critics: its language or, rather, its languages.

A recurrent complaint of movie reviewers was that *10ml Love*'s script suffers from having been conceived in English and translated into Hindi, and that the lead actresses—Tara Sharma and Koel Purie—do not speak a pure Hindi. But this criticism very much misses the point. Sharma and Purie's characters, who correspond to Shakespeare's Hermia and Helena, speak a recognizably class-specific version of Hinglish, as do their male counterparts. Their Hinglish is an English-saturated language of new money. (Neel, buying a saree for a discounted rate, tells Mini, 'It's called bargaining, darling. Yeh lo, tumhare liye'). This mixed language jostles with other impure variants of Hindi. Shweta is from a Punjabi family who speak a Punjabi-themed version of Hinglish ('Canadian dollars mein kitne hue?'). And her lover Peter Pereira is a mechanic from a Goan family; despite his relatively poor status, he too speaks a Hindi liberally sprinkled with an English that the film associates with the liturgy of his Christian community.

In contrast to the lovers' Hinglish, other characters speak in distinctive dialects that are specific to different communities. The mother of the Muslim apothecary Ghalib speaks a Bhojpuri dialect thick with poetic Urdu. Describing the love potion that Ghalib hopes to administer to his supposedly wayward wife, Ghalib's mother calls it 'josh-e-jawaani'

(Urdu for 'the vigour of youth') and reassures him that 'Dava peete hi jise pehle dekhegi ussiki ho javegi woh' (Bhojpuri for 'After drinking the potion she will become his on whom she first sets eyes'). Meanwhile, the ragtag group of lower-class street-actors speak a very different Hindi, one that contains both more rustic terms and, in their rehearsal of lines for a religious Hindu play, more Sanskrit (no matter how much they butcher it).

By using these polyglot linguistic markers, the film simulates the masala quality of *A Midsummer Night's Dream*'s diverse musics. Yet the film's different linguistic communities—upper middle-class and lower-class, Hindu and Muslim, Mumbaikar and Bhojpuri, Goan Christian and Punjabi—somehow negotiate these differences. When Ghalib speaks with Peter—whom he addresses, in Muslim–Christian portmanteau fashion, as 'Peter Miyan'—the exchange swerves between English, Hindi, Urdu, and Arabic: 'nice meeting you'; 'woh zuroor waapas aaegi'; 'insha'allah'.

The film's language is thus every bit as mixed as its potion, which we are told is a medicine that has to be mixed with sharbat. In this, *10ml Love* mirrors Shakespeare's own understanding of 'mixture'. In his plays, most of the instances of the word refer to a potion, whether medicinal or poisonous: in *Hamlet*, one of the players refers to 'drugs fit' for a murder and invokes a 'mixture rank, of midnight weeds collected' (3.2.233, 235); in *Romeo and Juliet*, Juliet describes the contents of the potion the Friar has given her as a 'mixture' (4.3.20). The '10ml love' of the film's title—a love that comes in small doses, but collates, in masala fashion, contradictory elements—is likewise a mixture. As its title suggests, *10ml Love* uses its potion as a metaphor for love. And in the process the film suggests that nothing can work without mixtures. These mixtures trace the patterns of both language and desire, each of which refuse to be contained within single communities. Just as *A Midsummer Night's Dream* allows us to imagine desire between characters of different cultures, tongues, and even species—Greek and Amazon, fairy and human, fairy and ass—so, too, does *10ml Love* persistently couple lovers and their languages across boundaries that conventionally divide poor and rich, Christian and Hindu, Muslim and Hindu, human and animal, human and god. But this is no longer Shakespeare's fantastical dreamworld: it is the stuff of everyday Bombay reality.

For me, the most powerful instance of masala mixture in *10ml Love* is a scene that develops the subplot of the village actors in *A Midsummer Night's Dream*. In the opening sequence, the street actors rehearse for their production of a Ramleela play. For an Indian audience, there is more than meets the eye about the choice of Ramleela, the folk theatre adaptation of the Ramayana. The epic of Ram has become a flashpoint for religious fundamentalists who regard the poet Valmiki's Sanskrit text as Hindu scripture, constituting, along with the Mahabharata, the sacred Sanskrit Itihasa. But the fundamentalists' desire for a singular Sanskrit Ramayana must contend with the fact that, as the literary critic A. K. Ramanujan has pointed out in a well-known essay, the Ramayana and the story of Ram exist in many local variations—within different languages, different media, and even different religious communities.

In 2011 Hindu fundamentalist student activists succeeded in getting Ramanujan's essay excised from the Delhi University curriculum on the grounds that it hurts Hindu sentiment. What particularly offended the activists was Ramanujan's insistence that the Ramayana has many iterations. There is, for example, a Malay shadow-puppet version of the Ramayana, performed by a rural Muslim community, which concentrates more on the monkey-god Hanuman and Ravan than on Ram. And there have been more than 300 Urdu renditions of the Ramayana, most of them written by Muslims, in Awadh alone. For the activists, these versions also raised the scandal of linguistic masala in ways that anticipated the VHP's opposition to the title of *Bajrangi Bhaijaan.*

This attitude has also shaped recent Hindu fundamentalist responses to the Ramleela play. The Bollywood star Nawazuddin Siddiqui announced in 2016 that he would act the part of Marich in the annual Ramleela play performed in his home village of Budhana, near Muzaffarnagar in Uttar Pradesh. However, he withdrew from the production after objections were raised with the police by the local Shiv Sena district head, who claimed that 'Our objection is with his name as well as the person... We will not allow this. For over 50 years, no Muslim has been a part of the production. Why should this be allowed now?' As this shows, the actor's Muslim name—of Perso-Arabic origin—was a vital part of the objection to his participation in the Budhana Ramleela. (Siddiqui has gained a revenge of sorts; he will play Shiv Sena strongman Bal Thackeray in an upcoming movie.)

Yet the objection rewrote history. Muslim actors have often performed in the Ramleela play, and Muslim artisans have contributed to the fashioning of its costumes and stage properties. The language of many Ramleela productions, moreover, is not chaste, Sanskritized Hindi but, as Rakhshanda Jalil has pointed out, '[an] immaculate Hindustani interspersed with flowery Urdu verses'. Jalil writes powerfully of her mother watching such a Ramleela performance in Lucknow. She also discusses a stage play, by the great Urdu poet Ufuq, called the *Ram Natak*. Ufuq's play contains couplets such as the following: 'Ajodha ko maatam sara kar diya/ Bharat ko qadam se juda kar diya (And Ayodhya was plunged into mourning/ As Bharat was separated from [Ram's] feet).' Nowadays, at a time when Urdu has become increasingly pigeonholed as a 'Muslim' language, such a couplet can sound jarringly discordant. Yet out of this discord, Ufuq and his audiences heard concord. Jalil has recommended that Ufuq's *Ram Natak* be restaged as a Ramleela play; she adds of the Ramleela play tradition that, 'written by both Muslim poets and non-Muslims at a time when inclusion and pluralism was the norm rather than the exception, they need to be revived and re-read, not merely for their evocations of communal harmony and goodwill, but also because many contain some fine poetry.'

Sharat Katariya's adaptation of a Ramleela play to take the place of 'Pyramus and Thisbe' daringly gestures in this direction. The play is dropped into a film whose lifeworlds include Muslim and Christian as well as Hindu characters. Yet, apart from a few lines spoken during rehearsal by the street-actors in the film's opening scene, we never see the Ramleela play performed in *10ml Love*. But the film does allow us to see the Hanuman-actor—like Nick Bottom, a hybrid of human and animal—coupled, thanks to the mixed love potion, with the Muslim apothecary Ghalib's wife Roshni, the film's counterpart to Titania. In a fashion that recalls the Sanskrit–Urdu conjunction of *Bajrangi Bhaijaan* and Kabir Khan's childhood memory of performing as Hanuman, the film daringly mates Hindu and Muslim in its Ramleela spin-off, desacralizing its Sanskrit epic source story and encasing it in layers of reference to other, syncretic Indian poetic traditions.

Indeed, the name of the Oberon character, Ghalib, is that of the quintessential Urdu poet of desire. In a particularly haunting couplet, Mirza Ghalib has written eloquently about how desire can cross borders of community, culture, and religion:

Khuda ke waaste parda na kaabe se uthaa zaalim
Kaheen aisa na ho yahaan bhi wahi kaafir sanam nikle.

(For God's sake, don't lift the veil from the sacred stone
Lest it turn out that here too resides the same infidel lover.)

These lines could easily be recited in *10ml Love* by Ghalib the apothecary to his wife Roshni about the Ramleela actor playing Hanuman. But such an expression of trans-communal connection with the monkey-god wouldn't be a radical departure from Indian performance traditions, as the Awadhi Urdu versions of the Ramleela play, Kabir Khan's childhood performance as Hanuman, and Salman Khan's performance as the Hanuman bhakt who crosses over into Pakistan in *Bajrangi Bhaijaan* all suggest.

Yet the romantic mixing that affects the Ramleela play in *10ml Love* is more complex than meets the eye. It is worth pointing out that the religious identities of Roshni and the Hanuman actor, who is named Chand, are by no means clearly established. Both 'Roshni' and 'Chand' are trans-communal names, used by Hindus and Muslims alike. We simply assume that Roshni is Muslim by virtue of her marriage, and Chand Hindu by virtue of the play in which he performs. But it is quite possible for each to belong to the other community. They can flip their identities just as easily as the upper-class and lower-class characters flip their languages in the concluding scene of *A Midsummer Night's Dream*. Behind the 'parda' or veil of the name, at least in these two cases, it is impossible to tell what lies. Yet the pairing of Chand and Roshni, of Moon and Light, creates a concord out of this discord.

In *10ml Love*, then, we see how Bollywood's masala language chimes with the linguistic syncretism of *A Midsummer Night's Dream*. And it does so in a way that resonates with but also crucially departs from many Indian theatrical adaptations of the play. From Dutt's Bengali/English *Chaitali Raater Swapno* to Tanvir's Hindi/Bastar Chhattisghari *Kamdev ka Apna Basant Ritu ka Sapna* and Datar's Marathi/Sanskrit *Jangal mein Mangal*, Indian regional language adaptations of *A Midsummer Night's Dream* understand language to be riddled with conflicts that are the legacy of colonialism and class or communal conflict. *10ml Love* seeks not to probe the class dimension of language but, rather, to suggest ways in which communities often pitted against each other might converse. And that is why it imagines finding the concord out of seeming discord between languages. In doing so, it doesn't offer a mythological linguistic history of India in the manner of *Jodhaa Akbar*. But with its many mixed languages it presents a vision of a masala Bombay—and, by implication, a masala subcontinent.

That vision can happen in large part because *10ml Love* is itself representative of another transcultural and trans-lingual jodi: the long-running flirtation between Bollywood and Shakespeare. And this flirtation is now as much second nature to Indian audiences as the trans-communal coupling of Romeo and Juliet.

ACT TWO SCENE THREE

'Jhalla Wallah'

In 2011, I moved to India from the US, where I had worked for twenty-three years after completing my doctorate. By this point I had been learning Hindi for some time. But the Hindi I had been taught bore scant resemblance to any language that north Indian people actually speak. It was instead a shuddh textbook Hindi, systematically purged of all 'foreign' terms, especially English and Persian. My teacher, a genial immigrant from Uttar Pradesh who had been living in the US for thirty years, overloaded our vocabularies with lapsed Sanskrit words. As a result, I learned a 'Hindi' that nobody actually speaks.

The insufficiency of the Sanskritized Hindi I'd been taught was driven home to me one day shortly after I moved to India. I was in Delhi University's north campus, looking for its library. I stopped a passer-by and asked him, in the finest Hindi my teacher had taught me, 'Kripya, mere mitr, bataaiye: pustakalaya kahaan hai (please, my friend, tell: where is the library)?' He looked at me with puzzlement and said: 'Hain????' And then, enunciating slowly, he asked: 'Tum kahaan se aate ho (Where do you come from)?' I told him I was from New Zealand, and repeated the question. He looked at me with furrowed brow, and said, enlightenment dawning: 'Oh, matlab, liberry kahaan hai (Oh, meaning, where is the liberry)!' And then he landed his killer punch: 'Bahut buri Hindi bol rahe ho, jhalla! (You speak really bad Hindi, you crazy person!)' That day, chastened by my experience but also curious about such colourful words as 'jhalla', I began unlearning my teacher's Hindi. I tried instead to acquire the mixed Hindustani and Hinglish I clearly needed to function in Delhi.

A major contributor to my re-education has been Habib Faisal's masala film *Ishaqzaade* (2012), which I saw a few months after the pustakalaya affair. *Ishaqzaade* tells the story of a Hindu boy and Muslim girl from my Hindi teacher's home state, Uttar Pradesh. As part of his clan's ongoing rivalry with a Muslim political family, Parma (Arjun Kapoor) cynically seduces one of its female scions, Zoya (Parineeti Chopra). Yet, after revealing to her that he did so simply to humiliate her family, Parma truly falls for Zoya. The couple elope; but they are persecuted by their families and killed. The Shakespearean in me quickly noted that there was something of *Romeo and Juliet* about the film's story. There was no Mercutio, no Nurse, no Friar; but the tale of star-crossed love between members of warring clans who meet at a big family party was clearly Shakespearean.

What made me prick up my Shakespearean ears while watching *Ishaqzaade*, however, was an item number that we see early in the film, at the party where Parma and Zoya meet. It is easy to dismiss item numbers as insignificant diversions, especially when they feature—as this one did—a scantily clad naach girl dancing while men wolf whistle and catcall. But the number's title, 'Jhalla Wallah' (literally 'Crazy Type'), took me back to my conversation with the passer-by at Delhi University, and not just because it featured the word 'jhalla'. 'Jhalla Wallah''s lyrics, written by the immeasurably talented Kausar Munir, were a world away from the Hindi I had spoken when asking the whereabouts of the library.

Unlike the Sanskritized Hindi I had been taught, its language is playful, colourful, and deeply impure. Who can forget lines like 'Jiske jaane se bum phate! Atom bum! (The one at whose departure a bomb/ bum goes off! An atom bomb/bum!)', or 'Aashiqon mein jis ka title "Titanic" (The one whose title among lovers is "Titanic")!', or 'Jisko mohabbat ka teacher kehte rahe/ Woh phateechar ek lesson mein fail ho gaya (The one I kept calling the teacher of love/ That useless guy failed in just one lesson)!'. The lyrics of the song swerve from Hindi into English and Urdu as surely as did the language of the passer-by who directed me to the 'liberry' and called me 'jhalla'. And as I tried to make sense of those lyrics in the weeks and months after I first heard the song, it occurred to me: more than *Ishaqzaade*'s plot, the impure lyrics of 'Jhalla Wallah' are the most Shakespearean aspect of the film.

But how so?

I had long known that English in the sixteenth and seventeenth centuries was not yet a standardized language. It was rather a simmering polyglot stew out of which neologisms—new terms—were constantly bubbling. French hadn't been spoken by the aristocracy for over two centuries, but it still provided fertile ground for new English words. Latin had only recently been disestablished as the language of the Church, and its vocabulary continued to permeate high as well as everyday English. Old Germanic and Scandinavian terms were also part of the mix, as were some newer words that made their way, along with the foreign merchants and the fashionable items they brought, from Italy and other parts of the continent.

Shakespeare's audience also spoke many different dialects. Indeed, 'English' as we know it did not yet exist, at least not in any standardized form. The language of the northeast was much more Scandinavian than that of the Anglo–Norman south, where a greater number of French terms were to be found. Even Shakespeare's own Stratford dialect contained terms that were incomprehensible to some of his audience members—such as 'geck', meaning idiot, or 'pash', meaning to pound someone with sufficient violence as to draw blood. (These Stratford terms are the best evidence that the author of Shakespeare's plays was Shakespeare, and not some pretender like the Earl of Oxford.) It was partly to accommodate his audience's differing dialects that Shakespeare's plays coin so many new terms. Take a term like 'dauntless', whose first recorded use is in *Macbeth*. It bangs together a root term from French—'daunt', to fear—with a Germanic suffix, 'less'. How is this masala linguistic invention any different from the mixed language title of a Hindi film like *Jab We Met* (2007)?

Sixteenth-century 'English', in other words, was a committedly impure tongue, repeatedly moving across borders of language. But it took several years in India, and countless conversations like the one I had that day with the passer-by at Delhi University, to make me realize how those movements play out in real life. I slowly began to understand how swerving between languages is necessary if one is to live with the differences, and *in* the differences, of a truly multicultural society. And I slowly began to understand how, in a country where people habitually swerve between different tongues in their everyday speech, puns are not just a type of joke. They are like metro hub stations, where many lines from different localities intersect. If one speaks several languages at home or on the streets, one is much more likely to pun, as a word in one language will inevitably sound like a word with a totally different meaning in another.

The Indian penchant for multilingual punning has made me re-understand *Romeo and Juliet*, a play infested with puns. Take, for instance, the opening lines of Act 1. The play starts with a famous, tightly structured sonnet—'Two houses, both alike in dignity'—which provides the play with its prologue. But then Gregory and Sampson, a pair of street fighters from the Capulet clan, enter. They proceed to have the following rapid-fire exchange:

SAMPSON: Gregory, on my word, we'll not carry coals.
GREGORY: No, for then we should be colliers.
SAMPSON: I mean, if we be in choler, we'll draw.
GREGORY: Ay, while you live, draw your neck out of the collar.
(1.1.1–4)

Their banter might be easily dismissed—like an item number in a Hindi film—as peripheral to the main play, little more than a moment of throat-clearing at the beginning of the performance while the audience settles down. Yet the exchange also assumes an audience that, even if not fully attentive, is capable of enjoying wordplay. That means not just understanding the individual meanings of 'carry coals (put up with insults)', 'colliers (coal-bearers)', 'in choler (angry)', and 'the collar (the hangman's noose)'. It also means revelling in the punning thread that links them all. This thread is the product of English's intercourse with many other languages in the streets of London: the Germanic 'coal' (compare kohl in German) sounds like the French 'collier', the Latin 'choler', and the Italian 'collare'.

In the much more monolingual United States, my students were often dismayed by Sampson and Gregory's exchange. They found its wordplay exceedingly difficult to understand, both in terms of the meanings of the individual words and the intent behind the passage as a whole. When I pointed out to them Shakespeare's string of puns on coals/colliers/choler/collar, some would groan; others ventured that perhaps Shakespeare was showing off to his audience, because he was still a young and un-acclaimed playwright when he wrote *Romeo and Juliet*. In any case, they thought the exchange was inconsequential. Many American theatre directors seem to have agreed with my students: in the more than two decades that I lived in the US, I saw six different productions of the play, and I don't believe a single one retained the opening four lines.

But Gregory and Sampson's street-wise exchange is not just a virtuoso, stand-alone display of trans-lingual prowess, although it is partly that. Their exchange also connects, if only at a subliminal acoustic level, to the main theme of the play. Puns make connections between different entities that are normally divided from each other. In the hustle-bustle of Gregory and Sampson's street banter, German flirts with French, or Latin, or Italian, just as in later scenes a Montague flirts with a Capulet.

The exponents of purity do all they can to insure that it is preserved in speech as much as love. They set up institutions to police the boundaries of language and community and to bar all promiscuous interlopers. But their attempts are always bound to fail, as Gregory and Sampson's exchange makes clear. No matter how much the two young men themselves seek to defend Capulets against Montagues, they speak an impure language into which foreign terms have intruded, in a spirit of exuberant and sexy playfulness. In other words, Gregory and Sampson's puns prepare us for Romeo and Juliet's first meeting, when Romeo the Montague breaks into the Capulet masque wearing a mask. Romeo is a pun here: two identities in one. Could there be a better dramatic personification of how a pun functions?

Hindi film adaptations of *Romeo and Juliet* cannot faithfully translate Gregory and Sampson's exchange. But after I first heard 'Jhalla Wallah', I realized that Bollywood has musical resources at its disposal that come close to replicating the effect of Shakespeare's trans-lingual wordplay. This is very true of 'Jhalla Wallah'. The song appears in a Hindi film. But its lyrics are not straightforwardly 'Hindi'. As is often the case in item numbers, the lyrics are sprinkled with English—'atom', 'title', 'Titanic', 'jubilee', 'matinee', 'teacher', 'lesson', 'hero'. The words are arguably part of a lower-middle-class aspirational vocabulary, and much of the song's humour derives from the fact that they are deliberately misused amidst Hindi words such as 'bisphot' (explosion) that hint at a village dialect rather than a supposedly more sophisticated urban Hindi. Yet they are also accompanied by poetic words of Persian origin that are associated with Urdu: 'shaamat' (problem), 'aafat' (trouble), 'qayamat' (apocalypse), 'mohabbat' (love). This poeticism is underscored in the last line, with the reference to 'Majnu', a famous lover from Persian and Arab legend.

The song traverses different linguistic and social registers: English malapropisms, designed to affirm an urban audience's superior knowledge of it; village Hindi, designed to lend a dash of rustic authenticity; and poetic Urdu, designed to impress a rural as much as an urban audience. Reinforcing this unexpected mating of high and low, Eastern and Western is a thread of puns. The English word 'teacher' is punned with 'phateechar', slang Hindi for useless. 'Bum' is the singer's rustic mispronunciation of 'bomb', though the scatological meaning of the former is clearly hinted at too. And, after I had listened to the song for the umpteenth time, I even started to wonder if the subliminal suggestion of 'bum' lends an extra trans-lingual meaning to 'bisphot' or explosion, which had begun to sound to my ears like bees (twenty) farts. Perhaps that passer-by at

Delhi University was right: I am a jhalla.

As these puns make clear, the song is less in Hindi than Hinglish, a mixture of Hindi and English. But its Hinglish is equally Urdlish too. The words stray across borders, ending up in places where they are not meant to be, and romancing strangers from forbidden households. This is driven home by the last line and its climax of affection, which passes through four languages—from Hindi to English ('mera hero') to Urdu ('mera aashiq' or my lover) to Persian ('mera Majnu') and finally to a term common to Hindi and Urdu ('mera saiyaan' or my lover)—to declare the singer's love.

For six years now I have been singing 'Jhalla Wallah'. Virtually everyone I sing it to laughs in recognition. Kausar Munir's memorable lyrics serve as a reminder that puns aren't simply occasions to make us groan in annoyance. Just like Gregory and Sampson's exchange at the beginning of *Romeo and Juliet*, the song's multilingualism creates a soundscape in which audience members can subliminally anticipate and celebrate the resistance of love to social control. This soundscape is not in and of itself subversive. Indeed, the practice of swerving between languages is part of the daily lived reality of most Indians. But in the current climate of Hindu–Muslim tension and violence, the language of 'Jhalla Wallah' has a topsy-turvy power. Just as *Romeo and Juliet*'s earliest audiences must have registered a similar power in Gregory and Sampson's puns, 'Jhalla Wallah' invites us to take pleasure in its acoustic bisphot, its explosive resistance to linguistic and communal division.

ACT TWO SCENE FOUR

Masala Lovers (*Romeo and Juliet*)

In March 2017, following the Bharatiya Janata Party's victory in the Uttar Pradesh elections, the controversial right-wing Hindu monk Yogi Adityanath was appointed the state's chief minister. His appointment also shone a searchlight on Shakespeare. Within days, 'anti-Romeo' police squads—as promised during the BJP's campaign—were set up throughout the state. The Uttar Pradesh director general of police announced that the squads' mandate was to reclaim public spaces and make them safe for women. They were ordered to keep a watch on universities, markets, shopping malls, cinemas, and other public spaces where large numbers of young women gather and incidences of 'eve-teasing' by young men are likely. Despite the directive to protect women, some squads took to haranguing female members of 'suspicious' couples. Even a woman who had travelled with her brother to her university in Meerut was needled by the police. The anti-Romeo squads, in other words, had become just as interested in targeting wanton Juliets as they were in cracking down on dangerous Romeos.

Why this heightened attention to Juliets? In many cases, the anti-Romeo squads' interest clearly went beyond prurient obsession with young women who might be sexually active: they were on the lookout specifically for young women whose desires had taken them outside the orbit of their fathers' and brothers' authority. Driving this crackdown was not just a patriarchal imperative to possess and control women, however, but also a fear of what their objects of desire might be. Without police intervention, it was possible such a woman's desires might cross boundaries of caste and—even worse—religious community.

In response to widespread expressions of concern about what seemed to have become a campaign of moral policing that harassed rather than protected women, the chief minister ordered the squads instead to target lone boys suspected of malign sexual intent. After all, these were anti-Romeo, not anti-Juliet, squads. Yet the chief minister's supposedly 'pro-woman' directive did little to stem the phobia about young Hindu women's desires. Still firmly in the grip of that phobia, the chief minister's order simply shifted the agency for Hindu women's unsanctioned desires from wanton Juliets to predatory, seductive Romeos.

The vastness of India means that, for every generalization one makes about it with absolute certainty, one can state the opposite with equal conviction. Just take India's attitude to cross-communal mixture. On the one hand, one can say with some justification: there are few nations globally that have as comprehensively embraced the ideal of pluralism. On the other hand, one can state with equal accuracy: there are few nations globally that are as horrified by mixing and impurity. This second position is especially true with regard to love. Despite India's long history of cultural syncretism, it witnesses very few mixed marriages or what we might call instances of 'masala love'—love relations that join people from different communities, castes or religions. The anti-Romeo squads are symptomatic of a deep-seated phobia throughout Uttar Pradesh—throughout most of India—about the coming together of Romeos and Juliets from different backgrounds. Women have often been made to bear the brunt of this phobia. Whether through so-called 'honour killings' or, more surreptitiously, the denial of their agency in love, Indian women are repeatedly reduced to being mere receptacles of their community's purity. The horror about masala love shades into a horror about the desires of 'our' girls as much as about the predations of 'their' boys.

For all the horror that the thought of masala love evokes throughout India, there is paradoxically a long-standing sentimental fascination with it too. It is an obsessive preoccupation of Bollywood. From *Mughal-e-Azam* (1960) and *Devdas* (1955 and 2002) to *Qayamat Se Qayamat Tak* (1988) and *Ishaqzaade* (2012), popular Hindi cinema invests in, even as it kills, young lovers whose parents or communities are opposed to their romantic choices. What is it about the masala movie—a genre defined by an inclusiveness that would seem to demand happy endings—that, when it comes to masala love, it reverts to tragedy? How, in short, is the tale of masala love in Indian film the tale not just of *Romeo and Juliet* but also anti-Romeo and anti-Juliet? And how does Shakespeare's play tell both tales?

◆

One thing should be noted from the outset: Yogi Adityanath's understanding of 'Romeo' bears scant resemblance to Shakespeare's. The original Romeo is certainly interested in women—but he is not an 'eve-teaser' or predatory harasser.

When we first meet Romeo he is something of a ridiculous character, but that's because of his serious devotion to a lost cause. We see him brooding and sighing about a woman named Rosaline. He expresses his unrequited love under the influence of the medieval Italian poet Petrarch, whose sonnets were to young lovers in Shakespeare's time what Arijit Singh's Bollywood love songs are to their modern Indian counterparts. Petrarch spent his entire adult life loving a woman, Laura, who was unattainable first because of her higher class and later because she had (somewhat inconveniently) died. The Romeo of the play's first scenes follows suit, agonizing over a woman whom we never see and who never returns his love.

Petrarch's poetry had, by Shakespeare's time, become something of a cliché. His distinctive language, widely reproduced to the point of parody, imagined love as an exquisite suffering induced by separation from a beloved who embodies a divine perfection. To capture the emotional intensity of this love, Petrarch favoured paradoxes—love is a heaven and hell, it makes a day of night and a night of day, it finds death in life and life in death, it derives pleasure from pain. All of these paradoxes became formulas among Petrarch's many imitators throughout Europe—including Romeo, who describes his passion for the absent Rosaline in a flood of Petrarchan clichés:

> Why then, O brawling love, O loving hate,
> O anything of nothing first create;
> O heavy lightness, serious vanity,
> Misshapen chaos of well-seeming forms,
> Feather of lead, bright smoke, cold fire, sick health,
> Still-waking sleep that is not what it is! (1.1.169–74)

Like the sonnet form itself, which always involved fourteen lines of rhymed iambic pentameter culminating in a final couplet, these formulaic paradoxes express a second-order paradox: the Petrarchan lover, convinced of his passion's uniqueness, cannot help but speak a script that has been uttered by countless others. Mercutio, Romeo's kinsman and best friend, laughs at his derivativeness: 'Speak but one rhyme and I am satisfied./ Cry but "Ay me!" Pronounce but "love" and "dove".' (2.1.9–10)—lines that seem to glance back at Thisbe's unforgettably ridiculous 'Asleep, my love? What, dead, my dove?' in *A Midsummer Night's Dream*.

Still, Petrarch's sonnets retained an extraordinary power for Shakespeare and his audiences precisely because of their association of love with paradox. To grab his audience, Shakespeare begins his famous love tragedy with a sonnet, as if to signal to them the kind of paradoxical world they will be witnessing. This sonnet is not a love sonnet; it simply tells the audience about the characters (Two households both alike in dignity), the setting (in Verona we lay our scene), and what is going to happen (misadventures and death). But it takes from Petrarch the form of the paradox—of two opposed concepts yoked within one—and transforms it into a social phenomenon. As the sonnet tells us, we will witness 'a pair of star-crossed lovers' who come from 'two households' divided by an 'ancient grudge' (Prologue, 6, 1, 3). The union of scions from these two opposing households, the Montagues and the Capulets, is the cross-communal embodiment of the Petrarchan paradox.

The anti-Romeo squads are in the business of policing such paradox. According to their mandate, a girl involved with a boy from another community is logically unthinkable—or thinkable only as the most profound violation of patriarchal order, an assault by a predator against not just the girl but also the men whose property she is. Yet Shakespeare's paradox-embracing lovers are a world away from the predatory eve-teaser and female victim imagined by the anti-Romeo squads. Romeo's love presumes humble longing rather than arrogant entitlement. This is true of his passion for the never-seen Rosaline. And when he does eventually interact with a woman who is actually physically present, not only does he not harass her; significantly, she also reciprocates his love. That is because Juliet, like Romeo, has the soul—and desire—of a poet. Upon first meeting, she and Romeo speak together an entire love sonnet, elegantly completing each other's rhymes with their concluding couplet:

ROMEO:	If I profane with my unworthiest hand
	This holy shrine, the gentle sin is this:
	My lips, two blushing pilgrims, ready stand
	To smooth that rough touch with a tender kiss.
JULIET:	Good pilgrim, you do wrong your hand too much,
	Which mannerly devotion shows in this.
	For saints have hands that pilgrims' hands do touch,
	And palm to palm is holy palmers' kiss.
ROMEO:	Have not saints lips, and holy palmers too?
JULIET:	Ay, pilgrim, lips that they must use in prayer.
ROMEO:	O, then, dear saint, let lips do what hands do:
	They pray; grant thou, lest faith turn to despair.

JULIET: Saints do not move, though grant for prayers' sake.
ROMEO: Then move not, while my prayer's effect I take. (1.5.90-
            103)

This sonnet is riddled with Petrarchan paradox. The sacred is mixed
with the profane, and the spiritual with the erotic, as is indicated by the
images of lips and hands alternating between prayer and physical intimacy.
Note in particular Juliet's pun on 'palm to palm' and 'palmers', a term
for religious devotees. As in Sampson and Gregory's opening exchange,
her pun links entities that are supposedly different and even opposed. It
also makes her an agent rather than object of desire. When, at Juliet's
instigation, these 'palmers' join 'palms', we witness the conjunction not
just of the spiritual and the physical, but also of male Montague and
female Capulet in reciprocal love. A border has been thrillingly crossed.

That border crossing—Juliet's as much as Romeo's—entails not just a
masala love, a mingling of communities. It also revokes the substantiality
of those communities. In this, Romeo and Juliet's union is in the grip
of a death wish. Not in the sense of a will to murder—that is the
prerogative of Tybalt, Sampson and others who seek to kill men from
the opposite clan. Rather, Romeo and Juliet's death wish is embedded in
the nature of paradox itself: it kills the substantiality of concepts whose
coherence is sustained through opposition. As Juliet says of Romeo: 'my
only love sprung from my only hate!' (1.5.135). If prayers can mingle
with kisses, if Montagues can mingle with Capulets, if love can mingle
with hate, then the identity of prayers or Montagues or love as the
opposite of kisses or Capulets or hate is both asserted and destroyed. This
is a version of the paradoxical death-within-life that typifies Petrarchan
desire, where opposing identities are simultaneously invoked and annulled.

Juliet's famous 'what's in a name' speech beautifully illustrates this
aspect of paradox:

O Romeo, Romeo, wherefore art thou Romeo?
Deny thy father and refuse thy name,
Or, if thou wilt not, be but sworn my love,
And I'll no longer be a Capulet...
What's Montague? It is nor hand, nor foot,
Nor arm, nor face, nor any other part
Belonging to a man. O, be some other name!
What's in a name? That which we call a rose
By any other word would smell as sweet. (2.1.74–7, 81–5.35–8, 42–6)

Peering from her balcony into the darkness of the night, Juliet seeks to erase Capulet and Montague as meaningful identities. The paradox is that the nameless world she wishes for depends on the names she erases: when she says, 'Romeo, doff thy name' (2.1.89), she invokes 'Romeo' as the one who must not be named. A 'rose by any other word'—say, 'gul'—might indeed 'smell as sweet'. But the rose's supposedly disposable name remains inescapable in the world she inhabits, as is proved by the fact that the word 'rose' seems to have been suggested to Juliet by the sound of 'Romeo'. Indeed, as the Nurse later asks Romeo, 'Doth not rosemary and Romeo begin/ Both with a letter?' (2.3.189–90). Names matter. And, in this play as in most of India, names matter with lethally divisive consequences. Juliet un-'Romeos' Romeo on her balcony; yet the social order of Verona cannot allow that un-naming to stand. The lovers may erase their divided identities by night but, in the light of day, that division is reasserted. In the last gasp of the night they have spent together, Romeo and Juliet rename a crying lark a 'nightingale', a bird whose song joins lovers. With the break of dawn, however, the singing bird reacquires the name of 'lark', which 'divideth us' (3.5.2, 29, 30).

This swinging between the erasure of identities in the shadow of the night and their violent re-assertion in the light of day finds a counterpart in Friar Lawrence's speech about the flower from his garden. The flower, in which 'poison hath residence and medicine power' (2.2.24), suggests the promise and the danger of paradox. On the one hand, the simultaneously poisonous and medicinal flower allows us to think across and against conventional boundaries. But if we try to resolve a paradox by extracting one purely 'healthy' element from it at the expense of the other, what remains is pure poison. And that is exactly what happens as a result of Friar Lawrence's machinations. The Friar, a celibate older man of the cloth, sees himself as Romeo's spiritual adviser and counsels him strictly against his 'violent delights' (2.5.9). Even though he marries Romeo and Juliet to sanctify what he regards as an otherwise inadvisable liaison, he ends up unwittingly ensuring the lovers' deaths by trying to distill medicine from poison. He gives Juliet the 'medicinal' potion that allows her to simulate death and escape marriage to Paris; yet she simulates death so well that Romeo, upon seeing her in her tomb, kills himself. The Friar's attempt to administer medicine, then, only insures the deadly triumph of the toxin—the violent passions—he has supposedly discarded. It is hard not to conclude that religious meddling in matters of masala love is a path to disaster.

I don't know if Yogi Adityanath would recognize himself in Shakespeare's Friar Lawrence. But if he were to study *Romeo and Juliet* closely, then he would learn from the Friar that the natural world, like language and love, conjoins elements that we have been conditioned to see as incompatible and even logically impossible. These conjunctions are not just inevitable; they also cannot be distilled from each other without deadly consequences. Attempting to assert the purity of what lies on either side of the verbal boundaries dividing 'medicine' and 'poison', 'Montague' and 'Capulet', or 'love' and 'hate' is more deadly than the identity-dissolving death wish of Petrarchan paradox.

To Indian audiences accustomed to caste, religious community and the scandal of mixed marriage, Friar Lawrence's desire for pure, differentiated categories is familiar. Medicine is medicine and poison is poison, and never the twain should meet. But, paradoxically, the impure world of Petrarchan paradox—in which every supposedly pure identity bears the trace of its opposite—can seem eerily familiar to Indian audiences too. Numerous traditions of Indian thought favour paradox as a means to assert the emptiness of identities that the mind has been conditioned to view as substantial. Buddhism asks us to recognize the illusoriness of duality, of the division between 'I' and 'it', inasmuch as both are suffused by shunyata or non-being. Tantric and Vedantic Hindu philosophy similarly insist on the illusoriness of being, and use paradox to illustrate the concept of anutpada, the not-coming-into-being of identity. Indeed, for all these traditions, identity is maya, or illusion.

The paradoxes of Petrarch's sonnets resonate most powerfully, however, with Indian Sufi poetry and its understanding of love. Like Petrarch's sonnets, Sufi poetry elevates an often distant beloved to the status of the divine, mingling not only the profane and the sacred but also a host of supposedly opposed categories. God and human, male and female, night and day, drunkenness and sobriety: in Sufi love, these worldly oppositions turn into divine paradoxes, conveying a sense of movement across supposedly insurmountable borders. And this movement destroys the substantiality of the identities that the borders supposedly circumscribe. Every worldly thing becomes no-thing.

This Sufi vision of love was first articulated in the Diwan poetry of medieval Andalusian poets such as Ibn Al-Arabi. Interestingly, Al-Arabi and his peers wrote in and for a multicultural Spanish world whose everyday existence involved the crossing of borders: throughout Al-Andalus, Jews spoke Arabic, Muslims read Greek philosophy and

Christians studied Hebrew. As Al-Arabi memorably noted in his most famous love poem, 'My heart can take on/ any form:/ A meadow for gazelles,/ a cloister for monks,/ For the idols, sacred ground,/ Ka'ba for the circling pilgrim,/ the tables of the Torah.' Perhaps paradox comes more easily to those who live in multilingual, multi-religious societies in which otherwise opposed ideas and identities co-exist and even blur into each other. In any case, the distinctive features of Al-Arabi's poetry migrated across the multicultural Islamic world, passing from Hafez in Shiraz to Khusro in Delhi. And with each geographical migration, Sufi love poetry acquired more associations with movement across boundaries of thought and community. The seventeenth-century Indian mystic poet Sai'd Sarmad, for instance, wrote Sufi rubaiyat inspired by his male Hindu lover that spoke of Sarmad's origins as an Iranian Jew and his subsequent initiation into Sufism and yogic knowledge. Yet what Sarmad's poetry repeatedly celebrates is the nothingness of all identity—a nothingness that is the ecstatic outcome of his love's movement across borders of space, language, culture and religion. As he writes: 'I follow the Koran as much as I follow Torah and Talmud/ But I am neither a Jew nor a Christian nor a Muslim.'

The Sufi idea of love, a migrant to the Persianate world born in the vibrant multicultural Spain of Al-Andalus, also migrated into neighbouring Christian cultures. The songs of the medieval Provençal troubadours, in which the poet devoutly worships an unavailable beloved, were influenced by Andalusian Sufi poetry. And the troubadours in turn inspired the early Renaissance Italian love poets, including Petrarch. The language of love that Shakespeare inherited from Petrarch was shaped by many factors, but its genealogy can be traced back in no small part to Al-Arabi. The distinctive Sufi Diwan metaphors of the beloved as a rose or gul and the lover as a nightingale or bulbul find uncanny echoes in Juliet's 'rose by any other name' and 'the nightingale' that Romeo and Juliet think they hear when they spend their one night together. And, in the manner of Sai'd Sarmad in particular, Shakespeare imagines a mutual love that allows both lover and beloved a subversive movement that traverses and dissolves the boundaries of supposedly opposed clans. As such, *Romeo and Juliet* retains, in Christian guise, much of the Sufi vision of love as a form of paradox.

In that vision there is a will to death that courts tragedy. But that will also marks a deep resistance to communal identities. Can we speak, as did Petrarch's predecessor Dante, of a 'divine comedy'—a tragedy that, in the ultimate scheme of things, could paradoxically usher in a new, more just order? Isn't that what is promised by the 'glooming peace' (5.3.304) of the feuding clans coming together at the play's end? If a tragedy ushers in a course correction against injustice, if it models a utopian dissolution of communal identities and the violence that sustains them, can it be called a tragedy at all?

Romeo and Juliet is a divine comedy of cross-communal love. And that is because Romeo and Juliet are not just lovers. They are also, paradoxically, haters. They are haters who, having internalized the violence of their viciously warring clans, redirect that violence against the substantiality of all identity, including their own. Just think of Juliet's mad desire to 'kill' Romeo 'with much cherishing' (2.1.228), or her fantasy of dying and cutting Romeo 'in little stars' (3.2.22). These 'violent passions' draw on but also ultimately destroy the clan antagonism of the Montagues and Capulets—anti-Romeo-and-Juliet squads in the guise of households who cannot tolerate the idea that children should act upon these passions, especially if doing so leads to inter-communal romance.

It's hard not to see Uttar Pradesh's squads as emerging from a similarly polarized and intolerant society, even if their vision of Romeo as a sexual predator has distorted beyond recognition Shakespeare's Sufi-like Diwan and his love poetry of identity-dissolving paradox.

◆

How has this distortion happened? Predictably, Romeo's name has entered many Indian languages as a term for a young would-be lover. In Marathi, for instance, 'Romeo' is a synonym for the male object of a woman's affection. A website that offers a crash course in romantic Marathi lines includes 'tu maza romeo (you are my Romeo/darling)'; it also prescribes 'tu mazi juliet' for those who wish to answer in kind. So far so mutually Shakespearean. This is, in fact, a rare and perhaps isolated instance of the word 'Romeo' acknowledging the desire of an Indian woman. It is an equally rare instance of 'Juliet' becoming absorbed into an Indian language with respect to female desire: in India, the dominant understanding of who is allowed to have sexual desire tends to exclude women.

But for the most part, the Indian equation of 'Romeo' with 'lover' has come to mean something less mutual, let alone romantic. From the north to the south, his name has become a synonym for a swaggering street Casanova. The Indian Romeo's love is not lasting, nor does he care for the hearts he breaks. Yet his behaviour is tolerated more often than not as a harmless, 'boys-will-be-boys' expression of masculinity. We find this meaning of 'Romeo' in the titles of many recent Indian films that have little to do with Shakespeare's play. *Roadside Romeo* (2008), an animated Hindi film about street dogs, features Saif Ali Khan doing the voiceover for a bratty, smooth-talking hound whose theme song announces that 'Main hoon (I am) Romeo, loving lovin' mera kaam ([that's] my job)/ Main hoon Romeo, I got these girls in my arms'. This Romeo may be an animated dog, but the lyrics of his song typify the cocky masculinity that Indian cinema associates with the name. The Bengali film *Romeo* (2011) features heart-throb Dev as a Casanova whose theme tune is 'Lady Killer Romeo'. And in the Hindi comedy *Raghu Romeo* (2004), Vijay Raaz plays a waiter named Raghu who pretends to be a go-getting playboy. Raghu fails to a hilarious degree, but the 'Romeo' tacked to his name is of the Indian rather than the Shakespearean variety, suggesting a swaggering sexual entitlement.

Similarly, *R… Rajkumar* (2013) features Shahid Kapoor as a brawling ladies' man whose first name is Romeo, and who spends most of the film baring his bloodied buff pectorals and bulging biceps. Revealingly, Romeo Rajkumar was originally named Rambo Rajkumar; his name was changed only when the filmmakers realized 'Rambo' was under copyright. But, as Shakespeare's Juliet asks, 'what's in a name?' A Rambo by any other name would still smell as sweaty—and be as much of a goonda. What this film makes clear is that 'Rambo' and 'Romeo' are somewhat interchangeable types in Hindi cinema's imagination: look at the gangster Romeo Suraj of *Shortcut Romeo* (2013), a good-for-nothing charmer, played by Neil Nitin Mukesh, who sexually blackmails women and resorts to extreme violence on his path to individual success. The Romeo–Rambo composite cuts two ways: on the one hand, he is a threatening, anti-social figure who spells trouble; on the other, he is something of an aspirational ideal, a charismatic badass who represents the pinnacle of male entitlement. A world away, in other words, from Shakespeare's comparatively effete Romeo.

This Indianized Romeo–Rambo has seeped so deep into the popular imagination that he has become a mainstay of recent Hindi and regional language film adaptations of *Romeo and Juliet*. More often than not, these films present their 'Romeos' as macho, swaggering lady-killers. It is hard to pull off this transformation, given the mutuality of Romeo's and Juliet's love in Shakespeare's play. But it is achieved in part by creating film Juliets bowled over by aggressive Casanovas whose sexual brashness proves irresistible.

In the Bengali film *Romeo vs Juliet* (2015), for instance, the small-town Romeo character is a lady-killer who refuses marriage to a fat and dark village girl (a version, one supposes, of Rosaline) because he has become infatuated with a photo he has seen on Facebook of a fair, urban Juliet, the daughter of the richest Bengali family in London. This village Romeo somehow makes his way to London, stalks his Juliet—creepy—and she obligingly falls in love with him at first sight—creepier. Hindi adaptations also Rambo-ize their Romeos. In *Ishaqzaade* (2012), the Romeo character is an arrogant, manipulative goonda from a political family who abuses his Juliet verbally when he first meets her, seduces her, then dumps her as a form of macho revenge. They later reconcile because Juliet loves what a badass he is. *Issaq* (2013) presents its Romeo as a sand-mafia gangster Casanova whose cocked gun, as it were, is irresistible to ladies. And in *Goliyon Ki Rasleela Ram-Leela* (2013), Romeo is a muscled, tattooed lady-killer who drives through town topless on the back of a jeep as women gaze at him with undisguised longing; even his scratching the back of his head drives them into mass fits of fainting as they snap photos of him on their mobiles.

So, on the basis of these films, we might ask: shouldn't we cheer the anti-Romeo squads? If the Indian Romeo has lent justification to a toxic masculinity rooted in gangster-machismo and sexual conquest of women, shouldn't we celebrate a concerted campaign to curtail his entitlements? But we might do well to check our cheers, because the anti-Romeo story is considerably more complex. As we have seen, its supposedly pro-woman mission blurs into an irrational conviction of the scandal of inter-community romance. This conviction also troubles countless Indian film adaptations of *Romeo and Juliet*, from *Ek Duuje Ke Liye* (1981) and *Qayamat Se Qayamat Tak* to *Ishaqzaade* and *Arshinagar* (2015). All these films display a tension between the utopianism of masala love—a love that, unlike in Shakespeare, receives the stamp of parental or grandparental approval—and, anti-Romeo squad style, the compulsion to punish the lovers for their scandalous desires.

There has been another uniquely Indian twist on the conundrum of masala love: the happy-ending version of *Romeo and Juliet*. Here, patriarchal approval is enough to erase the scandal of mixed romance and avert the need to kill the lovers. Take, for example, *Bobby* (1973), the musical tear-jerker directed by Raj Kapoor, starring his son, Rishi, and Dimple Kapadia as teen lovers from different communities—he from a Hindu Nath family, she from a poor Goan Christian family. Many of the elements of *Romeo and Juliet* are retained: the lovers meet at a party, elope, face intense pressure from their families, and will themselves to suicide (by jumpting off a cliff). But in the end, they are each saved by the other's father in a sentimental display of cross-communal harmony. *Bobby*'s happy ending seems to have inspired a Telugu adaptation of *Romeo and Juliet, Akkada Ammayi Ikkada Abbayi* (1996). Less a reimagining of *Romeo and Juliet* than of *Qayamat Se Qayamat Tak, Akkada Ammayi Ikkada Abbayi* allows its Romeo and Juliet to live after the Montague character saves the Capulet character from drowning in an abyss and everyone realizes the need for inter-clan peace, love and understanding—in terms acceptable to the film's fathers.

Also insisting on a happy ending is the Punjabi smash hit *Jatt & Juliet* (2012). This film, which presents us with a simple lady-killer Sikh Romeo and a sophisticated Anglophone Juliet, is the biggest grossing Punjabi movie of all time. And it finishes happily with the title couple coming together—in Canada, of course, the happy utopia of many a Punjabi dream. But there is also another dream towards which the film gestures. Arguably the real story of longing here is far bigger than that of Jatt for Juliet in Vancouver: it is the longing of all the characters for an undivided Punjab. Although the titular characters are Sikhs from Indian Punjab, their Pakistani Muslim landlady adds an extra edge to the film's oft-repeated, rather wistful mantra—'when abroad, all Punjabis look out for all Punjabis'. There is a happy ending for the lead couple in India, but the landlady—who comes from Multan—has long disappeared from the film by then, a reminder that some happy endings are unthinkable in the wake of 1947.

As *Jatt & Juliet* suggests, Indian adaptations of *Romeo and Juliet* sometimes hint at a historical trauma that they do not address explicitly: Partition and its aftermath. A now lost Urdu version of *Romeo and Juliet* was released in 1947. Starring Nargis, it featured a song—'Dono Jahan Teri Mohabbat Mein Haar Ke (Two Worlds Lost in Your Love)'—with lyrics by the poet Faiz Ahmed Faiz. Neither film nor screenplay has survived. But it is hard not to see Faiz's song of two worlds, and the film's engagement with Shakespeare's tale of warring households, as oblique responses to the traumatic events of that year.

The hope, and impossibility, of romantic rapprochement between Hindu and Muslim has been a feature of several subsequent Indian film versions of *Romeo and Juliet*. *Ishaqzaade* and *Arshinagar*, for example, present us with cross-communal lovers. Given the poetic bent of Shakespeare's character, one might expect to see a shayari-reciting Muslim Romeo versed in Khusro, Mir and Ghalib. But in *Ishaqzaade* and *Arshinagar*—indeed, in virtually all Indian film adaptations of the play—Romeo is Hindu. On this score, *Ishaqzaade* marches in lockstep with Bollywood depictions of Hindu–Muslim romance—for example *Bombay*, *Veer Zara*, or *Bajirao Mastani*—which invariably present the male lover as Hindu and the female as Muslim. The scandal of masala love becomes semi-acceptable, again in patriarchal terms, if a Muslim Juliet falls for (and implicitly submits to) a macho Hindu Romeo. But the cinematic union of a Muslim Romeo and a Hindu Juliet is something that, for now, remains beyond the horizon of possibility in Indian popular cinema.

The only time we glimpse the possibility of such a union is in Aparna Sen's brilliant Bengali/Urdu adaptation of *Romeo and Juliet*, *Arshinagar* (2015). This film gives us, like *Ishaqzaade*, a Hindu Romeo, Ranajit Mitra and a Muslim Juliet, Julekha Khan. But it also imagines that Julekha's father and Ranajit's mother were once in love. The parents' failed romance unfolds in flashback, acted out on a set that is manifestly artificial. Distancing the parents' romance further from the realm of possibility is that it appears within a tale that is itself self-consciously presented as fictional: the tale of Ranajit and Julekha is told in rhyming couplets by a female puppeteer, making it a kahaani-within-a-film. 'Arshinagar' means town of mirrors, and its male Muslim/female Hindu romance is the inverted mirror image of Ranajit and Julekha's. Indeed, the 'other' is shown throughout *Arshinagar* to be a misrecognized inversion of oneself in the mirror. This is brilliantly enacted at the tragic conclusion amidst a communal riot when a man, indeterminately Hindu or Muslim, sees his reflection and runs screaming from it. And it is suggested again when first the Muslim Julekha, disguised as a Hindu man, is killed by Muslim rioters and then the Hindu Ranajit, disguised as a Muslim woman, is shot by Hindu rioters. But as the film's carefully spun layers of artifice suggest, a Muslim Romeo and a Hindu Juliet is a cinematic possibility that recedes into the realm of illusion, as if it can be glimpsed only in a hall of mirrors as a reflection of a reflection.

And that is because, while the Hindu Romeo has been embraced in film as a charismatic badass, the Muslim Romeo has been demonized by the Hindu right as a sinister threat. He, too, has been Rambo-ized, but in a way that evokes horror rather than aspiration. This much is evident in the canard of 'love jihad', the right-wing Hindu fantasy of Muslim men scheming to seduce Hindu women, convert them to Islam, and impregnate them with Muslim children. And clearly 'love jihad' is the spectre haunting the anti-Romeo squads. Just as recent attacks on 'anti-nationalists' have provided cover for the expression of Hindu antagonism against Muslims, so, too, does the discourse of the anti-Romeo, which targets the love jihadi without having to name him. In the three years before and during the 2017 election campaign in Uttar Pradesh, Yogi Adityanath repeatedly mentioned 'love jihad' as a major menace in the state. With the anti-Romeo squads, he has managed to fold an anti-Islamic canard into a secular discourse of female 'protection'.

◆

Adityanath has ingeniously deployed a seemingly community-neutral figure from Hindi cinema, the macho Romeo lady-killer, to covertly target Muslim men. A recent masala film adaptation of *Romeo and Juliet* uses this same figure, but in a way that radically destabilizes the grounds of communal antagonism. This film's Romeo, like his Shakespearean predecessor, has a willing collaborator in Juliet. And both embody a death wish—a will to dissolve identities maintained through violent opposition—that draws on the energies of masala cinema as much as Petrarchan paradox.

Goliyon Ki Rasleela Ram-Leela is a typical Sanjay Leela Bhansali film. His brand of masala is distinctive: operatic, over-the-top love stories acted out on colourful, highly artificial sets with spectacular song-and-dance item numbers. 'I need to make my Taj Mahals,' he has said about his films. His remark describes to a tee the grandeur of his cinematic vision, as well as his persistent fixation with desire—and death. And this fixation has, in Bhansali's most recent work, returned repeatedly to the theme of masala romance. Saffron groups such as the Karni Sena recently got violently agitated about Bhansali's film *Padmaavat* (2018) to the point of dispatching goondas to beat him up on the film's set. They may claim to have been offended by his allegedly inaccurate presentation of historical events in Rajasthan. But it is hard to escape the conclusion that what the Karni Sena really objected to was the on-screen depiction of inter-communal Hindu–Muslim romance: it was rumoured (incorrectly) that a sequence in the film imagined the Hindu Rajput Rani Padmavati in a sexual liaison with Alauddin Khilji, the Muslim sultan of Delhi. Hindu–Muslim romance is something Bhansali explores in his previous film, *Bajirao Mastani* (2015), using the same film couple who play Padmavati and Khilji—Deepika Padukone and Ranveer Singh. And this pair are also the Juliet and Romeo of *Goliyon Ki Rasleela Ram-Leela*.

Goliyon Ki Rasleela Ram-Leela is the first in Bhansali's sequence of Deepika–Ranveer films about masala romance. But unlike *Bajirao Mastani* it does not present Ranveer and Deepika as belonging to different religious communities. Ram and Leela are instead scions of two opposing clans, the Rajadis and the Saneras, in the fictional village of Ranjaar. Still, the film is pointedly set in Gujarat, Bhansali's ancestral state, and the Hindu–Muslim violence of Godhra in 2002 casts a long shadow over the film. Communal warfare breaks out at the slightest provocation in Ranjaar, whose only business seems to be guns. A goonda remarks that there are 'sarhad ke uss paar bhi dushman…aur yeh gali ke uss paar bhi dushman (enemies on the other side of the border, enemies on the other side of the street)'. The line resonates eerily with the prevailing Hindutva tendency of equating local Indian Muslims with Pakistanis or Bangladeshis. And the phrase 'sarhad ke uss paar' is often used to describe cross-border terrorism in Kashmir.

In this violent setting, it is not surprising that Ram Rajadi, the film's hero, has acquired all the qualities of the Indian Romeo. He is a cocksure swaggerer and lady-killer: in his own words, 'Meri mardangi ke baare mein aap gaon ki kisi bhi ladki se poochh sakte ho…report achhi milegi (You can ask any girl in this village about my manhood… you will get a good report)'. Yet Ram is a lover, not a fighter, and refuses to bear lethal arms. His first meeting with Leela starts with their pointing guns at each other—hers a real one, his a Holi water pistol. Their confrontation beautifully illustrates the play's Petrarchan paradox of love born from hate: as Ram later says, 'Ab dushmani nibhaayenge, pyaar se (Now we will be enemies, lovingly)'. But that water pistol is a paradox itself—both a representation of violence and a refusal of it. It is also a shaping metaphor for their love, which both revokes and abides by the logic of 'goliyan' or bullets. One of the film's songs tells us that 'goli ko bhi goli de de yeh toh kare aisa kaam, Ram Leela (they do things that deceive even the bullet, Ram and Leela)'. The line's power derives from the pun on 'goli (bullet)' and 'goli de (deceive, fool)'. Even as Ram and Leela refuse the 'goli', they are also defined by it. This indicates how attentive *Goliyon Ki Rasleela Ram-Leela* is to the logic of paradox that shapes the play. And this attention is most apparent in the film's songs, composed by Bhansali himself with lyrics by Siddarth and Garima.

Bhansali's music often embodies the principle of mixture. His compositions for *Bajirao Mastani* include a song, 'Aaj Ibaadat', that plays through the closing credits. It is a bravura exercise in musical as well as cultural and linguistic masala. The song contrapuntally blends a Vedic prayer mantra with a Sufi qawwali; the formal fusion of Hindu and Muslim music is matched by lyrics that blend Sanskrit and Urdu. 'Aaj Ibaadat' is a profound homage to Bajirao and Mastani's masala love. Given that the signature poetry of masala love in *Romeo and Juliet* is the sonnet, a form connected to music, it is not surprising that Bhansali devoted special care to *Goliyon Ki Rasleela Ram-Leela*'s songs. It is in these that the most 'Shakespearean' masala element of the film is to be found.

Following from 'Aaj Ibaadat' as much as the sonnets of *Romeo and Juliet*, the songs of *Goliyon Ki Rasleela Ram-Leela* are riddled with paradox. More precisely, they are riddled with what Urdu terms 'ihamgoi', wordplay, and, more colloquially, 'yamak'—a coverall term for puns, rhymes and assonance. The term is Turkic in origin, and was once used to describe auxiliary foreign slave troops. Like these troops, 'yamak' are armed migrants: their meanings, if not their locations, keep shifting. And as they shift they violently destroy boundaries and identities we have been conditioned to regard as sacrosanct.

The clearest instance of yamak in *Goliyon Ki Rasleela Ram-Leela* is the hook line of the item number 'Ram Chahe Leela'. Sung by Bhoomi Trivedi and filmed with Priyanka Chopra performing a cameo as a naach girl, the song features a rap that pays its respects, in Gujarati, to the region's labouring classes and their music. Into this highly localized soundscape enters a song which, despite its modern dance-rhythm drums, recalls both Gujarati folk music and a Hindu sloka. This musical mixture is matched by the semantic mixture of the lyrical hook's hypnotic yamak: 'Ram chahe Leela chahe Leela chahe Ram'. 'Chahe' in its first and third instances means 'desires'; in the second it means 'whether'. This yamak is a brilliant demonstration of masala love, not just in its invocation of cross-communal desire between a Rajadi and a Sanera, but also in how it teases more than one meaning out of the Hindi–Urdu word 'chahe'. The song reminds us that masala love cannot help but cross borders, semantically as much as communally and geographically. Desire here is not a fixed entity that can be contained within the bounds of social and linguistic order. It is, instead, yamak—playfully unstable, conjoining opposites and, in the process, destroying their absolute difference.

The subversive power of desire as yamak reverberates throughout the soundtrack of *Goliyon Ki Rasleela Ram-Leela*. We can hear the yamak of desire not just in the lyrics' puns but also in their witty rhymes, as in the song 'Ishqyaun Dhishqyaun'. 'Ishq' means 'love', whereas 'Dhishqyaun' is the sound made by speeding bullets. The song's refrain, 'ishq yeh tera mera ishqyaun ki dhishqyaun ki', can translate as both 'this love between us is in the midst of speeding bullets' and 'this love between us is made of speeding bullets'. Desire both confronts and takes the form of bullets, every bit as much as 'ishqyaun' both semantically confronts and is lexically contained within 'dhishqyaun'. (Think again of the 'goli'/'goli de' pun.) In other words, love has the capacity to resist violence but also to inflict it. Here the rhyming yamak acquires the force of the Petrarchan paradox. More specifically, it acquires the force of paradox in *Romeo and Juliet*, where love and hate, medicine and poison, life and death are made dangerously close and even synonymous.

The closeness of seeming opposites is emphasized by the yamak that yokes the names of the lovers in the title of the Ramleela play. A version of the play is performed on the streets of Ranjaar near the end of the film. This Ramleela is a stunning tragic foil to the Ramleela that features in *10ml Love*. The latter imagines the union of lovers from different communities. But in *Goliyon Ki Rasleela Ram-Leela* the play becomes the pretext for a wave of communal violence in which the entire Rajadi clan, including the actor playing Lord Ram, is wiped out. In the murder of the Ram actor, Bhansali points to the tragic irony of how a Ramleela play, supposedly dramatizing the victory of good over evil, ends up murdering its divine titular character as if he were the devilish Ravan.

Goliyon Ki Rasleela Ram-Leela depicts the closeness of opposites with an acuteness I have not seen in any other Indian version of *Romeo and Juliet*. What we name 'good' and 'evil' become questions rather than self-evident truths. This problem of naming supposedly opposed entities is apparent also in the film's sustained reflection on the 'what's in a name' conundrum, which it sticks with more doggedly than any other recent adaptation of Shakespeare's play. And it does so in the register of yamak. Ram says of Leela that 'name toh kamaal che, par surname bawaal che (her name is great, but her surname is a problem)'. Note the rhyming yamak here, in the mixed Hindi/Gujarati/English of the line. Note also the yamak on 'bawaal', which means not only 'problem' but also 'riot'. Names are problems that cannot be discarded, and they lead to violence. And so Ram and Leela fantasize about a world in which names no longer lead to death but, rather, names suffer death.

This idea is picked up in the stunning song most associated with *Goliyon Ki Rasleela Ram-Leela*. 'Laal Ishq', hauntingly sung by Arijit Singh, appears twice in the film: first, briefly, after Leela has had her wedding ring finger chopped off by her mother; and then in full, over the closing credits, after a deadly wave of communal violence has hit Ranjaar during Dussehra. Ram and Leela, who at the time of the violence have become the dons of their respective clan gangs, make a suicide pact, assuming that their deaths will be the only way to end the violence. But their joint suicide is also an erotic act: they shoot each other in the chests while clasped in a tight embrace. We then see them both tumbling backwards, in slow motion, into the pond below Leela's balcony. They are dying; but they are also smiling, as if erotically aroused. The song's melody simulates this fall as it descends at the end of its chorus of 'mera naam, tera naam'.

'Laal Ishq' fantasizes the destruction of the social order that defines Ram and Leela through their opposed surnames, and it renames them both as 'ishq' or love. But this love is not an uplifting union of two as one. Love instead falls, joyously, into nothingness, drawing on the negative Sufi philosophy that underlies so many ghazals. Here love itself is defined not positively but through yamak, in terms of negatives—blood ('laal') morphs punningly into remorse ('malaal'), just as defect ('aib') acoustically echoes enmity ('bair'). All attempts to lend a singularity of substance to desire, and to the identities that desire supposedly joins and divides, fail.

Yet, as the smiles of the falling lovers suggest, that failure is desire's victory. Call this Bhansali's divine comedy. We return here once more to paradox, the basis of masala love for Bhansali as much as Shakespeare. The two men's vision of masala love not only joins people from opposing communities. Like paradox, it both presumes and cancels the logic of opposition that lends coherence to those communities. In the process, masala love also affirms and revokes the identities sustained by that logic. And that is why *Romeo and Juliet* and *Goliyon Ki Rasleela Ram-Leela* celebrate their lovers' names in their titles yet also dream of getting rid of them. It is, of course, an impossible dream: as the two entertainments' titles make clear, only the names of the lovers, not the lovers themselves, will survive the carnage of feuding clans. But if both film and play sing a song of 'anti-Romeo', they do so not to foment communal violence. They sing it to show us the price we pay for insisting on the purity of names and the communities to which they supposedly belong.

This song of anti-Romeo, so different from Yogi Adityanath's, is at once deeply Shakespearean and deeply Indian. It recognizes that all identity is a performance: that all the world's a stage or, as the title of Bhansali's film would have it, a rasleela (cosmic play). And the rasleela is integral to a masala sensibility. The term evokes Krishna's dance of divine love with Radha and her sakhis, a love that compulsively crosses borders between supposedly opposed states—god and human, dark and fair, male and female, one and many, earnestness and playfulness. In the rasleela, nothing can settle into a state of singularity or purity; its giddy dance makes all its participants mingle with what they are not. And that is why the rasleela dances a naatak (play) that laughs at all assertions of identity. We might also say, punningly, that the rasleela dances naa tak, 'until the no'. It dances until we can see the 'no' of no-thingness that is mixed within any seemingly substantial thing.

ACT THREE

naataks

CHORUS

The firangi and the desi twins mix up lineages, languages, and loves. They also mix up costumes. Their extensive wardrobes brim with manly accoutrements, but both also wear women's clothing at the drop of a hat. Or the fall of a dupatta. As we watch the firangi and the desi dress up—now as men, now as women—we find ourselves in the grip of a doubt: what if the twins are actually women, playing men who sometimes dress up as women? And then, hard on the (high) heels of the first doubt, another: what if even this is an act—what if these women, pretending to be men dressed up as women, are really men? Where does play stop and reality begin? Or is all reality simply play or rasleela?

To the firangi as much as the desi, being man or woman, aadmi or aurat, is the stuff of masala. It is an act, a naatak, which allows them to be both masculine and feminine—to be more-than-one—at the same time. The twins dress up in the knowledge that all the world really is a stage—sari duniya ek manch hai. Or, as a firangi master of song wrote, imagining himself in the mind of a female character from the city of his childhood just before he and his bandmates took a famous trip to Rishikesh: 'And though she feels as if she's in a play, she is anyway.'

ACT THREE SCENE ONE

'Woh Ladki Hai Kahaan?'

In 1996, I directed a production of *The Taming of the Shrew* at the Kitchen Theatre in Ithaca, New York. The production featured a cast of student actors, all of them theatre majors at Ithaca College, where I was teaching at the time.

The impetus for the production was my experience teaching the play. *The Taming of the Shrew* is, to most modern students and teachers, distastefully regressive. It presents us with a strong, articulate woman who refuses to do what society asks of her; she resists her father, speaks out against male authority, and insists on her right to do as she pleases. But the play punishes her for her behaviour. Her father marries her off to a man who promises to 'tame' her; the tamer's strategy includes denying her food, clothes and sleep—basically, torturing her. By the play's end, the strong woman has been broken down to the point where she does everything her torturer asks of her, including giving a long speech on how women must submit fully to their husbands' wills.

How on earth does one teach such a play to young students? As a case-study in the horrors of patriarchal ideology? Or is it possible to read against the grain of *The Taming of the Shrew*, to find moments in it that question or destabilize its misogyny?

In the classroom, I found my attention repeatedly captured by two aspects of the play. First, *The Taming of the Shrew* is self-consciously a play; indeed, the play is really an extended play-within-a-play, performed by actors who have been hired by a lord to play a trick on a drunken tinker. The lord thinks it will be a great prank to convince the drunk that he isn't really a tinker at all, but a nobleman who has fallen into a frenzy and hallucinated that he is lower-class. As part of the attempt to persuade the tinker that he is in fact a nobleman, the lord presents him with a play—after all, noblemen customarily watch plays in their households. And that play is *The Taming of the Shrew*. Once my students understood that the play is framed in this way, they began to reread its concluding speech about the supremacy of husbands. To them it suddenly seemed less like the words of a tortured wife and more like an act performed as part of the prank on the tinker, scripted at the request of a lord.

The second striking aspect of the play also involves the framing story about the tinker. The lord's attempt to persuade him that he is a nobleman starts by presenting him with a wife. And this 'wife' is a page boy who plays the woman's part, dressing up and feigning feminine behaviour—including using an onion to induce tears over her 'husband''s hallucinations. As a result, the students found it hard not to see femininity in the play-within-a-play as performed rather than natural. For all the women's parts are played by male actors hired by the lord. The tears cried by 'women' in the play-within-the play became for my students signs, not of 'real' feminine grief, but of ingenious performance techniques.

These two aspects shaped the production I directed. Unlike any production of the play I had seen up to that time, we retained the framing story of the tinker and the lord. The tinker remained in view of the audience as *The Taming of the Shrew* was performed, sitting in the front row, commenting on the action, falling asleep, and—later—being dragged on stage to play a part in the final scene. The point was to make the play-within-a-play seem as fake and staged as possible. But we also added another innovation: the play-within-a-play was completely cross-gendered. The tinker's page-boy 'wife', Mike Baugh, resurfaced as the sister of the shrew; the shrew herself was played by a brilliant young man, Caesar Samayoa, who subsequently went on to perform in an acclaimed off-Broadway cross-gendered production of *Romeo and Juliet*. And the shrew's torturer husband as well as 'her' father were both played by women, Sasha Statmore and Erin Maguire. The point was to show how both femininity and masculinity are products not of biology but of performance.

It was initially a struggle to get the actors to play their opposite genders. It wasn't because their biology was an obstacle; rather, they found it hard to get outside the gender scripts they had learned as part of their social conditioning. Mike, a lovely but very tall and muscular man, had to be coached into holding his elbows close to his body rather than in the man-spreading akimbo position that American boys learn. And Sasha initially found it hard to walk like a man in order to make her Petruchio terrifying; she had an inclination, like many American women of a certain class, to hold her groin back and walk tentatively as if on eggshells. The problem seemed intractable until I came to rehearsal with a rolled up sock and asked Sasha to put it in her pants. With this new 'centre' of gravity, she was suddenly able to walk like a cocksure tamer.

The big challenge was how to play that last speech of wifely submission. Drawing on the resources of the play—its framing of the play-within-a-play, its self-conscious representation of gender as performance—we took a bold decision. We set the speech in a Karaoke bar. And the tortured wife performed her speech at a Karaoke open-mic. The musical track playing in the background was the patriarchal country-and-western classic 'Stand By Your Man', sung by Tammy Wynette. But the lyrics 'sung' by Caesar as the wife were the words of Shakespeare's speech, pre-recorded by Sasha, the actress playing her husband. In other words, Caesar lip-synched to another's words, forcing the audience to recognize the speech as not the shrew's own but a man's. Of course, because a woman had recorded that speech, the words of the 'husband'—in a higher octave than that of Caesar's real voice—sounded more 'feminine' than anything else the wife had said in the play. But 'her' femininity was encased now in too many layers of performance to sound anything other than artificial. And, as a result, the contents of 'her' speech were every bit as artificial.

So, where was the 'woman' who uttered that speech? Woh ladki thi kahaan (Where was that girl)?

The production not only showed how all gender is performance. It also modelled how theatre can effectively foreground the gulf between the content and the form of a story. At the level of content, *The Taming of the Shrew* is conservatively patriarchal, outrageously so. At the level of form, however, the play is potentially quite subversive. And that subversive form can allow an audience to re-read the conservative content. This makes for a more-than-oneness of meaning that derives from the multiplicity of theatre itself, where representation is always double. The body of the actor might tell a slightly different story from that told by the character s/he is playing.

Shakespeare uses this doubleness to extraordinary effect in *A Midsummer Night's Dream*, where Ovid's tale of 'Pyramus and Thisbe' is hilariously butchered by the lower-class actors. The tragedy of the tale is punctured by the actors' bad rhymes, irregular rhythms, and inappropriate language (remember the bawdy double entendres accompanying the performance of the Wall). But Shakespeare allows us to keep both tragic and comic perspectives in view. As Theseus says, the audience's game will be 'to take what they mistake' (5.1.90)—to act as if the actors' farcical idiocy is, in fact, high seriousness. This is the masala of theatrical representation, where we can see more than one thing at once depending on our perspective: in this case, tragic lovers (Pyramus and Thisbe), comic village idiots (Bottom and Flute) and, if we choose, the brilliant actors who play idiots playing tragic lovers. Or, in our production of *Shrew*, brilliant actors playing women playing men and men playing women.

Five years after that production, I visited Delhi and saw *Lagaan*. I quickly became something of an Aamir Khan buff. At the Chanakya Theatre in June, I saw the trailer for his next film, *Dil Chahta Hai* (2001), which was due to open later in the year. Determined to see it even after I had returned to the United States, I tracked down and watched a pirated video at the end of the year. And I was spellbound. Not by the content of the film, but by its form, and in a way that resonated with how my students and I had come to understand *The Taming of the Shrew*.

This was the first of a breed of 'young generation' films that celebrated values associated with economic liberalization—upper-class urban youth were presented as cool, freedom-loving consumers decked out in designer brands, hip haircuts and facial furniture, and highly westernized in their nightclub-oriented musical tastes. There was a strong sense of the passing of a generational baton: the great Urdu poet and lyricist Javed Akhtar, father of the film's young director, Farhan Akhtar, wrote the words for the film's signature song, 'Koi Kahe Kehta Rahe (Let People Say and Keep on Saying)'. Its chorus goes, 'hum hain naye, andaaz kyun ho purana (we are new, so why should our style be old)?'. But for all *Dil Chahta Hai*'s militant embrace of novelty, this was in some ways a very conservative film. Its idealization of yuppie consumer culture was nothing to get excited about.

Formally, however, *Dil Chahta Hai* was exhilarating. Extremely aware of itself as a film, it kept drawing viewers' attention to its artifice through references to a rich array of cinematic and theatrical conventions. The Shakespearean in me noted especially *Dil Chahta Hai*'s self-conscious Shakespeareanism. Three young men, deeply invested in each other, find their friendships tested because of their relations to women; two of the three are paired off in marriage at the film's end. This scenario is highly reminiscent of the story of *Much Ado About Nothing*, and of the friendships among Don Pedro, Benedick and Claudio that are put to the test as two of the three fall in love with women. At one point in *Dil Chahta Hai*, we even see a boat whose name, *Much Ado*, is prominently emblazoned on its hull. And Aamir Khan's character, like *Much Ado About Nothing*'s clown-cum-hero Benedick, has to be trained into marriage through theatre—in this case an opera production of *Troilus and Cressida*. The film's performative self-consciousness in moments like these leaves us realizing that the so-called new generation that has supposedly dispensed with old styles is still acting out parts that derive from classical scripts.

The most self-consciously performative scene in *Dil Chahta Hai* is a brilliant musical number called 'Woh Ladki Hai Kahaan (Where Is That Girl)?'. Saif Ali Khan's character goes to a cinema with a girl. And what do they watch? A number in which the two characters appear on screen dressed up first in the costumes of sixties' and seventies' fluffy romantic musical numbers (think Rajesh Khanna and Zeenat Aman) and then do an eighties-style dance on a Himalayan mountain top (think Anil Kapoor and Madhuri Dixit). At the level of content, the sequence illustrates the seeming disconnection between a new age and older styles of cinematic romance. But at the level of form, it does something else. It makes us aware that gender in the new age of economic liberalization is just as scripted through conventions of performance as it was in older times. Saif Ali Khan and his girlfriend have simply exchanged one set of cinematic protocols—clothes, body language, acting styles—for another. This is not liberation from tradition; it is an ongoing capitulation to image.

As a result, the song's title, 'Woh Ladki Hai Kahaan?', acquires a double meaning. On the one hand, it is about Saif Ali Khan's girlfriend: where is she? (And the song answers, she is right next to him—this is when they realize they are truly in love.) On the other hand, it is about the location of women in general. Where are women? How do we recognize them as women? The song's picturization shows how our ideas of gender are derived from images, put together on and off the screen. This also allows us to read the title of the film in two ways. On the one hand, *Dil Chahta Hai* (The Heart Desires) refers not just to the love theme of the film but also to the anthemic desire of a new liberal age—'dil chahta hai', Farhan Akhtar has mentioned, is slang for 'because I feel like it'. In other words, it expresses the free will of the individual. But what the heart desires is also shown to be anything but free; it is shaped and conditioned by image, including cinema. The object of that desire, unspecified in the title, might change over time and place. The basic structure of desire remains the same, however, immersed in conventions of performance, costume, and image.

Dil Chahta Hai's idealization of consumer life in an upper-class bubble was in many respects depressing. But it was also bracingly smart in terms of its multilayered cinematic self-consciousness. In this it was hardly breaking new ground. Hindi film, like *The Taming of the Shrew*, has a long tradition of presenting stories-within-stories. Director Zoya Akhtar (Farhan Akhtar's sister) uses the device in her film *Luck By Chance* (2009); it is there in other films like *Billu Barber* (2009), but also dates back to early Hindi films. The device has a long history in South Asian traditions of stories about storytelling, as Sheherazade and her modern Indian descendants—Salman Rushdie, Arundhati Roy—make clear. But the device also has a partly Shakespearean provenance, given the Parsi theatre's adaptations of dramas that feature plays-within-plays: *A Midsummer Night's Dream* has 'Pyramus and Thisbe', *Hamlet* has 'The Murder of Gonzago', and *The Taming of the Shrew* has 'The Taming of the Shrew'. This convention is also part of a masala sensibility. The more-than-oneness that we see at the level of content is accompanied by the more-than-oneness of form, engendered by the realization that the story we are watching is a performance within another performance.

My classroom and onstage experience with *The Taming of the Shrew* prepared me for this dimension of Hindi cinema. But it took an ongoing engagement with the masala movie to better understand the politics of the more-than-one opened up by Shakespeare's plays-within-plays. Indeed, it is perhaps no coincidence that the story of the drunken tinker and the lord that begins *The Taming of the Shrew* is remarkably close to one of Sheherazade's stories in *Alf Layla wa-Layla*. It is only fitting that Shakespeare's play should have an Asian twin. And like *Dil Chahta Hai*, Shakespeare's play, too, asks, 'Woh Ladki Hai Kahaan?' Or, rather, woh shrew hai kahaan?

ACT THREE SCENE TWO

Masala Stories-Within-Stories (*The Taming of the Shrew*)

No self-respecting masala dish can do without the onion. Its acrid aroma might provoke tears from the stoniest face. But fried with oil and spices, its taste is irresistible. The mixture commonly known as onion masala—a blend of onion, garlic, tomatoes and aromatic spices, usually ginger, cumin, turmeric, and chilli—is the base for most north Indian dishes, from palak paneer to chicken korma. In the south, onion mixed with semolina and potato is the sine qua non of the masala rava dosa. The taste of onion blended with other ingredients is what I love most about Indian food. I didn't care much for Hrithik Roshan's masala blockbuster *Kaho Naa... Pyaar Hai* (2000), whose title translates to 'Do Say It Is Love'. If only it had been called *Kaho Naa... Pyaaz Hai* (Do Say It Is Onion), I might have given it a second look.

There is something masala about the form of the onion too. It may look like a singular bulb. But it consists of layers within layers. This quality contributes greatly to the onion's distinctive taste. The harder outside shells trap the onion's flavour within its softer inner rings; that is why the onion has also served as an enduringly powerful metaphor for a tasty, multilayered tale. Many of the best works of literature—most famously, perhaps, the Arabo–Persian marvel that is *Alf Layla wa-Layla*, also known as *A Thousand and One Nights*—are onions that consist of many layers of narrative, of tales within tales. These layers can also induce in us powerful experiences of the more-than-one: they prod us to adopt multiple perspectives on what we see and hear.

Take the Mahabharata. Ugrasrava's epic is, onion-like, full of stories within stories; indeed, it has been claimed that the Mahabharata pioneered this narrative technique. The story of the Kurukshetra war is narrated by a character in Vyasa's story of 'Jaya', which in turn is told by a character in Vaisampanya's story of 'Bharata', which is related by a character in Ugrasrava's Mahabharata. In other words, the epic's account of the Kurukshetra war, which is regarded by some as unvarnished historical reality, is actually a tale within three sets of quotation marks. The effect of those quotation marks is complex. Each tale acquires an aura of reality by framing another tale; but the repeated shift to a new fiction also reminds the reader of the fictionality of the frame. The onion-like encasing of many fictions within fictions can also point to a higher reality. After all, Hindu philosophy has repeatedly seen the world as a 'rasleela', a cosmic play, in which all seemingly substantial entities are in fact 'maya' or illusion.

In this the Mahabharata resembles the Maya Mahal or Palace of Illusions, where the Pandavas reside in Indraprastha after their marriage to Draupadi. This palace is a magnificently beguiling habitation: it is there that the Pandavas' Kaurava rival Duryodhana, much to his rage, mistakes a glossy floor for a pond, and a pond for a solid surface. But the Maya Mahal is also a metaphor for the Mahabharata itself—a vast, labyrinthine structure whose contents are made entirely of illusions that we believe to be real.

One of these illusions is gender. At times the Mahabharata can seem unalloyedly patriarchal. The story of the great warrior Bhima's wife, the alien witch Hidimba, is a good case in point. At first Bhima is reluctant to wed Hidimba as he is suspicious of her magic and her appetite for human flesh. (Marrying someone who wants to eat you is usually not the smartest move.) Yet Hidimba swears her deep love for Bhima, and he agrees to marry her, realizing he can easily dominate her and use her magic against his enemies. The tale could be renamed 'The Taming of the Rakshasi': it shows how a macho man can transform a powerful witch into a submissive wife, and turn her rakshasi magic into an asset for his patriarchal community.

Yet to assume that Hidimba and her submission represents the true ideal of women is to repeat Duryodhana's error and to mistake illusion for real substance. Other tales layered within the Mahabharata offer different perspectives. The tale of Shikhandi, for example, shows how the destiny of a woman isn't always to be submissive. Born in a past life as Amba, and seeking vengeance against the indestructible Bhishma who has humiliated her, she performs penance to Shiva; he hears her and she is born in her next life as Shikhandini who, after further austerities in the forest, morphs into the male Shikhandi. In some versions of the epic she becomes a eunuch; in others, she remains a woman but is trained as a warrior. In each instance, though, Shikhandi-who-was-Amba ends up killing Bhishma. A woman can, with the gods' support, become a vanquisher of the most powerful man. This is an illustration of how the Mahabharata's masala layering works. Hidimba's submission is not the necessary lot of women: it is a fiction—a story displaced by another story that shows how fluid gender can be.

Shakespeare's *The Taming of the Shrew* does something similar. A comedy grossly conservative in terms of content becomes potentially subversive in form: its female 'shrew' is exposed as a ridiculous fiction, a man in drag performed by an actor whom we first meet in a framing tale of a drunken tinker. But, despite *The Taming of the Shrew*'s closeness to the onion masala storytelling device of the Mahabharata, most Indian adaptations have dispensed with its framing tale. As a result, they have not fully appreciated the Maya Mahal that is Shakespeare's play. How, like Duryodhana, have they mistaken its insubstantiality for solid substance? Because for them the 'shrew', post-Independence, has shed her quotation marks. She is no longer a story-within-a-story. Instead she has come to be seen as the real face of what is oppressive about feudalism, colonialism, and globalization—and of what needs to be tamed in them. She is a reminder, therefore, of patriarchy's enduring power to shape Indian fantasies of gender, and make us believe that these fantasies are indeed real.

◆

Romeo and Juliet has become synonymous with an entire Indian subgenre of sentimental masala romance based on cross-clan desire. By contrast, *The Taming of the Shrew* has inspired a popular subgenre of misogynist horror-cum-comedy masala in which a virtuous Indian man overcomes a dangerous, suspiciously foreign woman. This subgenre has replayed the story of Bharata's scion Bhima and his taming of the alien rakshasi.

The first Indian-language adaptation of a Shakespeare play to have been performed was a Gujarati version of *The Taming of the Shrew*. Staged in 1852 in Surat, the script of *Nathari Firangiz Thekani Avi* (A Bad Firangi Woman Brought to Sense) no longer survives. But it is highly likely that, as was the case with most Victorian English productions of *The Taming of the Shrew*, *Nathari Firangiz Thekani Avi* did not include the framing tale of the tinker that begins Shakespeare's play. The Gujarati title is revealing: the 'nathari', or disreputable low woman, is a 'firangi' or foreigner, a character detail probably designed to reassure local audiences that shrewish behaviour is the preserve of non-Indians. As we shall see, this distancing of the shrew—the insinuation that she is in some profound way not truly Indian—has become part of the DNA of desi versions of the play.

The Taming of the Shrew also appeared in the repertory of the Bombay Parsi theatre. Many of its earliest productions were in Gujarati, and it is quite possible that the *Shrew* first seen by Bombay audiences was *Nathari Firangiz Thekani Avi*. In the following decades, as the Parsi theatre increasingly turned to other local languages, Marathi versions of *The Taming of the Shrew* also became popular on the Bombay stage. Musical sangeet naatak adaptations of the play were mounted in the 1880s by the Balvant Company [*Sangita Chaudave Ratna* (Song of the Fourteenth Jewel, an expression that also translates as 'to give a beating')] and the Patnakar Company [*Karakasdaman* (Shrew Taming)]. But the most popular Marathi adaptation was a prose version, *Tratika* (Female Fiend), first staged in 1891 in Bombay. Written by the Pune English professor V. B. Kelkar and produced by the Ichalkaranjikar Natak Mandali, *Tratika* continued to be performed for over four decades, and not just in Bombay. Productions toured the country: a performance in Dharwad in Karnataka in 1908 prompted a Kannada translation, *Tratikanataka* (Female Fiend Play), by Honnapuramath. Another Kannada version, *Candimardananatakam* (Crushing a Violent Woman Play), written by Lakshmanarao in 1910, may also have been influenced by the Dharwad performance.

None of these early versions of *The Taming of the Shrew* seems to have reproduced the play's framing tale of the tinker. Instead they focused more on the taming than the framing of the shrew. And their unframed taming stories often involved an odd mix of fictionality and reality. The shrew was no longer a character in an obviously fictional play-within-a-play, and to that extent became more real. But 'she' was still presented as a comically unreal scandal through the device of the cross-gendered actor. In the first performances of *Tratika*, for example, the play's female parts were played by men: Balwantrao Jog and Govindrao Supekar, two of the Ichalkaranjikar Natak Mandali's lead actors, played the 'shrew' and her sister. Jog's cross-gendering of the 'tratika' or female fiend in a farcical drama would have been over the top. The spectre of the quarrelsome woman who speaks back to men was thus presented as an outlandish apparition. It needed to be exorcized by 'real' men, including the man performing the tratika. As this suggests, the cross-gendering of the unframed shrew doesn't seem to have undermined the plays' misogyny—if anything, it enhanced it.

The Taming of the Shrew has been less popular on the Indian stage in the years after Independence. During this period, though, the play has repeatedly inspired film-makers. From the 1950s to the 1990s, audiences throughout the country witnessed a flood of masala comedies that derived inspiration from the play. There is more than simple misogyny at work in these films. They also lend voice to a populist anti-feudal and anti-colonial politics. The *Taming of the Shrew* films often represent the shrew as a high-class rani and her tamer as a simple village man who seeks not only to reform her behaviour and grind her into submission, but also to re-educate her about the iniquities with which she is complicit. In short, the films translate Shakespeare's comedy into the distinctively Indian genre of the 'social'. This translation suggests a gendered post-colonial fantasy—of the downtrodden subaltern reclaiming his dignity by gaining power over the daughter or sister of those who had once ruled and oppressed him. And this oppressor class is variously understood as indigenous (feudal and zamindari), foreign (capitalist and westernised), or both.

One of the templates for these socials is the iconic Hindi film *Aan* (1952). One of the first Indian movies shot in technicolour, it received a worldwide release; in America it was screened as 'The Savage Princess'. The English title aligns its temperamentally 'savage' woman with a culturally 'savage' people. The Hindi 'Aan', by contrast, ties together the hubris of a high-maintenance woman and a hereditary ruling class. The tamer is an upright villager, played by Dilip Kumar. His beloved childhood friend is killed by a predatory raja; as revenge, he uses the same skills of manly domination that he has previously used to subdue a horse and tames the raja's proud and arrogant sister. In this bizarre equine-themed melodrama, a fantasy of overcoming social oppression rides bareback on a fantasy of patriarchal domination. And, although the raja is the representative of a vicious Indian feudal system, it is hard not to see his downfall as standing in also for the demise of the British Raj just four years earlier. The princess, in this fantasy, becomes a gendered version of recently independent India, adapting to a new, more supposedly just, master who is a swadesi man of the soil.

This fantasy has been recurrent in Hindi film, especially in movies with heroes named Raju. In *Mard* (1985), for example, Amitabh Bachchan's Raju—the blacksmith-raised son of an anti-British fighter, with 'mard' tattooed on his chest—tames Amrita Singh's Ruby, the arrogant, westernised high-class daughter of the snivelling British collaborator Harry. And then there is *Laadla* (1994), a remake of the Kannada hit *Anuraga Aralithu* (1986), in which a mill-worker activist, Raju (Anil Kapoor), fights and eventually weds Sheetal (Sridevi), the arrogant, selfish mill company manager. Sheetal realizes the error of her ways, becomes a model stay-at-home wife, and lives happily ever after with him.

But neither Bollywood nor any other regional Indian cinema can rival the southern movie industry for its persistent mining of *The Taming of the Shrew*. Those early Kannada translations left a large footprint. For Kannada, Telugu and Tamil film adaptations of the play repeatedly resort to the formula of the haughty rani—often a suspiciously westernised rich bitch—and her principled man-of-the-soil tamer. Among Kannada films alone, *Veera Kesari* (1963), for example, mixes elements of Shakespeare's play and *Aan* by presenting its shrew as a princess and its tamer as an upright soldier. *Bahaddur Gandu* (1976) presents a tamer who, like Dilip Kumar's character in *Aan*, is a virtuous villager; its shrew is again an egotistical princess. Another Kannada version of *The Taming of the Shrew*, *Nanjundi Kalyana* (1989), likewise uses the device of the decent village tamer subduing an arrogant 'princess'—in this case, a rich urban girl who speaks back to men and is uninterested in marriage. Here, shrewishness has become associated once again with westernization and a refusal of all that is good—and patriarchal—about traditional Indian village life.

In the preceding decades, a slightly different take on *The Taming of the Shrew*—the double-shrew masala film—also proved to be a draw in southern cinema. Yet it, too, *Aan*-style, extolled the virtues of the common labouring classes over the decadent rich. This take owed more to another Kannada movie, *Mane Thumbida Hennu* (1958). The film was remade four years later as the Telugu box-office smash, *Gundamma Katha* (1962). Drawing on *The Taming of the Shrew* as well as *Mane Thumbida Hennu*, *Gundamma Katha* features a rich widowed termagant, Gundamma, and her arrogant daughter, Saroja, who is wooed by Raja. Gundamma also has a stepdaughter, the selfless Lakshmi, whom she forces to work as a maid. Raja 'tames' Saroja partly by acting as a drunkard, coaxing his servants to humiliate her, and making her do 'honest' toil as a gardener. As a result, Saroja transforms into a hard-working and polite model wife. And miraculously, even Gundamma comes round too, recognizing that docile Lakshmi is indeed the ideal woman.

Gundamma Katha was remade the same year in Tamil as *Manithan Maravillai* (1962). The remake retained all the plot elements of *Gundamma Katha*, including the double shrew story. It may not have been the big hit that its Telugu inspiration was, but it seems to have opened the floodgates for a sequence of other Tamil movies based on *The Taming of the Shrew*. The first of these was *Arivaali* (1963), starring the Tamil superstar Sivaji Ganesan as the tamer, Aalavanthan. Its plot is more in the *Aan* mode. Aalavanthan is an activist who fights for the rights of poor, virtuous farmers in his village against the evil zamindar, Azhagu Singam. Meanwhile, another landlord is so desperate to marry off his arrogant, spoiled daughter Manorama that he announces he will pay one lakh rupees and sixty acres in dowry to whoever is willing to wed her. Aalavanthan agrees to marry Manorama, in the hope of donating her large dowry to the poor farmers of his village. After their wedding, he inflicts endless domestic miseries on her; she repents, becoming his trusted adviser in the fight against the zamindar. Aalavanthan eventually sets up a cooperative farm in the village, aided and abetted not just by Manorama but also by the zamindar, who, too, has given up his wicked ways.

Arivaali was directed by the playwright A. T. Krishnaswami. Ten years previously, Krishnaswami had written a popular Tamil stage adaptation of *The Taming of the Shrew*, *Oh! What A Girl!*; it may have inspired the Kannada film *Abba Aa Hudugi* (1959). Krishnaswami's play starred future Tamil Nadu Chief Minister Jayalalithaa's aunt and mother as the shrew and her sister. This wasn't to be Jayalalithaa's only association with the play. She later starred in *Pattikada Pattanama* (1972), another adaptation in the *Aan* mode. Like *Arivaali*, the film starred Sivaji Ganesan as a village tamer, Mookaiyan, who is highly respected by his fellow villagers. Jayalalithaa played Kalpana, an arrogant and foreign-educated city girl who visits Mookaiyan's village. They fall for each other and, after overcoming various obstacles, they marry. But after their wedding, their class and cultural differences lead to conflict; Mookaiyan becomes enraged and beats Kalpana after seeing her drinking and dancing with her westernized hippie friends. She leaves, filing for divorce. Eventually, due to some ingenious theatrical maneuvering on Mookaiyan's part, Kalpana realizes the error of her westernized ways and is tamed. The couple reconcile and Kalpana becomes—no surprise—a model Indian docile wife and 'amma'.

Jayalalithaa certainly rebelled against this patriarchal script in real life, refusing marriage and eventually becoming Chief Minister of Tamil Nadu. But no matter how much Jayalalithaa refused to be a subservient 'amma' and morphed politically into the much more powerful 'Amma', her future constituents—and moviegoers across the south—flocked to see films that preached the virtues of wifely submission. What is it about *The Taming of the Shrew* that has resonated so much in the south? And what is it about southern film-makers' otherwise progressive fantasy of common men overcoming the injustices of colonialism and feudalism that has repeatedly lent itself to such a regressively patriarchal spin?

The popularity of the fantasy doubtless has much to do with the unique political situation in the southern states post-Independence. The Madras Estates (Abolition and Conversion into Ryotwari) Act of 1948 was implemented by the government of the Madras Presidency to dismantle the zamindari system; most feudal jagirs in what is now Kerala, Tamil Nadu, Karnataka, and Andhra Pradesh—though there were some holdouts in the latter—were dissolved by 1951. This is in stark contrast to the north, where there was fierce resistance to Nehru's 1956 Zamindari Abolition Act in Bihar as well as parts of Uttar Pradesh and Madhya Pradesh. Despite the widespread utopian commitment in the south to rooting out feudal oppressors—a kind of internal decolonization that followed in the footsteps of the anti-colonial freedom movement—patriarchal rule was not subjected to the same scrutiny. What resistance patriarchy encountered was stigmatized as the baneful effect of capitalism and westernization, and therefore easily dismissed in misogynistic fashion as non-Indian. Indeed, these foreign forces were seen as having emasculated the Indian man, who needed to reassert himself as an empowered swadesi agent. In the Hindi belt, that masculine reassertion has increasingly taken place at the expense of Muslims who supposedly commit love jihad. In the south, by contrast, it has walked hand-in-hand with a populist masculine socialism. Little wonder that there has been a vogue in Tamil Nadu for naming sons after anti-capitalist strongmen like Stalin.

Given their socialist sensibility it is a little surprising that the southern *Taming of the Shrew* films pay no explicit attention to the play's framing tale. After all, this tale allows a poor tinker to become a lord and enjoy a fantasy of domination by watching the taming play. Yet it is arguable that, in their own way, the films incorporate the tinker's mix of class mobility and patriarchal swagger. For they, too, fantasize that a common man can rule the roost. When the aam aadmi Sivaji Ganesan tames a zamindar's arrogant daughter or a westernized well-to-do city girl, something of the social elevation of Shakespeare's tinker can be seen in his triumph. But by shunning *The Taming of the Shrew*'s use of a framing tale, the southern films have also avoided the masala layering of story within story and the multiple perspectives this generates. They have instead reconciled framing and taming stories, to deadly patriarchal effect.

◆

A stark contrast to the southern films' refusal of stories-within-stories is offered by the Bollywood film *Isi Life Mein* (2010). It is the one Indian cinematic adaptation of *The Taming of the Shrew* that presents the story of the tamer and the shrew as a story within a story. And this onion-like technique has interesting consequences for how both the taming and the framing stories can be read by their audiences.

On the surface, *Isi Life Mein* is deeply conservative. And we would expect it to be so not just because of its taming plot but also because of the production house, Rajshri Productions, which made it. Rajshri films are notorious for their 'sanyukt parivaar' dramas—stories of undivided Hindu families who overcome all difficulties by remaining staunchly committed, in a spirit of high sentimentalism, to traditional religious and patriarchal virtues. And, in keeping with Rajshri Productions' brand image, *Isi Life Mein,* too, is an extended family production: the director, Vidhi Kasliwal, is the niece of Rajshri head Sooraj Barjatya. When interviewed in advance of *Isi Life Mein*'s release, Barjatya said he was confident that his niece had upheld the 'values' of his production house.

And that is precisely what we see in *Isi Life Mein.* A stern Rajasthani Hindu patriarch (Mohnish Behl) presides over a sanyukt parivaar that includes his imperious mother, homemaker wife, dutiful daughter, younger brother and sister-in-law. The patriarch, piously beholden to the counsel of his Swamiji, has enforced on his family his total distaste for everything foreign. He maintains that pizza and pasta are cultural contaminants; even western dress—forget western mores regarding drinking and sex—are completely unacceptable. So total is the patriarch's authority that his daughter Rajnandini (Sandeepa Dhar)—who, in the story-within-a-story, plays Shakespeare's shrew—is completely in thrall to him, to the point where she accepts, smilingly and uncomplainingly, his choice of a dowry-greedy family's son as her husband. This 'shrew' is in no need of taming: the sanyukt parivaar has already done a successful number on her. If *The Taming of the Shrew* preaches the danger of female resistance to patriarchal authority, *Isi Life Mein* seems to go one step further and show that female resistance is literally unthinkable. Its lead female character knows she has no choice but to be a docile daughter and wife. To be anything else would be scandalously non-Indian.

Yet there is much more than meets the eye in *Isi Life Mein.* The familiar spectre of the westernized woman haunts it. Made two decades after economic liberalization, however, the film does not share the swadesi parochialism of earlier Indian *Taming of the Shrew* adaptations. Instead it aspirationally embraces many of the trappings of western culture. This becomes apparent in *Isi Life Mein*'s opening dance-and-music item. 'Ramji Twenty-Four Seven', a song driven by a catchy western hip-hop beat, features Rajnandini and her friends dancing vigorously at a surreptitious rooftop pizza party, keeping vigilant watch so her father doesn't find out. Although she wears salwar-kameez and praises 'Ramji ka naam (Lord Ram's name)', she busts American-style dance moves; as we find out, her wardrobe also teems with western clothes.

It is no coincidence that Rajnandini is the state topper in English. And it is in English that dreams of deviation from her father's traditional Hindu-centric worldview are given voice. Appalled by his plan to marry her off as soon as she leaves school, Rajnandini's teacher informs her mother—in English—that the daughter can be successful like filmmaker Mira Nair and tennis-player Sania Mirza. The mother devises a deception in which the father is informed that Rajnandini will stay with her aunt in Bombay and take a cooking course to prepare her for future married life; in fact she will enroll for a course at an English-medium college of commerce and arts. Here, on the advice of the principal, Rajnandini ends up joining a dramatics society and playing the lead role in an adaptation of *The Taming of the Shrew*.

In sum, Rajnandini gravitates not just to the script of Shakespeare's play. She gravitates also to the westernized, independent behaviour identified with the figure of the 'shrew' in earlier generations of Indian *The Taming of the Shrew* movies. Yet *Isi Life Mein* seeks to exonerate rather than stigmatize this behaviour. It is instead the father who needs to be subdued by a tamer, through a mixture of coercion and strategic theatre, into accepting a new type of Indian woman who embraces some western values yet is never seen to question patriarchy. But here is the strange twist: Rajnandini also needs this tamer to initiate her fully in the virtues of this new westernized Indian femininity. *Isi Life Mein*, therefore, repeats one aspect of the earlier Indian *Taming of the Shrew* films: it presents the tamer as an educator who knows better than the 'shrew' what it means to be a good Indian woman and helps her achieve that goal.

This tamer is the leader of the dramatics society, Vivaan (Akshay Oberoi). Good-looking, English-speaking, and western in his fashion tastes, Vivaan is responsible for selecting *The Taming of the Shrew* as the society's entry in a national Shakespeare competition. At first his fellow student actors voice their doubts about the gender politics of the play.

Vivaan responds, in a mixture of Hinglish and English, that 'I think original ending bahut hi MCP-ish thi [was male chauvinist piggish]. Hum apna version karenge (We'll do our own version). No offence meant Mr Shakespeare sir, but we're going to do it our way!' And with the production renamed *The Taming of the Shrew Reborn*, in which the tamer does not subdue the shrew but instead teaches her 'to love herself and shine', Vivaan casts Rajnandini in the title role. This adaptation, which involves tacking on Broadway-style song-and-dance numbers to scenes from Shakespeare's play, ends up winning the national competition.

The film's performance of *The Taming of the Shrew Reborn* is formally closer to the conceit of Shakespeare's play: it nests the taming story as a tale within a tale. It presents this taming as artificial through the use of highly stylized mime, movement, and musical items. But it doesn't suggest, Mahabharata-style, that the shrew story is simply an illusion within its Maya Mahal. Instead, it uses that story as a parallel to its framing narrative, in which Rajnandini—like her onstage shrewish counterpart—is 'reborn' and learns to 'love herself and shine'. That rebirth is also shown to be less a discovery of a true self than a strategic performance. Post-liberalization, the film says, the conservative sanyukt parivaar can be made to accommodate westernization in a scenario where all the world's a stage.

Rajnandini's casting as the 'shrew' presents her with a serious challenge. To play the role, she has to learn how to shout—a skill that proves very difficult for the Indian daughter (even a daughter who loves pizza) of a Rajasthani sanyukt parivaar. Under Vivaan's tutelage, however, she comes into voice offstage as well as on. When she expresses timidity about departing from convention, he makes her eat with her left hand, defends divorce, endorses sex before marriage, supports gay couples, and tells her she needs to learn how to 'put up a fight'. To this end, he also renames her 'RJ' and gives her a western hair and wardrobe makeover—'happy new you!'—that receives sanction from Salman Khan, making a cameo as himself in a Being Human T-shirt. Flourishing under the tutelage of her male trainers, Rajnandini learns to play her new loud part well.

This 'happy new' RJ suggests how the title of the play she and Vivaan perform can be understood in two ways. In terms of its Shakespearean origin, it is '*The Taming of the Shrew*' *Reborn*; but in terms of its modern framing story, it is *The Taming of 'the Shrew Reborn*'. RJ has been, if not tamed, then trained to be a born-again 'shrew'—westernized, outspoken, prepared to fight. In other words, Vivaan has mansplained for Rajnandini how to be an empowered woman who can 'love herself and shine'. She later acknowledges as much, telling him 'you opened my mind'. But this 'opening' into a new reality is, like her theatrical training onstage, less about finding a truth than learning to play a part.

Vivaan's advice to Rajnandini during rehearsals becomes the film's repeated tagline: 'go into the character, solution mil jaaega (a solution will come)'. This applies off- as much as onstage. Rajnandini is disturbed by Vivaan's caustic words to his father, who wants him to leave university and become a chartered accountant; echoing Vivaan's earlier advice to her, she tells him he should speak more calmly to his father; 'go into the character, solution mil jaaega'. On the one hand, her remark might seem to be the kind of conservative statement a patriarchally raised child would make: the father must be treated with respect. On the other, it also suggests the modus operandi of the matlabi individualist who, post-economic liberalization, seeks to carve out a path for herself through the thickets of patriarchal convention by acting the part of a good Indian child. After all, one must do whatever one can to get what one wants. This more cynical view—in which Rajnandini's remark espouses what we might term, blending 'matlabi' with 'patriarchal', a 'patlabi' ideal of self-centred lip-service to patriarchy—demands that the will of the father be both respected and tamed. The device of the play-within-a-film allows us to see these two perspectives simultaneously.

It is only appropriate that Vivaan is a theatre director eyeing a career in commercial film. He directs Rajnandini towards excelling in this new patlabi script, all the while promising her profit from it. Her skill in performing this new script, as well as the profit it might yield, is put to the test in the film's second half. Immediately after her makeover, she and her friends—dressed in western clothes and drinking alcohol—return to her aunt's place to party. Her strict father turns up and, shocked by Rajnandini's transformation, drags her off back to Rajasthan to get her married immediately. This part of the film is the hardest to stomach. Not only does Rajnandini never once actively fight her father's will; she also submits to it happily. When Vivaan and the other actors follow her back to Ajmer and find out that she is to be married, she tells him cheerfully—in Hindi—that her husband-to-be 'accha hai; main Dilli mein rahoongi! (is good; I will live in Delhi!)'. Equally surprising, Vivaan and the actors accede to this development; they work tirelessly to help with the wedding plans, they pawn their expensive watches and jewellery when the father of Rajnandini's fiancé asks for more dowry, and Vivaan manfully lights the puja candle on the thali for the shaadi ceremony.

The layering of play within film allows us to understand these conservative gestures of submission to the father's will in two ways. On the surface, in accord with Sooraj Barjatya's promise, it represents the triumph of patriarchal family values. But to stick with the surface is to do what Duryodhana does, and to not recognize that what looks self-evidently solid may be anything but. It is here that the tagline of *The Taming of the Shrew Reborn* comes back to haunt the film's patriarchal story. 'Go into the character, solution mil jaaega': is Rajnandini simply respecting her father's will, or is she playing a part that will yield her profit? Likewise how genuine is Vivaan and the other actors' performance of respect for the father's wedding plan? Are they willing to give up on everything they have stood for? Or does their performance of docility uphold Vivaan's conviction that, by going into character, solution mil jaaega?

Solution indeed mil jaata hai (comes). Not only does Rajnandini's father, moved by the goodness of her friends, call off the wedding a millisecond before the bridegroom is to garland her. He also agrees—with Swamiji's blessing—to allow her to return to Bombay to perform *The Taming of the Shrew Reborn*. We next see him in the audience, smiling and applauding Rajnandini and Vivaan's performance. And the play suddenly seems less like a reworking of Shakespeare than of the father's prior treatment of his daughter. In *The Taming of the Shrew Reborn*, Vivaan's tamer does to Rajnandini's shrew exactly what the father has done to his daughter: deprive her of pizza and of western clothes. At first the performance seems to offer a pointedly cruel illustration of how patriarchal discipline can torture a wife or daughter. But then, in a final twist, we are told that the tamer has in fact all along loved the shrew, and his odd behaviour has been motivated simply by a desire 'to make her the woman she could be and should be'. In other words, the play-within-a-film deviously allows the father to be reframed as an enabler of, not an obstacle to, his daughter's liberty.

For this twist to stand, the father's value system has to be inverted. And this much is indicated by the song immediately before Rajnandini's aborted wedding: 'Apna Kaun, Paraaya Kaun (Who is ours, who is a foreigner)?'. The song troubles the strict boundary between family and outsider, Indian and western, which Rajnandini's father has sought to police so strictly. By giving the 'paraaya' licence to become part of 'apna', we see a version of the partition-busting that is the hallmark of the Bollywood masala sensibility. Yet from another perspective, this sentimentally inclusive ending underlines the contradictions that typify narratives of India post-economic liberalization. On the one hand, the film embraces a global 'development' whose benchmarks are western, whose values are supposedly egalitarian, and whose local icons (Sania Mirza and Salman Khan) are Muslim; on the other it still respects the primacy of the Indian father and the Hindu Swamiji.

In sum, *Isi Life Mein* appeals to several ideological communities at once. It is and is not cosmopolitan. It is and it is not patriarchal. It is and it is not Hindutva. (Indeed, it's striking that, swimming against the tide of current film practice, the opening credits show the title in Roman, Devanagari, and Nastaliq scripts.) No matter how much of a commercially shrewd cop-out—or cash-in—all these compromises might be, they are enabled in large part by the multilayered masala onion of a play within a film. *Isi Life Mein's* use of this device allows us to understand better the masala qualities of *The Taming of the Shrew* itself. And its onions.

◆

The Taming of the Shrew is widely regarded as one of Shakespeare's earliest plays. Its coarse physical humour lacks the depth of character associated with his more mature drama. And its gender politics can seem a world away from those of later plays; just take the cheeky Beatrice in *Much Ado About Nothing*, whose taunts against men are received in good grace, or the outspoken Emilia in *Othello*, who advocates convincingly for women's right to do everything that men do. Adding to the suspicion that *The Taming of the Shrew* is an 'immature' play are the opening scenes' references to English villages such as Burton Heath and Wincot, adjacent to Stratford-upon-Avon. Clearly the haunts of his childhood were fresh in Shakespeare's memory as he wrote *The Taming of the Shrew*. This has led some to assume that it was his first play and written as early as 1588, just after he left Stratford for London.

But I suspect a later date of composition. Like the travelling actors who visit the Lord's house in the opening scene, Shakespeare's company may have performed the play on tour; an anonymous play called *The Taming of a Shrew* survives, and its script—which includes the framing tale of the drunken tinker—was quite possibly patched up by Shakespeare during the plague year of 1594, when the London theatres were closed and his company was forced to perform in the provinces. Indeed, the local references to Burton Heath and Wincot may have been added for a special performance in his hometown. In any case, *The Taming of the Shrew* shows signs of Shakespeare's mid-career fascination with the idea that all the world is a stage. And as I shall argue, its seemingly shallow characters and regressive gender politics should be understood in relation to that fascination. I am inclined to place *The Taming of the Shrew* closer to the fertile six-year period when Shakespeare experimented most with the device of the play-within-a play, from 'Pyramus and Thisbe' in *A Midsummer Night's Dream* (1595) to 'The Murder of Gonzago'—also performed by travelling players—in *Hamlet* (1601).

An even later date, 2010, additionally inflects my sense of *The Taming of the Shrew*. That is the year in which Vidhi Kasliwal chose to embed her 'reborn' version of Shakespeare's play in a film about an undivided family. Kasliwal's film has changed how I see the play. But what does it mean to view *The Taming of the Shrew* in light of *Isi Life Mein* rather than the other way round? There are three ways in which the film has transformed my understanding of Shakespeare's play and helped me recognize its masala more-than-oneness.

First, *Isi Life Mein* has helped me see how Shakespeare's play is ambivalently haunted by the spectre of consumerism. Katherina the shrew, like Rajnandini, longs for fashionable items. Petruchio the tamer may not deprive Katherina of pizza and pasta. (And if he were to do so, it wouldn't mean quite the same thing as it does in *Isi Life Mein* because, in the play's Padua setting, pizza and pasta would be local rather than exotic fare.) Yet during the scenes of torture he inflicts on her at his house, he pointedly deprives her not just of basic human necessities such as sleep and food but also of the modish items of prêt-à-porter clothing that she craves. As in *Isi Life Mein* and other Indian adaptations, being a shrew is not just about speaking back to men but also about being a dedicated follower of cosmopolitan fashion.

Yet in masala style, *The Taming of the Shrew* offers two competing perspectives on consumerism. As he begins his torture of Katherina, Petruchio invites a tailor and a haberdasher to exhibit their wares in her presence, only to tear the well-designed dress she likes and stamp on the chic hat she wants. Consumerism is presented here as a shrewish no-no. But the play's first audiences could not have helped but gaze admiringly upon these items, which were held up for their loving scrutiny as much as Katherina's. Shakespeare's contemporary, Thomas Dekker, complained that London audiences often paid more attention to eye-catching costumes than to playwrights' lines. And in London's nascent consumer society, where imported luxury goods were available in unprecedented quantities due to the rise of joint-stock trading companies that would ultimately bankroll Britain's colonial adventures, the playing companies had to adapt accordingly. It is some indication of their priorities that they would usually pay a writer three pounds for a new play, but they would pay up to twenty pounds for a lavish new costume. In short, the play creates a masala perspective on fashion, both ridiculing it—Petruchio insists that 'to me she is married, not unto my clothes' (3.2.110)—and bowing to it.

Second, *Isi Life Mein* has impressed on me how *The Taming of the Shrew* is a manifesto for what I'm calling patlabi performance. By staging scenes where women submit to patriarchal authority in order to get what they want, the play both respects and disrespects fathers. We see this doubleness with Bianca, Katherina's sister: she may tell their father, 'sir, to your pleasure humbly I subscribe' (1.1.81), but her humility is manifestly an act that wins her privileges at her sister's expense. Katherina, too, eventually acquires the skill of the patlabi. Petruchio asks her to address Lucentio's father Vincentio as if he were a beautiful young woman; she complies. Her obedience to Petruchio seems to mark her successful taming. But it also allows her to do what she has done in the past—mock a father—albeit now with patriarchal sanction. Her lines drip with sarcasm: 'Young budding virgin, fair and fresh and sweet,/ Whither away?' (4.5.38–9). The wicked pun on 'whither'/'wither' mocks Vincentio's age under the guise of paying him respect. And Petruchio's scolding response, even as it seems to put her in her place, also heaps scorn on Vincentio in ways that wink at her pun: 'this is a man, old, wrinkled, faded, withered' (4.5.44). Katherina and Petruchio are here both a depressingly conventional patriarchal couple and a subversively mischievous tag-team mocking fathers in unison.

Arguably Katherina's best patlabi performance is saved for the play's last scene. Petruchio and his two friends, Lucentio and Hortensio, make a gambling wager with each other to see whose wife will come when called. All bets are on Lucentio winning the wager; after all, he is married to Bianca, Katherina's 'good' sister. But she refuses her husband's call, as does Hortensio's new wife, the Widow, who has already been outed as a second shrew. Much to everyone's surprise, Katherina comes when called, and obeys Petruchio's command to take off her hat and stamp on it. The coup de grâce is provided when she delivers the longest speech in the play—a hideous jeremiad to the other wives about their duties in marriage:

> Fie, fie, unknit that threat'ning, unkind brow,
> And dart not scornful glances from those eyes
> To wound thy lord, thy king, thy governor...
> Thy husband is thy lord, thy life, thy keeper,
> Thy head, thy sovereign, one that cares for thee...
> And craves no other tribute at thy hands
> But love, fair looks, and true obedience,
> Too little payment for so great a debt.
> Such duty as the subject owes the prince,
> Even such a woman oweth to her husband,
> And when she is froward, peevish, sullen, sour,
> And not obedient to his honest will,
> What is she but a foul contending rebel,
> And graceless traitor to her loving lord? (5.2.140–2, 150–1, 156–64)

The speech drearily intones the patriarchal mandates of Elizabethan conduct manuals for wives, which understood marriage on the analogy of feudal obligation to a lord. Yet Katherina's homage to lordly husbands hardly embodies the virtues it praises. She condemns women who are 'froward', which is to say contrary and outspoken; yet her speech is the quintessence of frowardness in its testiness and its length. Notably, Katherina's speech also wins Petruchio—and presumably herself—a lot of money. In keeping with *Isi Life Mein's* repeated refrain of 'go into the character, solution mil jaaega', Katherina's speech can be understood in two very different ways: as a performance utterly in lockstep with patriarchal convention and as a wickedly subversive route to personal profit.

Third and most importantly, *Isi Life Mein* has underscored for me what the masala device of the story-within-a-story does to Shakespeare's taming story. The device's most immediate effect is to make that story and its shrew appear outlandish, in the manner of *Nathari Firangiz Thekani Avi* and subsequent film versions that present their shrews as somehow un-Indian women who need to be Indianized. Unlike Shakespeare's many other plays set in Italy—most of his comedies from *The Two Gentlemen of Verona* to *As You Like It*, as well as his tragedies *Romeo and Juliet* and *Othello*—*The Taming of the Shrew* throws the taming tale's Italian setting into theatrical relief with its pointedly English framing tale. For film and play alike, the shift from the main story to the performance of the taming tale represents a shift from a supposedly 'real' world to a manifestly 'theatrical' setting. In *Isi Life Mein*, that theatrical setting includes Broadway-style tap-dancing and orchestration as well as a nod to the Hollywood musical *Kiss Me Kate*. Likewise, *The Taming of the Shrew* theatrically estranges its characters by aligning them with stock figures from the popular Italian theatrical form known as commedia dell'arte. Gremio, for example, is a match for the old miserly character of Pantalone, Grumio is the typical Zanni or servant, and Petruchio is the Harlequin clown.

But the framing tale doesn't simply make the taming story theatrically outlandish. Shakespeare's likely source play, *The Taming of a Shrew*, closes by returning to the framing story of Christopher Sly the tinker. This serves to remind the audience of the fictionality of the taming story. By contrast, Shakespeare's version allows the audience to forget the taming tale's fictionality because it abandons Sly and the framing tale after Act One. As a result, Katherina's speech at the end of the play can be read both as fictional and credible, thanks to the suspension of disbelief that the framing tale's absence encourages. Her speech acquires something of the paradoxical aspect of the contents of the Maya Mahal: illusory yet real.

This masala paradox is a product of Shakespeare's artful abandonment of the framing tale. But it is also due to how the framing tale predisposes the viewer to see theatre not simply as an illusion but as fundamentally constitutive of reality. We can see as much from the speech in which the Lord enlists his page, Bartholomew, to act as the tinker Christopher Sly's noble wife:

...see him dressed in all suits like a lady.
That done, conduct him to the drunkard's chamber
And call him 'madam', do him obeisance...
And say 'What is't your honour will command
Wherein your lady and your humble wife
May show her duty and make known her love?'...
And if the boy have not a woman's gift
To rain a shower of commanded tears,

An onion will do well for such a shift,
Which, in a napkin being close conveyed,
Shall in despite enforce a watery eye. (Induction, 1.102–4,
111–13, 120–4)

The Lord's speech serves as a reminder that all the 'real' women in the taming story, including Katherina, are played by male actors who require the kind of fashionable costumes ('dressed in all suits like a lady') that Petruchio theatrically rejects. As in *Isi Life Mein*, femininity, consumerism, and 'going into the character' walk hand-in-hand.

The fashionably attired Bartholomew—no doubt wearing one of those lavish twenty-pound costumes that enraged Dekker—also lays bare how femininity is the result of onions: layered play-within-play onions, and tear-jerking onions. Batholomew's onion-induced tears arguably provide a model to the actor playing Bianca in the taming story: when her character weeps, Katherina's quip—'it is best she put finger in her eye,/ An she knew why' (1.1.78–9)—could draw attention to an onion in Bianca's hand. Kaho Naa... Pyaaz Hai, indeed.

Bartholomew's performance of femininity again seeps into the taming play in light of his remark to Sly: 'My husband and my lord, my lord and husband;/ I am your wife in all obedience' (Induction, 2.103–4). These lines eerily echo Katherina's in her last speech. When we hear her say that 'thy husband is thy lord' and is owed 'true obedience' (5.1.150, 157), we might recall how, in Bartholomew's earlier speech, these words are likewise performed rather than authentic. How they too are coerced by a Lord. And how they, too, result in profit—the 'love' that the Lord promises him (Induction, 1.105). In short, an audience's response to Katherina's speech can be affected by Bartholomew's performance. Conversely, we might think afresh about the framing tale in light of the taming tale: the Lord's direction of Bartholomew and tricking of Sly the tinker is as coercively nasty as Petruchio's taming of Katherina.

To understand the play's gender politics simply in terms of plot content, then, is to miss something about the power of masala layers. *The Taming of the Shrew*, like *Isi Life Mein*, clearly lacks the socialist politics of the un-framed, misogynist southern film adaptations. Yet formally, Shakespeare's play and Kasliwal's film offer their audiences more room for interpretation. Like the Mahabharata, their onion-like narratives allow for shifts of perspective that refuse what the Nigerian writer Chimamanda Ngozi Adichie calls 'the danger of the single story'. And that is why 'the Framing of the Shrew' has just as much power as *The Taming of the Shrew.*

ACT THREE SCENE THREE

'Zindagi Ek Naatak Hai'

In 1997, a year after directing the cross-gendered production of *The Taming of the Shrew*, I accidentally saw my first Hindi film. I had gone with two friends to an arthouse cinema in London's Leicester Square to catch a movie one of them had recommended. Yet when we arrived at the box office, all tickets for the show had sold out. So we were forced to pick another film. Earlier the same day we had seen an exhibition in east London about Krishna. Exhilarated by the idea of the musical love-god and his dancing gopis, we took a chance on an Indian film we knew nothing about other than that it, too, would feature song and dance. I can no longer remember which movie we had initially hoped to see at Leicester Square. But oh my goodness, do I remember *The Square Circle* (1997).

The Square Circle was, in fact, the English title for an unusual masala Hindi film, directed by Amol Palekar and scripted by Timeri N. Murari, called *Daayraa*. I knew no Hindi at the time; so I didn't know that daayraa meant 'circle', although more in the theatrical sense of a circular performance arena. The English title, 'Square Circle', evokes something of the masala quality, the mix of contradictory opposites, embodied by each of the film's two lead characters: a hijra nautanki performer from coastal Orissa (Nirmal Pandey), who is 'baahar se mard, andar se aurat', and a village woman (Sonali Kulkarni), who dresses as a man after being sold into prostitution and raped. Yet the Hindi title captures more fully than 'Square Circle', the theatrical movement between genders that the two lead characters trace, coming full circle in their reverse journeys between male and female. The film completely won me over. I wasn't surprised to learn later that it had won a National Award, and was nominated by *Time* magazine as one of the 10 Best Films of 1996. But it was never released theatrically in India. Perhaps the film upset the Victorian sensibilities of its distributors.

A masala film never screened before an Indian commercial audience is itself something of a square circle, a contradiction in terms. Yet despite its lack of a release, it had clearly been crafted to appeal to a mixed audience. *Daayraa* contained the predictable plot improbabilities and song-and-dance numbers—including 'Bolo Kya Tum' and 'Palkon Pe Chalte Chalte', performed by Asha Bhosle singing Gulzar's lyrics—of a Bollywood movie. But its music derived largely from popular folk tradition, especially nautanki, the operatic theatrical form of north Indian villages. I knew nothing at the time of the nautanki convention of the cross-dressed actor. Nor did I know about hijras or the mythic tales that regard Hindu gods not as having only one gender but as moving cyclically between male and female avatars. Take, for instance, Vishnu, who turns into the enchantress Mohini, becomes the object of Shiva's sexual infatuation, and gets pregnant before reverting to his male avatar. *Daayraa*'s masala vision of gender, as a fluid movement that encompasses seeming opposites, is fully immersed in these subcontinental traditions. To my Western eyes, however, what the film magically conjured in its treatment of gender was Shakespearean paradox.

The English title of the film, and its teasing contradiction, reminded me of Shakespeare's love of paradox. I was reminded of the flower in *Romeo and Juliet* that Friar Lawrence describes as poisonous yet medicinal. I was reminded even more of how the play-within-a-play of 'Pyramus and Thisbe' in *A Midsummer Night's Dream* is described as 'hot ice' and 'tragical mirth' (5.1.58, 5.6.55–6). These paradoxes are augmented by the apparition of the young bellows-mender Francis Flute, who is cast as Thisbe despite his insistence that he has a beard coming. Flute's performance of Thisbe draws attention to how all the other female characters in this and every Shakespeare play were played by young males.

As I watched *Daayraa*, it occurred to me that the paradoxical 'Square Circle' of the English title—with its sexual hint of both a square peg and a round hole—was a perfect description of Shakespeare's recurrent fascination with the figure of the man who is also a woman. The paradoxical 'master–mistress' of Sonnet 20, supposedly born a woman but then 'pricked out' by nature with 'one thing to my purpose nothing', is both male and female. So are a string of female characters who assume male guises: Julia in *The Two Gentlemen of Verona*, Portia and Nerissa in *The Merchant of Venice*, Rosalind and Celia in *As You Like It*, and Viola in *Twelfth Night*. Then there is Cleopatra in *Antony and Cleopatra*, who enjoys dressing as a man while making love to Antony, drunk, dressed in Cleopatra's clothes. And there are also the androgynous bearded witches of *Macbeth*. Of these characters, *As You Like It*'s Rosalind provides the most wonderfully layered version of the cross-dressed square circle. Played by a boy, Rosalind is a girl who disguises herself as a boy named Ganymede.

And in this male disguise, Rosalind-as-Ganymede acts as a girl so that her witless boy-love Orlando can practise wooing a girl.

But it is *Twelfth Night* that stands as Shakespeare's most far-reaching inquiry into the square circle of the cross-dressed male–female. When Viola, separated from her identical twin Sebastian, dresses up as the male Cesario, Olivia—wooed by Orsino—falls for her/him. Viola, however, loves Orsino. And Orsino develops feelings for Cesario. Once Olivia pledges herself to Viola's identical twin Sebastian, whom she believes to be Cesario, Orsino doesn't hesitate to commit himself to Cesario even though he says he would like to see him/her wearing a dress. So Viola–Cesario's gender in the play is presented as a paradox, a square circle, that blurs our sense not only of his/her gender but also of other characters' sexuality: is Olivia heterosexual or lesbian when she falls for Cesario? Is Orsino heterosexual or gay when he proposes to Viola dressed in Cesario's clothes? Conventional categories of sexuality fail us in *Twelfth Night*, just as they do in *Daayraa* when the 'baahar se mard, andar se aurat' Nirmal Pandey falls in love with the cross-dressed Sonali Kulkarni.

The resonance between *Daayraa* and *Twelfth Night* struck me again in 2015. Two years earlier I had joined Ashoka University, a new liberal arts college in Haryana, as its founding Dean of Academic Affairs. My colleagues and I had been tasked with devising a brand new English literature curriculum, and we resolved to approach Shakespeare rather differently from how he tends to be taught in both the West and in India. We didn't want to focus narrowly on the meanings of Shakespeare's plays, whether in isolation or in relation to the society in which they were written and performed. Instead we opted for a more creative approach that took into account how Shakespeare was an imaginative reader of other stories. The students would be asked to transform his plays into narratives of their own, and in a variety of media: short story, play, film, dance, music, art, graphic novel. In sum, we wanted the students to imaginatively interfere with Shakespeare's texts in just the same way that Shakespeare had interfered with his own sources, from Ovid's *Metamorphoses* to stories that can be traced back to *Alf Layla wa-Layla*. To that end, we pioneered a new pedagogy that would first require students to read texts Shakespeare had himself read and reimagined. And then they would reimagine Shakespeare's plays in conjunction with other reimaginings of them by writers and artists from around the world.

In my Shakespeare class, I taught *A Midsummer Night's Dream* side by side with Ovid's tale of 'Pyramus and Thisbe', the English graphic novelist Neil Gaiman's reinterpretation of the play, and Sharat Katariya's Bollywood film *10ml Love*. I taught *Othello* with the Perso-Arabic tale of the 'Slave and the Apple' from *Alf Layla wa-Layla*, the Sudanese novelist Tayeb Salih's *Season of Migration to the North*, and Vishal Bhardwaj's Hindi film *Omkara* (2006). And I taught *The Tempest* with Ovid's tale of 'Medea', the Martiniquan playwright Aime Cesaire's *A Tempest*, the Indian storyteller Suniti Namjoshi's *Snapshots of Caliban*, and the Sierra Leonean poet Lemuel Johnson's 'Calypso for Caliban'. My aim was to make the students aware of how stories are migrants whose meanings change as they move through different communities of readers. There can never be a single, timeless reading of any Shakespeare text; rather, one always reads it from a specific location in space, time, culture and language. Each interpretation of a Shakespeare play is, therefore, a creative reimagining from a new vantage point that allows the play to have more than one meaning and speak afresh. The students' final assignment was not to write a formal academic paper on Shakespeare, or to take an examination on his works, but to creatively reimagine one of his texts, reflecting on how their own cultural and historical locations have influenced their interpretation of it.

In 2015, as part of the Shakespeare Society of India's national seminar at Ashoka University on 'Shakespeare and the Street', a group of twenty Ashoka students performed a pair of creatively reimagined scenes from *Twelfth Night* that built on the new pedagogy we were developing. Drawing on Hindustani folk theatrical and music forms, especially nautanki, they picked two 'street' scenes: the early sequence in which Viola decides to disguise herself as the male Cesario after initially proposing to pass as a eunuch; and the later scene in which Antonio is arrested as he declares his love for Sebastian to a startled Cesario. With these two scenes, the students found elements in Shakespeare's play that correspond to north Indian folk theatre's presentation of gender as a cross-dressed performance. And they also made these scenes speak to the then-recent ruling of the Indian Supreme Court to uphold Section 377 of the Indian Penal Code that outlaws sexual acts 'against the order of nature'. The students' creative reimagining, then, made allies of Shakespeare and nautanki in order to question the 'natural/ unnatural' distinction drawn by Indian law. As I watched, I couldn't help but remember the words of the hijra in *Daayraa*, who calls himself a 'kudrat ka karishma', a phrase that translates both as a freak and a marvel of nature: which is to say, the hijra is simultaneously perverse yet natural, a masala square circle.

Yet I remained ignorant of the nautanki lens through which the Ashoka students had reimagined *Twelfth Night*. By focusing on Shakespearean paradox alone, I had missed one important aspect of nautanki: its cross-dressing is not simply about trans-gendering. It is altogether more capacious in the circles it draws. The daayraa stage of nautanki performance is both all-encompassing and traces the shape of a zero: it suggests that everything in its ambit is empty rather than substantial, in a state of protean movement rather than of static identity. The Ashoka students understood this fundamentally masala philosophy of nautanki. Their production of *Twelfth Night*'s street scenes *moved*: not just in the energetic dancing of its actors, or in its movements across boundaries of gender and sexuality, but also in its swerves between high poetry and street-theatre, English and Hindi. And as I watched the scenes I experienced a movement of my own, in time, back to *Daayraa*, making me revisit the film to try to understand it better.

Daayraa and *Twelfth Night* are about far more than just the celebration of mixed male/female identities. Each also opens up to embrace a multiverse of unexpected intimacies, wanton dalliances between phenomena that we otherwise regard as separate. Masala Shakespeare, in film and in theatre, often treats gender in this capacious and dynamic fashion. In particular, masala Shakespeare adaptations influenced by nautanki—a theatrical form in which not only have men traditionally played women but also more recently women have played men—underlines Shakespeare's old adage from *As You Like It*, 'all the world's a stage'. The title of *Daayraa*, alluding to the open-air stage on which its hijra nautanki actor performs, hints at the theatrical nature of the world depicted in the film. All the world's a stage indeed. Or, as *Daayra*'s playback singer Asha Bhosle sings elsewhere, in an iconic number from the 1970s blockbuster *Natak* (1975), 'Zindagi Ek Naatak Hai'. The masala of nautanki, then, runs rings around gender paradoxes, revealing the dynamic naatak that beats at their heart.

ACT THREE SCENE FOUR

Masala Genders (*Twelfth Night*)

Vikram Seth's 1993 novel, *A Suitable Boy*, imagines an Indian student performance of *Twelfth Night* staged in the fifties. Two of the novel's main characters—Lata Mehra and Kabir Durrani—play significant parts in the production. Earlier, offstage, they have acted out an intense, failed masala romance. For Lata is Hindu and Kabir Muslim, and their relation is star-crossed. Yet their onstage avatars are not Romeo and Juliet. Now estranged from each other, Lata and Kabir play the parts of Lady Olivia and her puritanical yet amorous steward Malvolio. The two are scrutinized closely by Lata's mother and grandfather, who respond to the performance in markedly different ways.

Mrs Rupa Mehra—a rather prim type—has long been suspicious of a production that brings her daughter Lata into contact with boys. And, as it dawns on her who has been cast as Malvolio, she is utterly scandalized by 'that' boy's presence. Twenty minutes into the performance, however, she finds herself placated by the play, which flatly denies Malvolio any hope of romance with Olivia. Mrs Rupa Mehra is sufficiently mollified that she even awards Shakespeare, if only in her mind, honorary Indian citizenship. But when Olivia innocently asks her steward, 'wilt thou go to bed?' (3.4.30), Mrs Rupa Mehra responds with her trademark spluttering red-nosed indignation. She revokes Shakespeare's recently acquired Indian citizenship, and prepares to walk out. Yet the second half of the play, in which Malvolio is comprehensively humiliated by Olivia's uncle Sir Toby Belch in cahoots with her maidservant Maria and clown Feste, allays Mrs Rupa Mehra's anger. Shakespeare is restored to his position as an honorary desi.

Lata's grandfather, Dr Kishen Chand Seth, views the performance rather differently. Despite his stern, patriarchal demeanour, he is an aficionado of sentimental Hindi movies such as *Deedar* (1951), which never fail to leave him weeping profusely and noisily banging his walking stick in grief-stricken sympathy with their heroes' sad plights. He responds in kind to *Twelfth Night*. While his daughter is delighted to see Malvolio punished, Dr Kishen Chand Seth is moved to tears by the steward's humiliation. And he reacts as if he were watching a Hindi film: he bangs his stick and howls in raucous grief, attracting the attention of the audience. 'Kishy,' hisses his embarrassed wife, Parvati. 'This is not your *Deedar!*' But to no avail: Dr Kishen Chand Seth is lost to his anguish.

Vikram Seth gently satirizes two standard Indian responses to masala entertainment. The first, shaped by a prudish Victorian attitude to sexuality, bristles with outraged indignation at supposed moral impropriety. The second, lacking any emotional filter, sheds tears at the slightest whiff of injustice. There is a double joke here. Mrs Mehra and Dr Seth are themselves characters straight from a masala story: even as *A Suitable Boy* channels nineteenth-century British fiction, it also has deep roots in classic Hindi film, down to its musical interludes, broad social canvas, prodigious length, and emotional over-the-top-ness. But the second joke concerns Shakespeare. For all the seeming inappropriateness of Dr Kishen Chand Seth's reacting to *Twelfth Night* as if it were *Deedar*, Shakespeare's play, too, contains many of the elements of a masala film: comedy, tragedy, romance, song and dance, witty wordplay. As such, *Twelfth Night* is also a mirror image of popular Indian entertainment.

There is something odd, however, about *A Suitable Boy*'s production of *Twelfth Night*. Seth has us focus on Olivia and Malvolio; he diverts our attention from Viola, the play's main character. Mrs Rupa Mehra and Dr Kishen Chand Seth are outraged by Malvolio—she by his desires, he by his ill-treatment. But they pass in silence over moments in *Twelfth Night* that others might see as more outrageous: in particular, the many homoerotic episodes occasioned by Viola dressing up as a young man named Cesario. Mrs Rupa Mehra is not bothered by Olivia's attraction to Viola-as-Cesario, or Orsino's love for a woman whom he only sees dressed as a man, or Antonio's love-struck response to Viola-as-Cesario in the mistaken belief that she is his beloved Sebastian, her twin brother. This indifference—all the more striking for an out gay writer who elsewhere in *A Suitable Boy* explores the complexities of same-sex attraction—works in two ways. It brushes something about the play under the carpet. But it also serves to make *Twelfth Night*'s treatment of Viola's gender topsy-turviness literally unremarkable.

Arguably *Twelfth Night*'s gender confusions *are* unremarkable for most Indians. Men who are women, and women who are men, are commonplace in Indian life. They feature in Hindu mythology, hijra kothas, and popular dramatic forms such as nautanki, where male actors have traditionally played female parts. Even Dr Kishen Chand Seth's tear-drenched response to *Twelfth Night* crosses the border dividing conventional masculinity and femininity. And although Section 377 of India's outmoded penal code (read down by the Supreme Court of India in September 2018) regarded 'sexual acts against nature' as illegal, the law of the land also recognizes what it calls the third gender. Which is to say, it does not blink at an idea of a gender that is more-than-one. Little wonder, perhaps, that the sight of the lady Viola dressing up as the male Cesario should pass without comment from masala aficionados Mrs Rupa Mehra and Dr Kishen Chand Seth.

As we shall see, though, modern masala Indian versions of *Twelfth Night*—on stage and on screen—have played in remarkable ways with the otherwise unremarkable convention of the (man who is a) woman who is a man (who is a woman). In this they chime with Shakespeare's play, which also uses the cross-dressed actor to present a remarkable view of the world.

◆

In January 1602, the London lawyer Sir John Manningham attended the first recorded performance of *Twelfth Night*. Like Mrs Rupa Mehra and Dr Kishen Chand Seth, Manningham enjoyed the performance, which took place at the city's Inns of Court. And like them, he seems to have found the play's gender confusions completely unremarkable; what arrested his attention far more than Viola's transvestism was *Twelfth Night's* genre. In the notes he jotted down in his diary after the performance, he said that the play reminded him of *The Comedy of Errors*. He probably had in mind the shared device not just of the twins, but also of the shipwreck that divides them. But Manningham may have been thinking too of the stylistic mix of both plays. He characterizes *Twelfth Night* with a striking phrase: 'It is,' he says, 'a mingled comedy.' A masala entertainment, in other words.

What exactly did Manningham mean by 'mingled'? *Twelfth Night* is, as he says, a comedy. But it also—like *The Comedy of Errors*—contains elements of tragedy. A brother and sister separated in a shipwreck, believing each other dead; a grieving woman who, having lost her brother and father, vows never to love a man; a man who loves another man and risks great danger—even capital punishment—to be with him; a man who dares to love someone above his social station, is made the victim of a cruel practical joke, and is confined to the darkness of a lunatic asylum. That darkness might serve as a metaphor for the shadows that haunt much of this supposedly comic play. Even its clown, Feste, is a sombre character who concludes *Twelfth Night* with a depressing song about death and the rain. The very title of the play suggests something of this mingling of comedy and darkness. On the one hand, the Twelfth Night festival is the last day of Christmas and, as such, an occasion for raucous celebration. On the other hand, it falls on 5 January at the coldest time of the year, when the days are at their shortest. An afternoon performance of *Twelfth Night* timed to coincide with the festival, such as the one Manningham saw, would have certainly ended in frigid darkness: the fickle English January sun sets at around 4 p.m.

Twelfth Night's mingling of warm cheer and winter chill, reminiscent of *A Midsummer Night's Dream's* 'hot ice' (5.1.58), is just one instance of how the festival is immersed in paradox. So many of the rituals of the Twelfth Night celebrations in Shakespeare's time involve some kind of paradox. The social order is symbolically inverted, creating paradoxical compounds: a common man who discovers a bean in his Christmas cake is elected King, a poor woman who finds a pea is elected Queen, religious observance is channelled into wassailing, i.e. feasting and consumption of alcohol. These inversions find counterparts in *Twelfth Night*: a noble knight who is forever drunk (Sir Toby Belch), a maidservant who rules the roost (Maria), the eclipse of Malvolio's puritanical zeal by Sir Toby's nocturnal revelry. The festive mood is best expressed in the boozy knight's famous question to the steward: 'dost thou think, because thou art virtuous, there will be no more cakes and ale?' (2.3.103–4).

The festival's logic of ritual inversion also finds expression in the play's central preoccupation with transvestism. Sir John Manningham had no cause to draw attention to the profound gender confusions of *Twelfth Night's* 'mingled comedy'; these confusions were ubiquitous in the theatre of the time, when all female parts were played by boy actors. But how did a boy become a credible woman on the Shakespearean stage? How in particular could a boy assume the guise of Viola, who in turn has to become the male Cesario, who nonetheless retains some elements of femininity? And how might Manningham's comment about the 'mingled' quality of *Twelfth Night* potentially shed light on the play's gender confusions in a way that goes beyond mere festive inversion?

Boy actors' voices had yet to break. So the actor who played Viola would have sounded something like a woman. But he was also able to present the illusion of femininity in ways that had nothing to do with accidents of biology. Instead, like the Lord's page-boy Bartholomew in the framing tale of *The Taming of the Shrew*, he was made feminine through the addition of objects. Bartholomew's accessories—dress, onion—exposed the profound theatricality of what Shakespeare in *Cymbeline* calls 'the woman's part' (2.5.20). The woman's part is not just a role in a play (the 'part' was so named because every actor was given only the 'part' of the script containing his character's lines). It is also a prosthetic part added to an actor, by means of which male body and feminine object are mingled.

This prosthetic mingling is apparent in the case of Viola. We do not see a boy actor dress up to play her in the way we see the page-boy Bartholomew before he dresses up as Sly's wife. But *Twelfth Night* emphasizes, as does *The Taming of the Shrew*, how much gender is stitched out of clothing. Viola first appears in a dress—the 'part' that transforms the boy playing her into a woman. We refer to this boy as 'she' because he wears female dress. But this 'she' quickly changes into men's clothes, at which point the play's pronouns become far trickier. What should we call Viola–Cesario? He? She? S/he?

Twelfth Night uses the word 'habit' for what Viola wears to become a man: when Duke Orsino, in love with Cesario, sees Sebastian and Viola–Cesario dressed identically, he says

> one face, one voice, one habit and two persons!
> A natural perspective, that is and is not! (5.1.208–9)

The twins are a 'natural perspective', which is to say an optical illusion. But their masculinity too is equally an illusion. And it is sustained or broken through their 'habits':

> Cesario, come,
> For so you shall be, while you are a man.
> But when in other habits you are seen,
> Orsino's mistress and his fancy's queen. (5.1.372–5)

Note how Viola–Cesario's gender identity here is fully tethered to his/her clothes. Orsino insists that the person he is addressing remains 'a man' as long as s/he doesn't wear the 'other habits' of a woman. This makes gender a 'habit' also in its more familiar sense: an act that one repeats over and over to create the illusion of a 'natural perspective.'

Twelfth Night is radical in making Viola's masculinity as much of a 'habit' as the boy-actor's femininity. And in this, it differs a little from the earlier plays. For all the subversiveness of their transvestite scenes in which male characters dress up as women, plays like *A Midsummer Night's*

Dream and *The Taming of the Shrew* can easily cleave to a patriarchal understanding of gender. They make it seem as if femininity is a secondary condition, a dress-up act comically performed by a man. The male, therefore, remains the primary biological truth while the female is a fabrication. This is one of the consequences of the all-male stage. But it is also related to the pre-modern patriarchal conception of the female as an imperfect version of the male, in which the womb is simply an ingrown version of the penis thanks to a lack of heat. According to this view, the man is the biological starting point and the woman, like Eve, always follows as a secondary, fallen condition.

Twelfth Night, by contrast, allows us to see maleness not as the biological starting point but, rather, as simply yet another theatrical performance. After her shipwreck and separation from her beloved twin brother Sebastian, Viola initially declares that she will disguise herself as a eunuch—presumably to harmonize her high female voice with that of the castrato. Instead, she simply adopts the attire of a man. In her guise as Cesario, Viola complicates the idea that the 'male' is the anatomical reality underneath the 'feminine' performance—despite the fact that she is performed by a boy. Being a man is just as dependent on the addition of a prosthetic 'part' as is femininity.

Shakespeare has a great deal of fun with this twist. Viola–Cesario is challenged to a duel by Sir Andrew Aguecheek, her/his 'rival' for Olivia's hand; but s/he cannot fight effectively. At first, this suggests that the truth of Viola's female sex trumps the charade of Cesario's masculinity: 'A little thing would make me tell them how much I lack of a man' (3.4.268–9). Yet Sir Andrew proves to be as ineffectual a swordsman as Viola–Cesario: his masculinity—or lack of it—is likewise at odds with his sex. Even a man playing a man, then, is a mingled performance of body and habit. Just because Sebastian proves to be a good swordsman doesn't mean his identity is any less mingled; his manly skill emerges not from his biology but from his performative prowess with a prop. So when Viola–Cesario says, 'I am not what I am' (3.1.132), her sense of self-contradiction applies as much to Andrew, Sebastian, or any other character whose gender derives from a mingling of body and object, 'I' and 'it'.

And this shows how *Twelfth Night's* experiments with masala gender are not confined to the 'habit' of cross-dressing. Everyone in the play offers a mingled performance of the self and its gendered parts. This mingling happens even with the part we most think of as indispensable to the self: one's name. Take 'Viola'. The name is a feminine version of 'violet', both flower and colour. But it refers also to a musical instrument, and as such seems to respond to Orsino's famous opening line: 'If music be the food of love, play on!' (1.1.1). Viola, in name and in person, gives Orsino what he hungers for, as is only to be expected in a play that so relentlessly associates music with both food and love. And this music is seemingly in a heterosexual key: the feminine Viola provides the sentimental string accompaniment to the bearish Orsino's longings. Yet not all is as it seems. For there were two types of violas in Shakespeare's day. The 'viola da braccio', or viola of the arm, was what we are more used to now: a viola played by, and resting on, an arm. But equally popular was the 'viola da gamba' or viola of the thigh, which was played at groin level. (Toby refers to the 'viol de gamboys' at 1.3.21). As such, the 'viola' became a winking synonym for the male sexual instrument. Which means that, in her role as Orsino's musical extension, 'Viola' is both feminine and phallic.

But the power of the name 'Viola' in *Twelfth Night* extends beyond its musical meanings. It also haunts the names of the other main characters. 'Olivia' is an anagram for 'I, Viola'. And 'Malvolio', too, contains all the letters of Viola's name: a keen Malayali crossword-cracker will be quick to see the steward's name as an anagram for the decidedly feminine 'Viola Mol'. It is hard to believe that a wordsmith of Shakespeare's calibre, even one who didn't speak Malayalam, wouldn't have been aware of these anagrammatic echoes. Indeed, Shakespeare invites us to see them when he has Maria play, as part of her prank on Malvolio, with the letters of his name: the love letter she forges conjures as Olivia's true love someone whose name contains M, A, O and I. Malvolio sees his name in these letters. We equally can see the gender-confused Viola's name in those of Olivia and Malvolio.

These letter-based confusions are part of a larger vision of mixture and movement that suffuses the play. Nothing in *Twelfth Night* can be fixed with certainty in one place: everything is dynamically tugged by the spectre of a double that opens up to alternative ways of being, doing, and meaning. Just as for every Olivia and Malvolio there is a ghost of a Viola—and, thanks to her cross-dressing, for every Viola there is the ghost of a Cesario and a Sebastian—so does every single utterance in the play potentially move towards more-than-oneness. For words can never quite mean one thing. The clown Feste remarks, with a metaphor of movement, that 'A sentence is but a cheverel glove to a good wit, how quickly the wrong side may be turned outward' (3.1.10–12); to which Viola replies, 'they that dally nicely with words may quickly make them wanton' (3.1.13–14).

Lurking in Feste's remark is a hint of Shakespearean paradox. The cheverel glove is like 's/he': a masala creature in which seeming opposites—inside and outside—are forever transforming into each other. We can also recognize in Feste's remark the idea of a turning world in which supposedly singular entities keep 'wantonly' shifting into new forms. 'What country, friends, is this?' asks Viola when she has been shipwrecked (1.2.1). The seemingly singular answer, 'Illyria' (1.2.2) is a red herring. For this exotic 'Illyria', initially populated by the Italianate crew of Orsino, Viola, Olivia and Malvolio, wantonly morphs into a more diverse space populated also by English-named characters such as Toby Belch and Andrew Aguecheek. Illyria, like the gender of Viola–Cesario, like the meaning of any word, is not a singular location but, rather, a plural space of restless movement.

And this movement is highly theatrical. This is not quite the theatricality of the play-within-a-play—the masala onion—that we find in *The Taming of the Shrew*. It is, rather, a theatricality grounded in an intuition that 'reality' is composed of artfully costumed, ever-changing performances. It is not for nothing that Feste's powerful shaping metaphor, the cheveril glove, derives from a piece of clothing. Virtually everyone in this play is, in a sense, an improvisational transvestite, dressing up to become another. Not only does Viola dress up as Cesario. Bumbling Sir Andrew Aguecheek dresses up to play the part of Olivia's suave suitor. So does grasping Malvolio, in his yellow cross-gartered stockings. Feste dresses up as Sir Topas, the priest who ministers to mad Malvolio. Even Olivia, wearing her black mourning clothes, plays a theatrically costumed part. All identity in *Twelfth Night* is a changeable habit that makes any character, in the words of the play's subtitle, 'What You Will'.

All the world's a mingled stage, and all of us mingled players. And this is how *Twelfth Night*'s masala vision of gender blurs into its masala treatment of genre. On the one hand, comedy—in the old sense of a play with a happy ending—is the conventional genre for heterosexual couplings in which, as Puck says in *A Midsummer Night's Dream*, 'Jack shall have Jill and nought shall go ill' (3.3.45–6). Yet *Twelfth Night* swerves not just from comedy into tragedy but also from heterosexuality to something else. The play's two main romantic couples—Olivia and Sebastian, Orsino and Viola—may give the audience two versions of Jack and Jill. But both these Jacks and Jills are the result of gender misrecognition: Olivia falls for Sebastian because she believes him to be Cesario who is really Viola, and Orsino falls for Viola even as he believes her to be Cesario and himself to be in love with Olivia. Misrecognition is the currency of a world in which, as Viola says, 'I am not what I am.' As that doubled 'I' suggests, we rush to impose singular identities on forms that are, in fact, irreducibly masala, or mixed, because they are irreducibly mingled. Manningham was right: *Twelfth Night* is a mingled comedy—about a mingled world.

◆

Let us now move forward 300 years to another audience member's response to a production of *Twelfth Night*. In about 1910, three centuries after Sir John Manningham saw the play, a British visitor to Bombay attended an Indian performance of *Twelfth Night*. And he was confounded by what he saw. Unable to determine whether the production's Viola was played by a woman or a man, he demanded a private meeting with the actor to determine the truth of his/her sex. The actor turned out to have been a man, as was customary in sangeet naatak performances of the time.

What a difference 300 years make. For this early twentieth-century spectator, the masala gender of Viola was now a problem in need of solution rather than an unremarkable theatrical convention. And this is symptomatic of a historical shift in Britain that, in 1910, had yet to take full effect in India. In English playhouses, the convention of the transvestite boy actor had been superseded more than two hundred years earlier by the new phenomenon of the actress. The change has been celebrated by theatre historians as a progressive development, granting women a voice on the hitherto all-male stage. But it also contributed to an increasingly narrow view of identity grounded in the body: it was now expected that the actor's sex should align with the gender of his or her character. In stark contrast to what was conventional on Shakespeare's stage or in transvestite Indian theatrical forms (from sangeet naatak in Bombay and nautanki in the Hindi belt to therukkuttu in Tamil Nadu), sex in British theatre had become a 'truth' anchoring the reality of the performance.

The increasingly global equation of sex and gender in performance has arguably been facilitated by the rise of cinema. It is less that film is an intrinsically realist medium than that it has produced a particular assumption about the reality of sex and gender, in which biology is the ultimate truth. Almost without exception, the biological sex of the screen actor is the same as that of the part s/he plays. Yet this wasn't always the case in Indian films. When the first Indian silent movie *Raja Harishchandra* (1913) was made, there was considerable stigma attached to the idea of women being made objects of audience scrutiny. To circumvent this, the film's director Dadasaheb Phalke resorted to the sangeet naatak convention of the transvestite actor and cast his male cameraman, Anna Salunke, as the Raja's love interest Taramati. Anna obviously did a very good job: Phalke cast him again in his film *Lanka Dahan* (1917), where he played both Ram and Sita.

Many early Indian film actors were recruited from the ranks of the sangeet naatak companies. What has been forgotten is that long after the rise of cinema these companies continued to cast men in female roles, and several of their specialist female character–actors graduated into film. Bal Gandharva, the star of the Gandharva Sangeet Mandali, was renowned for his performances as women and his aptitude for singing in an androgynous timbre. In 1935, he was cast as the sixteenth-century saint Eknath in the devotional film *Dharmatma* (1935); Eknath's poetry, like that of many social reformer Hindu saints, emphasized gentleness and softness in ways that valorized androgyny, and Gandharva's performance drew on his lifetime as a female-character actor. Similarly, the Marathi female character-actor Vishnupant Pagnis was cast as the titular character of the devotional film *Sant Tukaram* (1936), and deliberately played the saint's love for god on the model of a woman pining for her lover.

The gender ambiguity of these saint films stands in stark contrast to the 'mard' masculinity valorized in post-Independence cinematic adaptations of *The Taming of the Shrew*. This newer masculinity has been boosted by the rise of Hindutva, which seeks to empower Hindu men supposedly emasculated by long-ago Muslim 'invaders'. Men looking for such empowerment will find little to enjoy in *Twelfth Night*. But in the transitional period mid-century, when sangeet naatak's transvestism was still fresh in audience memories, *Twelfth Night*'s gender fluidity proved a vibrant resource for Indian filmmakers. A Hindi film, *Uran Khatola* (1955), begins with a premise that seems to have been lifted straight from the play. A plane crash takes the place of the play's opening shipwreck; it is followed by a love triangle between an imperious lady, a music-loving hero, and the heroine, who disguises herself as a man, Shibu, in order to serve him. The music-loving hero falls for the cross-dressed heroine, with the result that their love scenes are enacted largely in male costume. (Interestingly, the gender-bending heroine and her hero are played by two of the same actors—Nimmi and Dilip Kumar—who appeared in *Deedar*, the film that shaped the response to *Twelfth Night* of Vikram Seth's gender-fluid Dr Kishen Chand Seth.)

Uran Khatola was successfully dubbed into Tamil as *Vaana Ratham* (1956). The success of *Vaana Ratham* is perhaps not surprising given that, six years earlier in 1949, Tamil audiences had turned a masala film version of *Twelfth Night* into a huge hit. *Kanniyin Kaadhali* (1949) is in many ways a faithful Indianized version of Shakespeare's play, full of memorable songs that survive on YouTube. Prince Adiththan and his sister Princess Chandrika are separated at sea; she disguises herself as a man named Kalaimani, and serves a local prince named Vasanthakumaran, who is in love with Megala Devi—a haughty woman who, under the pretext of grieving for her dead brother and father, forswears the company of men. Vasanthakumaran employs Kalaimani as a go-between to woo Megala Devi, who falls for 'him', even though Kalaimani has, of course, fallen for Vasanthakumaran. The love triangle complication is resolved with the reappearance of Adiththan, allowing for a happy ending with two couples. Left out of this adaptation, interestingly, is the Malvolio character.

Kanniyin Kaadhali's most significant choice involves its casting. It does not feature a man playing the Viola counterpart. Instead, a woman acts the part of a man. The remarkable Rajasthani-origin actress, Madhuri Devi (still alive today, and living in Kolkata), plays both Chandrika/Kalaimani and her brother Adiththan, with a male playback actor doing the voiceover for the latter. If the Marathi sangeet naatak female-character actors brought femininity into their cinematic performances as men, Madhuri Devi suffused her film roles with masculinity, playing a series of androgynous women. By casting her, the directors disrupted what we now regard as the conventional relations between actor's body and character, sex and gender. Instead, like Shakespeare, they allowed us to see sex and gender as fluid states.

The casting of Madhuri Devi as both the Viola and the Sebastian characters was no doubt partly inspired by Shakespeare's own experiment with masala gender. But it may have been influenced also by the popular Tamil theatrical form of therukkuttu. Indeed, therukkuttu—Tamil for street performance—seems to be tailor-made for *Twelfth Night*. And that is because it epitomizes what Manningham termed 'mingled' comedy. It takes old tragic stories from the Mahabharata, especially of beleaguered women such as Draupadi, and mixes them with music and clowning. It tells tales of marriage riddled with darkness and confusion. And, most importantly, it always involves cross-gendered actors. It is hard not to see Madhuri Devi's performance in *Kanniyin Kaadhali* and her androgynous appeal in Tamil film as having emerged from a culture in which therukkuttu had helped normalize an appreciation of gender as a masala mingling. This appreciation faded after Independence, as the many southern *Taming of the Shrew* adaptations suggest. But Madhuri Devi's performance in *Kanniyin Kaadhali* underscored *Twelfth Night*'s insistence that masculinity as much as femininity is performed, not biological.

◆

Has Indian folk theatre's gender fluidity survived in modern Hindi cinema? On the one hand, the masala movie genre continues to be fascinated by transvestism. Films in which men dress up as women are a dime a dozen: Amitabh Bachchan in *Laawaaris* (1981) and Govinda in *Aunty No. 1* (1998) are only two instances. But these films do very little to unsettle ideas of gender: Bachchan's and Govinda's masculinity is the reality, their femininity a (supposedly hilarious) performance. And men are in total control of that performance—in much the same way as they are in *The Taming of the Shrew*. Occasionally we also see women playing men, such as Saira Banu in *Victoria No. 203* (1972). But here, too, there is no uncertainty about what is the truth of the body beneath the performance. The intricate, multilayered performances of gender that distinguish nautanki, sangeet naatak and therukkuttu have by and large not served as a resource for modern Hindi cinema, which—like its global counterparts—has increasingly tended to presume on the biological truth of the actor's body.

One exception is *Dil Bole Hadippa!* (2009). Like that other transvestite-themed exception, *Daayraa*, it evokes two theatrical conventions of cross-gendering: nautanki and Shakespeare. *Dil Bole Hadippa!*, directed by Anurag Singh, is a second-order adaptation of *Twelfth Night* by way of the Hollywood film *She's The Man* (2006). The latter was made at the tail end of a brief American fad for high-school reimaginings of Shakespeare, such as *10 Things I Hate About You* (1999), a version of *The Taming of the Shrew*, and *O* (2001), a version of *Othello*. *She's The Man* turned *Twelfth Night* into a coming-of-age sports movie, where Viola dresses up as her twin brother Sebastian to make the school football team at Illyria Preparatory School, and tries to woo the male sports star Duke (his last name is Orsino). There is no Malvolio in *She's The Man*. And that is because the film is not interested in cross-class desire; rather, it is invested in a brand of feminism-lite, the idea that women can do anything that men can do.

Dil Bole Hadippa! preaches much the same message. The film relocates *She's The Man* to a Punjabi setting, replacing the school football theme with a village cricket story. Viola is now Veera Kaur (played by Rani Mukerji), a humble Punjabi nautanki dancer-actress who also happens to be an unusually gifted cricket player. In the film's opening sequence, she effortlessly lofts six sixes—five right-handed and the last left-handed—off six deliveries from a champion male fast bowler. But there are few opportunities for a gifted female cricketer in the fiercely patriarchal environment of Punjab. To achieve her heart's dream of playing for a championship team, Veera is forced to dress up as a young male Sikh cricketer named Veer. In this guise she not only wins a cross-border championship game for her Amritsar team against their rivals from Lahore; she also wins the heart of the handsome Anglophone NRI cricketing star Rohan (Shahid Kapoor).

The film creatively reimagines many aspects of *Twelfth Night*. Veera-as-Veer is a version of Viola–Cesario; s/he also embodies the Viola–Sebastian relation, as Veer presents 'himself' as Veera's brother. Rohan is a counterpart to Orsino, a cricketing prince (he plays professional county cricket in England) who is attracted to a cross-dressed woman in ways that are ambivalently hetero- and homosexual. There is an Olivia figure of sorts, a Punjabi princess whom Veera-as-Veer counsels about Rohan. Notably, as in *Kanniyin Kaadhali*, there is no counterpart to Malvolio. The tale of cross-class desire that Malvolio embodies is not absent from the film, however. In Veera's class mobility—she is a simple villager who comically murders the English language but lands a sophisticated Anglophone shehzada—there is also something of the Maria/Sir Toby Belch liaison.

But *Dil Bole Hadippa!* mines *Twelfth Night* most in its masala treatment of gender. Unlike Hindi transvestite movies that present femininity as a performance controlled by men, *Dil Bole Hadippa!*—like *Kanniyin Kaadhali*—follows *Twelfth Night* in presenting masculinity as a performance. And, as in Shakespeare's play, masculinity is a matter not of biological sex but of prostheses. As Rohan says, 'cricket mein player nahin, uska bat bolta hai (in cricket the player doesn't talk, his bat does)'. This bat is presented as a sign of masculinity. Veera quips early in the film that a rolling pin rather than a bat is what distinguishes the hand of a Punjabi girl. Refusing the rolling pin and donning a bat, Veera has no choice but to morph into Veer. Which is to say, she cannot be Veera and hold a bat: the chowkidar at the ground where she trials for the Amritsar team tells her that the day girls start playing cricket, boys will have to start wearing bangles. As this suggests, *Dil Bole Hadippa!* is insistent that gender is conferred by objects rather than biology. And that is why 'Veer'—the name is a cross-lingual pun that means 'brave' in Hindi and 'to go off-course' in English—is the product of a host of prostheses: bat, beard, pagdi, and brown contact lenses. The gender confusion embodied by Viola's 'I am not what I am' is loosely approximated by Veera's 'mera sapna hai toh main hoon, nahin toh main kuch bhi nahin hoon (if my dream exists then so do I, if not then I am nothing)'. Her dream can become a reality only if she wields a bat; if she doesn't, there can be no 'she'. So she must be a 'he'. Echoing the title of the Hollywood film, she's the man, indeed.

Dil Bole Hadippa! is closer to *Twelfth Night* than either *She's The Man* or *Kanniyin Kaadhali* in its explicit fascination with the relations between gender and theatrical transvestism. And here *Dil Bole Hadippa!* suggests that the 'habit' of gender is not just confined to clothing. It extends to theatrical forms of movement—acting and, in particular, dancing—that, to be learned successfully, need to be practised over and over again. Veera performs Veer by drawing on these practised skills. She has cultivated them during her years as a performer-dancer in the Jigri Yaar Dance Company, a nautanki group. Indeed, the idea of assuming the guise of Veer comes to her only after she steps in for a drunken male actor during a dance routine. The climax of the routine is her vigorous performance of an item number, 'Bhangra Bistar (Bhangra Bed)', to unforgettable Punjabi–Hinglish lyrics.

The song is a hilarious performance of swaggering Punjabi masculinity. This masculinity again emerges from objects: to be male means to consort 'with bhangra, bistar, beer, bater (bhangra, bed, beer, quail)'. But what is most striking about the song's mise-en-scene is not just how convincingly Rani Mukerji pulls off the requisite masculine movements. Equally striking is how close these movements are already to her vigorous dancing film persona as a woman, showcased in masala films from *Bunty aur Babli* (2005) to *Om Shanti Om* (2007). The film plays with the fact that the line between Rani's Veera and Veer is porous:

both are given to boisterous twirls and vigorously waving arms. The song's lyrics delight in this gender ambiguity. The metaphorical accessory of the tumescent Punjabi male is the pressure cooker, an instrument of the supposedly female kitchen. This 'Bhangra Bistar' is indeed tailor-made for a 'Bi-Star', a showstopper who is equally hero and heroine.

Veera's turn as Veer draws on the musical dimension of nautanki. When she comes back to her company dressed as Veer, she is asked 'aap kaun hain (who are you)?' And she replies: 'main Jagjit Singh hoon (I am Jagjit Singh)', the name of a famed ghazal singer. But if Jagjit Singh's ghazals are the music that will provide the food of love for Rohan/Orsino, Veera here suggests also a self-love: early on Veera-as-Veer intends, 'he' says, to marry Veera because 'cross-connection hai, ji (there's a cross-connection, sir)'. Because this 'cross-connection' is a direct connection, the film unsettles any stable distinction between the female actress and her male part. Instead, what we see is gender mingling. When made to run in training, Veera-as-Veer complains that while waiting to be 'Sachin' (i.e. Tendulkar, the famous cricket batsman), 'he' has instead become 'P. T. Usha' (the champion female runner). And when Rohan spies Veera–Veer's deception, he says: 'I couldn't imagine that you were such a good actress—or should I say actor?' The confusion is allowed to stand.

This confusion is of a piece with the film's typically masala dream of partition-busting. Two scenes take place in the cross-border zone at Wagah, where dear friends Vicky (Vikramjeet Singh) of Amritsar and Lucky (Liyaqat Ali Khan) of Lahore meet each year to begin the annual cricket competition between their two cities. And even though 'winning is winning and losing is losing,' as their two captains like to say, the film's impulse is not to choose one side over the other but to allow for something more-than-one, something masala. As Lucky says, the match is just an excuse—'the idea is to wipe out differences, whether it is across borders or across chairs.' Or across male and female, as Veera's final speech demanding that women be allowed to play in the same teams as men makes clear.

Veera's 'cross-connection' skills—what Sir John Manningham might have called her talents in 'mingled comedy'—are explicitly linked to her nautanki background. After all, nautanki, like sangeet naatak and therukkuttu, has traditionally featured transvestite actors. In the past, nautanki cast men in female roles; recently, women have also started playing male parts. It is perhaps no surprise, then, that a much acclaimed

JONATHAN GIL HARRIS

nautanki production of *Twelfth Night* has most successfully captured the masala gender elements of Shakespeare's play. More than Hindi cinema, in which the effects of cross-gendering tend to depend on the 'truth' of the actor's body, it is transvestite folk theatre that most successfully communicates the radically masala vision of gender that *Dil Bole Hadippa!*, like *Kanniyin Kaadhali* and *Twelfth Night*, purveys—the idea that all identity entails a mingling of parts, objects, and 'habits.'

◆

In 2015—more than 400 years after Manningham saw *Twelfth Night* in London and a hundred years after that other British spectator saw its sangeet naatak adaptation in Bombay—I first experienced a nautanki version of the play at the Kamani Auditorium in Delhi. This reimagining too was a mingled comedy, but in a new way. When I entered the darkened theatre, I spied a near-bare stage set that consisted of a mounted platform for a nautanki 'mandli' (a company of actors) and, at stage-right, a carpet with a harmonium and a dholak drum. The one slightly elaborate component of the set was a large garlanded cut-out of a devta's face hanging at the back: an Indian god-like figure who, upon closer inspection, turned out to be the familiar face of Shakespeare, made unfamiliar in an Indianized form. Yes, this was a culturally cross-dressed Shakespeare: masala Will, simultaneously English and desi. 'What You Will', if you like.

Piya Behrupiya (Multifaced Lover) is not the first nautanki version of *Twelfth Night*. That honour belongs to a Marathi play from the 1960s called *Madanachi Manjari* (Madan's Friend). But *Piya Behrupiya* is the most successful, with more than 200 performances since it was first devised in 2011. I have now thrilled to it three times. The play is directed by Atul Kumar, who did his Shakespeare apprenticeship with Rajat Kapoor in a series of mixed English-language-gibberish clown adaptations. *Piya Behrupiya* has something of the harlequin exuberance of Kapoor's adaptations. But the play draws less on Kapoor's Western clowning styles than on Indian folk traditions of comic performance.

Piya Behrupiya is in many ways a typical nautanki. It may have been performed largely in urban proscenium stage auditoriums such as the Kamani Theatre. But it employs many of the conventions of outdoor village nautanki performance. It makes extensive, often hilarious use of music played on traditional folk instruments, coupled with exuberant dance. It adapts the convention of the sutradhar, turning Sebastian—

performed by the playwright, Amitosh Nagpal—into a wise-cracking narrator (he mocks his director, saying 'he wanted me to do it in gibberish'). Its actors do not leave the stage; when they are not acting, they rejoin the 'mandli' in the middle of the daayraa, from where they comment—often irreverently—on what is being acted before them. Its language is a colourful folk Hindi, spiced with elements of Punjabi, Urdu, Bhojpuri and English. And, most importantly, it employs cross-dressed actors.

Viola is played by the firecracker actor Geetanjali Kulkarni. She enters in a ghaghra-choli, but is quickly reclothed by the other actors in traditional village male attire, including a turban and a painted moustache. She flexes her biceps, swaggers convincingly, and dances with masculine ferocity. But Kulkarni's Cesario is not the only cross-dressed character. The Feste of *Twelfth Night* has been transformed into the androgynous Phool Singh, played by Neha Saraf. The cross-gendering of Shakespeare's iconic clown speaks volumes about the vision of masala that is at the heart of this nautanki 'mingled comedy'. As in Shakespeare's play, cross-dressing is simply an exemplary instance of a world in which mixture is the defining element.

The title of Nagpal's adaptation, *Piya Behrupiya*, insists on the masala multiplicity not just of Viola or Phool Singh but also of Shakespeare. The garlanded face that hangs at the back of the stage is both English and Indian; he is also revered and mocked in a fashion that recalls the ambivalent treatment of the Shakespeare face in *Angoor*. On the one hand, this face is the performance's muse, to whom the actors peform adaabs at the start. On the other, Sebastian complains to, and of, the devta that he has been given hardly any lines ['Shakespeare ne neend mein likha pehle hi mera character (Shakespeare wrote my character in his sleep already)'], and moans that, because Antonio has been cut from this adaptation, he has to perform his boyfriend's lines too. *Piya Behrupiya* is thus both dependent on Shakespeare and resistant to his authority. Nagpal's bravura performance also demonstrates the masala more-than-oneness of the actor, who morphs into Sebastian, Antonio, and even Shakespeare himself ['Toh main jaldi se Sebastian ban jata hoon aur aapko Shakespeare sunata hoon (I'll quickly turn into Sebastian and perform Shakespeare for you)'].

Piya Behrupiya's title not only describes the play's masala multiplicity. It also enacts it. The repetition of the 'piya' sound in the title performs something of Feste's remark about how a word resembles a cheverel glove turned inside out—it means something different as it is twisted into a new shape. This conviction that words' meanings will wantonly morph, that they themselves are 'multifaced lovers', is at the heart of *Piya Behrupiya*'s immense theatrical charm. The wantonness of words is evident everywhere in its script. The play is in Hindi, but with a myriad linguistic variations. Some characters resort to Urdu when they sing qawwalis or Kabir's dohas. When Orsino (Sagar Deshmukh) speaks of love, he does so in a Lucknowi Hindustani. Phool Singh speaks in a heavily Bhojpuri dialect. The Olivia character (Mansi Multani) is a princess who speaks in a thick Punjabi Hinglish—telling Viola that she has 'kaisi kaisi mithi awaaz (such a sweet voice)! I'm sure you belong to bast family'—and performs (siyapa!!) a show-stopper of an item number about Cesario, lustfully bellowing his name as 'Say-jar-ee-oh.' The class aspirationalism of Malvolio (Saurabh Nayyar) takes the form of a tutta-phuttah English. Andrew Aguecheek (Mantramugdh) has become Andrew Da-da, a surrealist bhadralok Bengali fop. And Sir Toby Belch (Gagan Singh Riar) wears a lungi—though his language does not have the southern inflections one might expect.

The play is multilingual. But it is, more accurately, trans-lingual: the script is loaded with wordplay that swerves brilliantly between languages, particularly when it comes to names. We are invited to admire Orsino's 'aur seena (extra big chest)'. Toby Belch tells Maria that 'I am Toby and you are my Gobi (cauliflower).' And Maria's name morphs into multiple Hindi forms. Toby transforms it into 'mariada (convention)'; Andrew greets Maria as 'madam Malai (cream)'; and she corrects him with another pun on her name: 'mera naam Mera hai (my name is mine)' [in Nagpal's Hindi script, Maria and 'Mera' (my) are written the same way].

These linguistic morphings are accompanied by rapid-fire, utterly ingenious theatrical transformations. The actor who plays Malvolio, for reasons known only to the production, does a bravura cameo turn as a confused blind qawwal in the scene involving the mock duel between Viola and Sir Andrew, transformed here into a musical show-down between Sufi songs and Hindu bhajans. And the actors playing Toby and Sebastian suddenly transform into two corrupt priests. [The play's energetic mocking of Hindu fundamentalism includes a winking translation of Andrew Aguecheek's blasphemous claim to be 'a great eater of beef' (1.3.73–4).]

What *Piya Behrupiya* offers is not just the most achingly funny two hours of Indian theatre I have seen. It also enfolds its audiences in a comprehensive masala vision of the universe. This vision derives from the theatrics of Viola's gender confusion, but it then radiates outwards. Sebastian asks Olivia: if she had married Viola, 'kaun banta mister, kaun banta missus (who would become mister, who would become missus)?' Sebastian's question, at once side-splitting and totally serious, resonates with his earlier wry remark to the audience: 'comic play hai, tragic character hoon, bahut confused hoon (it's a comic play, I'm a tragic character; I'm very confused).' Everything in this play—gender, genre, language, Shakespeare, the actors, the audience—is 'behrupiya', multifaced.

It is because of this pervasive multifacedness that *Piya Behrupiya* is a more thoroughly masala adaptation of *Twelfth Night's* 'mingled comedy' than Vikram Seth's novelized production in *A Suitable Boy*. Vernacular nautanki more than Anglophone literature is invested in the cosmic theatrical play—the rasleela—that erases the fixity of any identity, twisting it like a cheveril glove into something more-than-one. The rasleela of gender is particularly useful to remember at a time when a newly rampant Hindutva is provoking mass outbreaks of beards and chhappan-inch chests in a collective fantasy of mard wapsi. The desire to be a pure man is time and again fuelled by a consuming sense of emasculated inadequacy. Little wonder the desire expresses itself in violence against women, Muslims and Dalits who supposedly deprive higher-caste Hindu men of the pure masculinity they once possessed in an imagined perfect past. Geetanjali Kulkarni's comically flexed biceps, like Rani Mukerji's raucous bhangra bi-star gyrations, present a powerful masala corrective to today's noxious dreams of shuddh mardangi. In this, Kulkarni and Mukerji are not just cousins of Viola. They are the reincarnations of Shakespeare's Witches, those 'bearded hags' from *Macbeth* who see a future, now, in which all dreams of singular masculinity are shattered by their impossibility.

Poster for Sohrab Modi's 1935 film Khoon ka Khoon,
his Urdu adaptation of Hamlet

Saed-e-Havas, *Sohrab Modi's 1936 film adaptation of
Shakespeare's* King John

Deven Verma (who plays both the Bahadur twins) with director/screenplay and dialogue writer/musical director Gulzar on the set of Angoor *(1981)*

Rajat Kapoor (Ghalib) and Tisca Chopra (Roshni) in 10 ml Love, *dir. Sharat Katariya (2010)*

Ranveer Singh (Ram) and Deepika Padukone (Leela) in Goliyon ki Rasleela Ram-Leela, *dir. Sanjay Leela Bhansali (2013)*

Sandeepa Dhar (Rajnandini) and Akshay Oberoi (Vivaan) in Isi Life Mein, *dir. Vidhi Kasliwal (2010)*

Rani Mukerji *(Veera / Veer)* and members of the Jigri Yaar Dance Company in Dil Bole Hadippa!, *dir. Anurag Singh (2009)*

Geetanjali Kulkarni *(Viola / Cesario)* in Piya Behrupiya, *dir. Atul Kumar (2011)*

Saif Ali Khan (Langda Tyagi) in Omkara, *dir. Vishal Bhardwaj (2006)*

Salman (Sumit Kaul) and Salman (Rajat Bhagat) in Haider, *dir. Vishal Bhardwaj (2014)*

The first page of Purvai Aranya's unpublished graphic novel The Return, *written and drawn in 2014*

The cast of Hera-Phericles *(2018), from left to right: Purvai Aranya, Ira Sen, Udeshi Basu, Sreya Muthukumar, Zico Saigal, Goutam Piduri*

dardnak kahaanis

CHORUS

The firangi and the desi twins recognize that the world of masala mixture isn't always a happy one. It is frequently beset by internal disruptions that threaten to destroy it. In this world, as the firangi says, nothing is but what is not. The more-than-one is simultaneously the less-than-one: in the masala universe, a thing cannot help but mix with other elements that make of that thing a nothing, neither this nor that. Widespread acceptance of this mixed state of affairs is at best a utopian hope. And when singularity is valued over mixture, when we insist that masala more-than-oneness be purged of all impurity to create a shuddh oneness, terrible violence can ensue. Tragic violence.

Ek dardnak kahaani hai, the desi says. It's a painful tale. There is no precise word for 'tragedy' in Hindi or Urdu. But both languages express a deep understanding of pain.

The firangi, who sometimes answers to the name Will, understands that although a tragedy is often caused by what its name means—desire—it is always willy-nilly haunted by Will's opposite which is also its outcome, Nil. And the desi, who sometimes answers to the name Vishal, understands that although a dardnak kahaani-themed film can match the meaning of its name—grand—it is always visually haunted by Vishal's vice-versa which is also its outcome, Shunyata, nothingness. In short, the twins both know that the single is shadowed by the double, the pure by the impure, being by non-being. They know too that the hero who picks the first term in each pair at the expense of the other quickly becomes what he most fears: a zero.

144

ACT FOUR SCENE ONE

'Koi Ahmak Jaise Sunaaye Afsaana'

In early 2018, I interviewed the director, writer and musician Vishal Bhardwaj at a literary festival in Chennai. The invitation to talk with him was for me a dream come true: Bhardwaj is more responsible than any other filmmaker for the current popularity of Indian Shakespeare, thanks to his critically acclaimed trilogy of adaptations of *Macbeth*, *Othello*, and *Hamlet*. But the festival organizers informed me that Bhardwaj didn't want to speak about his films. He wanted instead to talk about *Nude*, his recently published collection of ghazals and nazms. My heart sank. How was I to engage Bhardwaj about two poetic forms I know only a little about, written in a language in which I am at best only haltingly proficient?

I was relieved to discover that the collection of poems is bilingual. On the left pages, Bhardwaj's ghazals and nazms are printed in Devanagari script; on the right, they are printed in an English translation by Sukrita Paul Kumar. Her translation has helped me savour the distinctive flavour of Bhardwaj's poems. In particular, Kumar has helped me see how his ghazals and nazms *veer*. They veer (as so much classical north Indian poetry does) between anguish and wit, between the personal and the political, between the erotic and the spiritual, between the generic impersonality of poetic form and the confessional reveal-all impulse suggested by the collection's title.

But something strange happened as I began to read the poems. I, too, found myself veering, as my eyes kept straying from Kumar's translations to the Hindi originals. Or, I should say, Hindustani originals. Because I couldn't help notice that the language of Bhardwaj's poems, despite being printed in Devanagari, was a lively mixture of Hindi, Urdu and English. Indeed, the English title of the collection—*Nude*—was not a translation of a Hindi word, even though one ghazal speaks memorably about how 'aankhon mein dil ke mansoobe nange hain,/ sab apne kapdon ke neeche nange hain/ panch sitara hotel ke chaurahe par,/ kitne saare bacche bhuke-nange hain/ gahre gol hamaam si sansad ki building/ sab ke sab hi jiske andar nange hain (Naked are the heart's motives in the eyes/ Naked are we all beneath our clothes/ At the crossing of the five-star hotel/ Many children starving and naked/ Circular, hamam-like, the Parliament building,/ Inside, everyone is naked, all of them)'. The collection's title is taken instead from a ghazal that commands 'gaur se dekhe nude painting ko/ kitni pakizagi jhalakti hai (Look at the nude painting closely/ What purity radiates from it)'. The single-language translation of this couplet cannot do justice to the trans-lingual scope of the original. Despite the 'pakizagi' (purity) of the nude painting, the lines express the idea in a masala rekhta, veering between Hindi and Urdu and English. Linguistic mixture is the paradoxical medium, then, of Bhardwaj's vision of purity.

I asked Bhardwaj why he used the English 'nude' rather than the Hindi/Urdu 'nanga' as the title of his collection. He replied that Gulzar, his friend and mentor, had advised him to title his collection *Nude* because the word conveyed a different shade of meaning from 'nanga'. If the latter suggested something stripped down and shocking, the former implied an artistic vision. And, of course, Gulzar's own artistry, too, is a rekhta that crosses linguistic and cultural boundaries. But as Bhardwaj reminded me, mixed language not only serves an artistic purpose. It also captures the idiom of everyday speech in northern India, where even in the poorest villages Hindi is supplemented by terms from English, Urdu, and other bhashas in order to lend expression to thoughts that cannot be completed in just one language. He cited as an example a line from one of his ghazals—'mujhko lagaa ki network tootne lagaa (the network seemed to be breaking, I felt)'. In a new age of mass mobile phone and internet dependency, the English 'network' is, in fact, a resonant and distinctively Indian metaphor with which to think about the disconnections between two people.

Nude's poems speak in the many tongues of Hindi, Urdu and English. They speak also in the many voices of Bhardwaj's poetic influences. His early inspiration, Dr Bashir Badr, is lauded in the preface. Mirza Ghalib and Gulzar are the subjects of two nazms, both of which slyly capture the two poets' distinctive personalities. Ghalib appears as a character in one, scolding Bhardwaj in typically contrarian fashion for his worthless poetry. And Gulzar—who always wears starched white kurta pajama—is memorably described in the other, with cheeky trans-denominational alliteration, as 'Santa Claus sa saccha safed Sufi (like Santa Claus a true white Sufi)'.

But as I read through the poems, I noticed another Sufi poet haunting Bhardwaj's words—a Pir. Or, rather, a Sheikh's Pir. In a particularly eerie ghazal that describes a mysterious figure 'jisne apna chehra theek se pehchana (who recognizes his own face well)', Bhardwaj writes:

Itne dheeme dheeme waqt guzarta hai
Koi ahmak jaise sunaaye afsaana.
(So slowly does time drag
Like a tale told by an idiot.)

The identity of the figure is unclear. But the reference to the tale told by an 'ahmak (idiot)', at least to the ears of any Shakespearean, is very clear. Bhardwaj has adapted, into a concise couplet, the theme of Macbeth's famous speech:

Tomorrow, and tomorrow, and tomorrow
Creeps in this petty pace from day to day
To the last syllable of recorded time,
And all our yesterdays have lighted fools
The way to dusty death. Out, out, brief candle.
Life's but a walking shadow, a poor player
That struts and frets his hour upon the stage,
And then is heard no more. It is a tale
Told by an idiot, full of sound and fury,
Signifying nothing. (5.5.18–27)

Bhardwaj omits Shakespeare's 'sound and fury' and 'out, out, brief candle'. But he elegantly compresses the burden of Macbeth's existential ennui into his couplet, with two lines that potentially communicate his own self-critique as an 'ahmak (idiot)'. Just as Bhardwaj has the English phrase 'nude painting' interrupt a linguistic mix of Hindi and Urdu, so, too, does the English poet interrupt a mushaira comprising Badr, Ghalib and Gulzar. When I asked Bhardwaj about the reference, he laughed and said he wanted to pay homage to the poet who has enabled so much for him in his film career. In other words, like that poet, Bhardwaj, too, deals in mixed lineage and language.

Yet mixture is also a source of anxiety for Bhardwaj, at least in his untranslated introduction to *Nude*. There he writes: 'adhaa adhaa sa lagta hai mujhe. Lagta hai ki zindagi mein agar sirf ek hi vidha pe kaam karta toh shayad behtar hota. Na pura musician hua na writer aur na hi director. Aur ab adhi shayari lekar haazir hoon (I feel a little half and half. It might have been better if I had stuck with just one mode in life. I did not become a full musician, writer, or director. And now

I present myself as half a poet).' Gulzar says in his prefatory note to *Nude* that 'Vishal ki creative shaqsiyat (Vishal's creative persona)' combines 'mausikar bhi…filmmaker bhi aur kayi mediums mein apni baat ka izhaar karta hai (musician, also filmmaker, and someone who expresses himself in many mediums)'. Taking my cue from Gulzar, I asked Bhardwaj whether his many vocations have been an asset rather than a liability. His mixed languages have given him a greater vividness of expression, and his mixed poetic lineages have given him more inspiration. Similarly, his mixed skills as musician, writer, and director are a large part of why his film conversations with Shakespeare are so uniquely memorable. I asked him: Doesn't your experience as a musician give you a special ear for the sound of poetry? Doesn't your experience as a director give you a special eye for the arresting poetic image? And aren't your films augmented by your musician's and writer's sensibilities? In typically modest fashion, he demurred. But at least I had sneakily managed to change the subject from *Nude* to his Shakespeare films. And I had located in *Nude*'s recurrent interest in mixture—linguistic, poetic, musical/directorial/writerly—the basis of what has long fascinated me about Bhardwaj's version of masala Shakespeare.

'Koi ahmak jaise sunaaye afsaana': Bhardwaj's reimagining of the line from *Macbeth* may be ironically aimed at himself and his poetic as well as cinematic tales. Elsewhere Bhardwaj writes with some fierceness about how 'sab kehte hain filmon vale nange hain (film-wallahs are naked, say all)'. But by speaking confessionally in the translated language of Shakespeare, Bhardwaj tells us something about the masala flavour of the ahmak ka afsaana—the idiot's tale that is both Shakespeare's and his own, foreign and desi. That is why his masala Shakespeare is somewhat different from the instances I have discussed in earlier chapters. Bhardwaj draws on the cinematic vocabularies of foreign directors—Francis Ford Coppola, Akira Kurosawa, Quentin Tarantino, Krzysztof Kieślowski—as well as Indian auteurs such as the artful Satyajit Ray and the more populist Ram Gopal Varma. Yet because of his gifts as a composer and playback singer, Bhardwaj's films always boast distinctive musical interludes—and occasionally full-blown item numbers—that tip over into the style of Bollywood. As a result, Bhardwaj's films fall somewhere in the grey area between so-called 'parallel' art cinema and mass masala entertainment.

Born in 1965 in a village near Bijnor in Uttar Pradesh, Bhardwaj has always had an ear for the sounds of both rural India and Bombay cinema. His father was a sugarcane inspector who also composed Hindi film songs. The younger Bhardwaj evidently inherited his father's skill; without formal training, he effortlessly picked up the harmonium while accompanying ghazal singers. And a song he wrote in his teens, thanks to his father's musician connections, made its way into a little-known 1985 Hindi movie. Bhardwaj properly entered Bollywood in the early nineties as a musical director. He quickly captured attention for his songs, especially 'Chappa Chappa Charkha Chale' and 'Chhod Aaye Hum Woh Galiyaan' in Gulzar's film, *Maachis* (1996), about the 1980s Sikh insurgency. Shortly after, he scored Ram Gopal Varma's gangster movie *Satya* (1998). These two films have greatly influenced Bhardwaj's Shakespeare adaptations, which perform a balancing act between politically sensitive socials and genre gangster movies. And Bhardwaj's musical compositions—with lyrics by Gulzar—continue to be one of his films' most distinctive features, serving as conduits between Shakespeare's poetry and the masala formulas of Bollywood item numbers. Indeed, Bhardwaj says he became a filmmaker primarily to give himself more scope to write music.

I suggested to Bhardwaj that, more than any other factor, his musical sensibility is responsible for the extraordinary power of his cinematic reimaginings of Shakespeare. It is not just that he adapts Shakespeare's stories or the psychology of his characters—though he does both ingeniously well. It is also that he has a unique ability to hear the musical dimension of Shakespeare's language. He was appreciative (if a little bemused) by my suggestion that his use of an ominous melodic dip in a song for *Omkara* (2006) perfectly matched Shakespeare's equally ominous falling rhythm in a line from *Othello*. But even if Bhardwaj is not trained in the prosody of Shakespearean metre, as a musician he can hear something in the sound of Shakespeare's language that more story- or character-oriented adaptors cannot. And that is why, when he imagines 'koi ahmak jaise sunaaye afsana', Bhardwaj recognizes that the idiot's tale is one that is spoken or sung out *loud*, like a ghazal. Even the afsaana of an ahmak possesses a music that propels it.

Vishal Bhardwaj: half-musician, half-director, half-writer. By my maths, a mixture who is more-than-one. A mixture who not only creates but also embodies masala. As he himself writes in a haunting nazm 'Main hi tha woh main hi hoon' (an earlier, much shorter version of which appears in *Haider* (2014), his adaptation of *Hamlet*), he is both 'dair (temple)' and 'haram (harem)', Sunni and Shia and 'panditon ke haat mein (in the hands of Pandits)', 'Qaziyon ke mathe pe/ Sajde ka nishan (a mark of obeisance on the forehead of a Qazi)' and 'padre ke seene pe/ Jhoolti saleeb (a swinging cross on the chest of a Pastor)'. The 'main (I)' of this nazm traverses differences, as does Bhardwaj himself. This isn't simply a cheerful celebration of diversity. A sadness, even a quiet anger, pervades the poem. Bhardwaj said to me about this nazm that he hates organized religion: he hates its claim to a single monopoly on the truth at the expense of other ways of being, seeing and doing. Within the wondrous multiplicity of this nazm's 'main', then, are embedded the seeds of tragedy. It is not just the Pandit or the Qazi or the Pastor who is tragically flawed: it is anyone whose will to singular truth violently refuses the many that make up the 'main'.

If *Macbeth*'s idiot's tale haunts Bhardwaj's poems, this nazm might allow us to glimpse the more-than-oneness of the play as a whole. For *Macbeth*, like the 'main' of the nazm, keeps reminding us that every seemingly singular entity is always shadowed by multiplicity. And that to insist on one's singularity is not simply to tell a tale that signifies nothing. It is also an act of violence that guarantees a dardnak kahaani.

ACT FOUR SCENE TWO

Masala Time (*Macbeth*)

You could call Holi masala time. Not only does the festival involve a riot of colours, in which its participants—often under the influence of bhang—vigorously daub each other with multihued rang (colours). It is also celebrated across communities. Muslim and Sikh as well as Hindu, all take part, discharging the contents of pichkaris or lobbing water-filled balloons at all and sundry. In recent years, Holi has become an occasion for violence, as young male celebrants find ever more aggressive ways to throw their rang and their balloons. And that's why, these days, I lock myself indoors for its duration. Yet whatever misgivings I might have about how it is celebrated, Holi is rarely if ever a time of communal violence. Inclusiveness remains its central tenet, and that's why it has been Bollywood's go-to festival in countless films from *Mother India* and *Aan* to *Silsila* (1981) and *Goliyon Ki Rasleela Ram-Leela*. And Holi is masala time in another, more literal sense. It is a time of many times: a spring ritual that recalls an old tale of tyranny overcome and celebrates the imminent arrival of the harvest. In Holi, then, past and future crowd joyously into the present and make it more-than-one.

Holi comes in part from an ancient legend that is itself a tale of masala time. It is a tale that, even when commemorated by a bhang-addled ahmak full of sound and fury signifying nothing, can strike readers of Shakespeare with uncanny force. The festival derives its name from Holika, the demoness sister of the evil asura Hiranyakashipu. Their story is told in the Bhagavata Purana. Hiranya, as he is also known, is an ambitious fighter who becomes a king. He is granted a seeming promise of invincibility by a supernatural power: Brahma informs him, in riddling fashion, that Hiranya cannot be killed by human or animal, during the day or the night, indoors or outside, on the earth or in the air. In Hiranya's riddling masala present, the future seemingly co-exists as an assured immortality. Overconfident, he turns increasingly tyrannical and murderous: his victims include his sister Holika. Yet he has failed to read the riddles properly. The future-in-the-present is indeed correctly described by Brahma. But it entails death rather than everlasting life, for Hiranya is eventually slain by the half-human half-lion Narasimha (who is neither human nor animal), at twilight (which is neither day nor night), at the threshold of a courtyard (which is neither indoors nor outside), in Narasimha's lap (which is neither on the earth nor in the air).

The tale of Hiranyakashipu is, of course, uncannily close to the story of *Macbeth*. So much so that some scholars have even speculated about a distant genealogical link between the Bhagavata Purana and Shakespeare's Scottish play. But we now read the two stories very differently. Since the nineteenth century, in India as much as in Britain or New Zealand, students of Shakespeare have been trained to read *Macbeth* as a tragedy of ambition. By contrast, the story of the feckless asura is about how to inhabit masala time. For it is, fundamentally, a story about the perils of thinking in terms of the logic of 'either/or': it warns against seemingly black-or-white choices that admit no possibility of mixture. To read Brahma's prophecies correctly, one has to recognize how they abide by the logic not of 'either/or' but of 'both-and'. The future that is prophetically mixed within the present is itself a time of mixture, in which the human and the animal, the outside and the inside, the day and the night, and the up and the down all blend. In the tale of Hiranya, the present is plural because it contains a future that is also plural in its many possibilities.

What lessons can be drawn from this *Macbeth*-like tale of masala time? Had Hiranya allowed mixture into his understanding of the world, he may have escaped death. More importantly, he would have had to give up his sense of absolute singularity, invincibility, and supremacy. He would have had to concede that the world is full of in-between spaces of mixture. And he would also have had to recognize that, in the masala time of the now, the future resides in the present as a myriad new possibilities for thinking and behaving. Everything must and will and does change. Yet change is not just a distant point on a line that extends from present to future. It is here, now, in this masala time where futures radically different from what we think of as the present already exist.

Something of that vision of time survives in Holi. After all, the festival celebrates not so much the past burning of Holika—this is no cheerful homage to sati or jauhar—as the present promise of mixed colours and communities. That's why its presiding deity is the deep-blue Krishna, whose lover is the fair Radha. The time of the tyrant admits no mixture: it is one line, obeying one will. Holi by contrast imagines a now of many times, in which the mixtures missed by Hiranya and embodied by Radha and Krishna continue to predict, in their more-than-oneness, deliverance from tyranny. The colourful utopianism of Holi seems a world away from the darkness of *Macbeth*. But how is Shakespeare's play, like the Bhagavata Purana's tale of Hiranya, also steeped in a vision of masala time?

◆

When I first studied *Macbeth* as a teenager in New Zealand, I was taught that it was the tragedy of its titular character's ambition. This had much to do with the trend, popular since the English Romantics and strengthened further by the early twentieth-century scholar A. C. Bradley, to read tragedies as stories of *one*, of a single tragic hero foiled by a single flaw. But even a fairly superficial reading of the play exposes cracks in this narrative. For *Macbeth* is a play in which the titular character is not one but two. Macbeth is doubled by his wife, whose name is also Macbeth—Lady Macbeth. As if to stress the point, the first lines Shakespeare gives her are the words of her husband: she reads out his letter about the Witches' prophecy that he will be king. Which Macbeth is speaking here: Thane or Lady? But to pose the question this way is to follow Hiranyakashipu's error and to pose as an 'either/or' problem what is, in fact, a 'both-and' reality. Both Macbeths speak here. Or rather, both speak through each other. And both are possessed of deep ambition. But lurking in their joint tragedy is another dardnak kahaani often unwittingly re-enacted by their readers: a desire for singularity in a world that, like the two Macbeths themselves, is inescapably plural.

From the outset that plurality is embodied by the Witches. The three Weird Sisters, as Shakespeare calls them, are often regarded by readers as singularly evil. But from the moment of their entry on the blasted heath, they represent a principle of multiplicity that cannot be so easily pinned down. As their name suggests—'weird' is a Scottish version of 'wayward'—they refuse any singular, straight and narrow path. The Witches embody paradox. They are bearded hags. They are three beings who speak as one. They are immoral connivers who are amoral fates. They are solid entities who dissolve like bubbles into the earth. Their riddling language, too, is distinctively paradoxical. Their most memorable lines—sung in the trochaic music that Shakespeare had used for the otherworldly Puck—refuses the either/or logic that Hiranya succumbs to: 'Fair is foul and foul is fair,' they chant (1.1.12).

The Witches' plurality is of a piece with the mixed world described by Brahma in his prophecies. But the Witches differ from Brahma in one respect, and in a way that augments the vision of masala time in the story of Hiranya. The Witches are of the present, and predict the future. But they are also of the past. Unlike Brahma who continues to rule in the present, the Witches are supernatural beings who belong to a long-ago age: a pagan time that, for its original audience, had been supposedly superseded by Christianity. In their powers of divination, they not only recall the classical Greek fates. They also hint at an older Celtic faith that has supposedly been relegated to the past in an island now blessed by the light of Christian gospel and the healing powers of the saintly English King, Edward the Confessor. And that is why the time the Witches inhabit is also more-than-one: they embody a past-in-the-present that cracks open the singularity of the 'now' to reveal tantalizing glimpses of many futures. As Macbeth says after his first meeting with them, 'nothing is/ But what is not' (1.3.140–1).

There are three Witches. But the number—or rather, numeric operator—we might most associate with them is 'double.' As they stir their cauldron, boiling over with eye of newt and toe of frog, they mutter their most famous incantation thrice:

> Double, double, toil and trouble
> Fire burn and cauldron bubble. (4.1.10–11, 20–1, 35–6)

That repeated 'double, double' reverberates through the play. But what does it mean? It is easy to assume that it is a rhyming synonym for 'trouble' and therefore simply refers to something evil. But 'double, double' has a double meaning. 'Double' is both adjective and verb, meaning 'twice as much' and 'deceive.' Both meanings are at play in the Witches' incantation: twice as much toil and trouble; deceive duplicitously while the cauldron is bubbling. Neither one is the exclusively correct meaning of 'double', just as the Witches are neither singly male nor female, neither singly fair nor foul.

Even when we first hear the word 'double' in the play it has something of the duality the Witches give it. Lady Macbeth tells the unsuspecting King Duncan, whom she and her husband are about to murder, that

> All our service,
> In every point twice done, and then done double

Were poor and single business to contend
Against those honours deep and broad wherewith
Your majesty loads our house. (1.6.14–8)

It is clear that Lady Macbeth wants Duncan to think that she is doubly obliged to him, and that she will work doubly hard to look after him while he is her guest. But the other, menacing meaning of 'double' also lurks here, like a snake in the grass: Lady Macbeth's 'service', deceptive to the core, will indeed 'contend' against King Duncan's 'honours deep and broad'. Her language resonates with that of the Witches here, as it has earlier when she invokes 'spirits' to 'unsex' (1.5.38–9) her. Little wonder many readers regard her as the fourth Witch.

Yet the double meaning of 'double' does not work quite the same way for Lady Macbeth as it does for the Witches. Her use of the word presumes an evil meaning hidden beneath its surface. 'Look like the innocent flower,' she tells her husband, 'But be the serpent under't' (1.5.63–4). This is the doubleness advocated by Lady Macbeth—a doubleness that conceals a single, true evil. But it is not the doubleness of the witches. Their 'double, double' does not presume a hidden meaning. It is instead, like the mixture cooking in their cauldron, a more-than-oneness that refuses a final, singular essence.

This quality extends in particular to the Witches' famous riddling predictions. Their Brahma-like prophecies speak the language of 'both-and': Macbeth will be both Thane of Cawdor and King of Scotland. His close friend Banquo will be both more and less happy than Macbeth. Banquo both won't be king and will produce a line of kings. More famously, Macbeth will be killed only by a man of no woman born, and only when Birnam Wood rises up against him. The Witches' predictions suggest both Macbeth's indestructibility and the certainty of his death. Macbeth indeed dies at the hands of Macduff, who has been born from his dead mother through a caesarean section, after Malcolm's army, disguised as Birnam Wood, has moved against him. And Banquo, though murdered by Macbeth, lives on in his escaped son Fleance who will be the forefather of a line of kings culminating in Shakespeare's monarch and patron, King James VI of Scotland and I of England.

Macbeth denounces the doubleness of the Witches' predictions as he prepares to meet his death:

And be no more these juggling fiends believed
Who palter with us in a double sense. (5.10.19–20)

Macbeth's use of 'double' resonates with his wife's; he believes that, beneath the illusory assurance he has received from the Witches' predictions, there is an essential deceptiveness responsible for his destruction. But Macbeth, like Lady Macbeth, misconstrues doubleness by understanding it simply in terms of appearance and reality. For the Witches' predictions typify an idea of masala time that has eluded Macbeth. He thinks the future is a singularity that can be known correctly. But the 'double sense' of the Witches' predictions, neither right nor wrong, suggests that the future be understood differently. It is not something that can be known with absolute certainty in advance, captured through cunning like a stolen answer to a Board Exam question. The future, rather, is a matter of radical uncertainty *in the present*. It exists, in the present, as a riddle. And even though we can intimate something from that riddle, *we* are the ones who transform the riddle of the future into a new present by interpreting it this way or that. It is not the Witches' double meanings that are evil; rather, our deeply ingrained compulsion to resolve doubleness into singularity—as surely as our brain resolves the double signal provided by our two optic nerves into one object of vision—is what gets us into trouble. We are all Hiranyakashipus, to our peril.

This longing for singularity, far more than ambition, is Macbeth's tragic flaw. But it is also the flaw of so many of the play's characters. *Macbeth* keeps showing us the costs of this longing. From the first act, Macbeth has been invested in maintaining 'my single state of man' (1.3.139); yet his very first line, 'so foul and fair a day I have not seen' (1.3.36), channels the doubleness of the Witches. No matter how much he may try to wrest singularity from the Witches' riddling predictions, his 'single state of man' is presented, like the dagger he hallucinates, as a mirage that will lead him to murderous tyranny and then his doom. This tell-tale choice of phrase suggests how Macbeth's wished-for singularity is repeatedly gendered as masculine, just as the Witches' double, 'both-and' state is presented as transgendered. Macbeth fantasizes a masculinity that is rock-solid, phallic 'marble'. Raging over the escape of Fleance from the murderers contracted to kill him, he says 'I had else been perfect,/ Whole as the marble, founded as the rock' (3.4.20–1). By contrast, the Witches are represented as *both* solid *and* gas, evaporating into thin air like bubbles.

But Macbeth is not singular in his desire for rocky masculine singularity. Lady Macbeth, who herself wants to lose all traces of her sex, sees her husband as too full of the feminine 'milk of human kindness'

JONATHAN GIL HARRIS

(1.5.15). No wonder that she keeps screaming at him to be a man. Goading him into a singular course of murderous action requires baiting him with his fantasy of perfect, whole masculinity: 'When you durst do it, then you were a man' (1.7.49). That Macbeth is susceptible to such baiting is not his weakness alone. Macbeth pressures the murderers to kill Banquo and Fleance by asking them to prove they are men, not in the 'worst rank of manhood' (3.1.104); Malcolm does the same to Macduff by telling him to 'dispute' the death of his wife and child 'like a man' (4.3.221); when Macduff says he will kill Macbeth, Malcolm responds with 'This tune goes manly' (4.3.237). Macbeth, Lady Macbeth, the Murderers, Malcolm, Macduff: all united by the initial M, which stands for Murder as much as Manliness. Because, in this play, to acquire a 'single state of man'—a single identity, a single meaning—means massacring one's way out of multiplicity.

This murderous desire for singularity also affects Macbeth's sense of time. He wants time to extend from him in the form of a massive 'swelling' (1.3.139), through which his single state of man will extend itself indefinitely by becoming king and producing a line of Macbeth successors. His laughable fantasy of phallic hugeness into the future is marred almost as soon as he is enthroned: he blames the Witches for putting 'a barren sceptre in my grip' (3.1.62). Macbeth's sceptre cannot extend through time the way Banquo's line seems to, no matter how many murders he commits to secure his future. And so, time for Macbeth becomes an endlessly repeated and incomplete present, a sequence of Groundhog Days in which every day mirrors, and doubles, the inadequacy of the previous one: this is the time of 'tomorrow, and tomorrow, and tomorrow', the time of 'a tale/ Told by an idiot... Signifying nothing' (5.5.18, 25–6, 27). Taking a cue from his fruitless sceptre, we might describe Macbeth's despairing vision of empty meaningless 'tomorrows' as barren time.

This vision is a long way away from the celebratory masala time of Holi. But *Macbeth* gives us other ways of thinking about time that don't involve the 'either/or' of phallic lines and barren repetitions. Importantly, it also gives us a 'both-and' vision of time: what it calls the 'untimely'.

The word 'untimely' appears twice in *Macbeth*. It is often glossed over as 'premature'. But it more accurately suggests something out of time: an event that goes against the grain of a predictable development, that happens at the 'wrong' time, and that brings the future into the present. Macduff tells Macbeth that he was 'untimely ripped' (5.10.16) from his mother's womb. And Macduff says that 'Boundless intemperance' is 'a tyranny' that has occasioned 'the untimely emptying of the happy throne/ And fall of many kings' (4.3.69–70). Revealingly, both instances of the untimely are associated with an end to tyranny—or, more specifically, an end to the singular, linear time of the tyrant.

The Witches are untimely in this sense. By seeing the future as well as the past in the present, they interrupt time. The eeriest illustration of this power comes when they stage a procession of kings descended from Banquo, the last holding a mirror that presumably catches the reflection of Banquo's descendant, King James, sitting in the audience in the play's first performance staged for him in early 1606. This is more than prophetic omniscience about events that play out to humans as the unfolding of linear time. Like Brahma, the Witches see the untimely more-than-oneness that lurks in every moment. And they recognize that the wish to extract oneness from that multiplicity is deadly. Rather than attempting to resolve doubleness into singularity, as the Macbeths do, the Witches—who survive a play full of carnage—fully embrace the multiple. Even the mirror image of the future king conjured by the Witches doubles the monarch sitting in the audience. (It would have been a potentially risky piece of stage business too, given that King James had a notoriously short attention span and may well have been fast asleep by the time the mirror reflected his image.)

There is one other character who embodies the untimely. And that is the Porter. He is a drunken lout whose bawdy quips in his one-scene cameo about the effects of alcohol on nose colour, bladder, and sexual prowess come at totally the wrong time: King Duncan has just been gruesomely murdered, and the Porter—speaking cheeky prose in a play that has been hitherto entirely in poetry—enters from a totally different universe, performing a black comic stand-up show in Hell. For the play's original audiences, the Porter's entrance would have felt untimely not just in relation to his generic inappropriateness. It would have felt untimely in another, more literal way. The play is set in medieval Scotland. Yet the Porter's frame of reference is contemporary England. He refers obliquely to the recent Gunpowder Plot of November 5, 1605, in which a group of Catholics—associated with a priest whom the Porter mentions, Henry Garnet—attempted to blow up the House of Parliament while King James was in attendance. This reference makes chilling sense, given Macbeth's own attempt on the life of a King. The Porter thus belongs to two times in one, to both medieval Scotland and

Shakespeare's London. And in his cheeky straddling of two times, the Porter is surprisingly irreverent about the authority of kings troubled by murderous plotters. He represents an untimely interruption that raises questions about the singularities of power and violence.

The Porter is a character whose references to the events of the Gunpowder Plot, at least for the other medieval characters onstage, embodies a future-in-the-present. For the members of the audience in 1606, however, he would have also conjured up a recent past-in-the-present. Indeed, the Gunpowder Plot would have hung heavily in the air, quite literally, since the beginning of the performance. The opening thunder and lightning—a high-tech special effect for the time—was staged through the detonation of squibs, small fireworks that created both a clap of noise and a spark of light. They also left a pungent smell of gunpowder in the playhouse. That untimely smell, quietly evocative of the recent plot, would have placed the audience simultaneously in the past and the present, the medieval time of the Scottish play and the recent scandal in England. Like a Holi celebrator, then, Shakespeare flung powder in the faces of his audience, giving them a powerful experience of masala time.

In a theatre company with a limited number of actors having to play numerous roles, it is likely that the Porter would even have been played by one of the three actors who played the Witches, and who are absent from Act One Scene Four to the end of Act Three. Every production I have seen of the play casts a male actor dressed in black as the Porter. In my production, he would be performed by all of the Witches. They would also be caked in rang, as noisy, bhang-taking Holi celebrants who refuse the tragic tyranny of Hiranya-style singularity. Such singularity can belong to king, murderer, and audience member alike. But masala time makes fools of them—of us all.

◆

The masala time that the Witches inhabit can be disconcerting to those Western readers who want unity of place and time in their entertainments. But living in two times at once is not at all a strange proposition to most Indians. My partner's grandmother, born in 1913, was a highly educated Malayali woman who had completed an advanced degree in science and worked for years as a high-school teacher and principal. She was the model of a modern Indian woman. Yet she was also a committed practitioner of horoscope casting. She drew up elaborate charts on the basis of which she made regular predictions, with deepest conviction, about her equally well educated granddaughters' marital and reproductive futures. That these predictions were continuously proved wrong dimmed neither her ardour in making them nor her family members' deep interest in them. Their interest was often ironic: her predictions could be the occasion for disbelieving laughter. Yet to this day—more than a decade after her death—her daughter and granddaughters still credit her powers of prognostication. In short, they as much as she have somehow managed to straddle two very different times simultaneously, one of rational modernity and another of superstitious tradition. And this straddling has never struck them as contradictory. Because 'hum toh aise hain, bhaiyya (we are such, brother)': masala time, blending the primitive and the modern, the superstitious and the scientific, is the lot of most Indians.

This is not surprising in a subcontinent whose inhabitants simultaneously fetishize technology and have faith in supernatural arts of prediction. Thousands, even millions, of Indians make careers out of reading animals' entrails, examining tea-leaves, or drawing up raashiphal (horoscopes), janampatri (birth charts), and kundli (astrological charts). Many more buy their services. To gain admission into the country's hallowed temples of scientific modernity—the Indian Institutes of Technology (IITs)—would-be engineers and their families will routinely consult astrologers, soothsayers, and prognosticators of various stripes.

Indian versions of Macbeth's Witches have often embodied something of this contradiction. And by simultaneously inhabiting two times these Witches have often been the most Indian part of the adaptations in which they appear. To represent them, writers and directors have mined ancient Indian cultural traditions that are now stigmatized or even illegal. So in Maharashtra, for example, the state assembly passed the Prevention and Eradication of Human Sacrifice and other Inhuman, Evil and Aghori Practices and Black Magic Act Bill in 2013. Sponsored by rationalist activists, one of whom was murdered the same year by a fringe Hindu fundamentalist group, the bill's impossibly long name gives some indication of the persistence of a wide range of old magical practices in Maharashtra. Marathi adaptations of Macbeth have repeatedly put these practices on stage. The Shahu Theatre Company in Pune mounted a highly successful reworking of the play in 1896, Manajirava, in which the Witches were bearded Hindu practitioners of ancient black magic. And the Marathi film Jalwa (1938) had its Macbeth-inspired lead character, Angan, kill a king after his future has been predicted by a sinister 'chetakya' or black witch.

English-language Indian productions of *Macbeth* have likewise tapped into old indigenous traditions of supernatural prognostication. So a 2007 production by the Bombay director Alyque Padamsee transformed Lady Macbeth into a tantrik who conjures up the Witches to provoke her husband into becoming King. Another English-language production by the Pandies' Theatre in New Delhi, 2013, began with a Hindi-language frame, in which poor women labourers resort to necromancy and jaadu magical rites to protect themselves from exploitation by upper-class bosses; the women resurface in the play as the Witches. And a 2015 South Asian production in England by the Tara Arts company, directed by Jatinder Verma, transformed the Witches into fortune-telling hijras.

These Anglo-Indian Witches represent an untimely power that arguably surpasses that of the Weird Sisters. They pointedly occupy two worlds and two times simultaneously—English and Indian, modern and traditional. Something of this untimely doubleness is apparent also in a plethora of non-English *Macbeth* reworkings from three distinct cultural zones in India, each of which are distinguished by powerful indigenous traditions of the supernatural: Bengal, Manipur and Kerala.

In Bengal, pre-colonial village life was in thrall to rupkatha, myths populated by ghosts and supernatural characters. Under the influence of British colonialist enlightenment thought, however, the upper-class bhadralok culture of Calcutta came to regard these myths as antiquated curiosities. Yet rupkatha's enduring power is clear from a late nineteenth-century Bengali stage adaptation. Girish Chandra Ghosh's otherwise faithful translation of *Macbeth* in the 1890s drew on stock images from the rupkatha tradition—snakes and graveyard fir trees—to illustrate the world of the Witches. That world came across as an untimely Bengali past-in-the-present, one that interrupted the modernity of British colonialism.

The untimely power of rupkatha endured well into the twentieth century. In 1954, Utpal Dutt experienced the power of these old superstitious myths when he directed a Bengali translation of *Macbeth*, by Jatindranath Sengupta, for performance on rural open-air stages. Although it was not itself a traditional folk jatra—it was apparently performed 'straight'—this Bangla *Macbeth* appealed hugely to audiences for whom the play's supernatural ingredients resonated. Dutt noted how the Witches connected with villagers used to the idea, familiar from rupkatha, that the world was controlled not by explainable rational laws but by supernatural forces. As a Marxist, Dutt was disturbed by this fatalism, and his subsequent adaptation of *Macbeth* in 1975 minimized the Witches' importance.

Bengali versions of *Macbeth* have tapped into an untimely mythic otherworld belonging to stories associated with the past. By contrast, Manipuri adaptations of the play draw on present tribal practices that are equally untimely. These have survived despite the conversion of much of the majority Meitei tribe to Vaishnavite Hinduism in the eighteenth century and Christianity in the nineteenth. Even though 90 per cent of Manipur's population is now Hindu or Christian, tribal culture has played a large part in forming a new sense of indigenous identity independent of the Indian state, whose presence in the lives of Manipuris has been sharpened by the imposition of the Armed Forces (Special Powers) Act (AFSPA). Much of the region's vibrant performance traditions, including shumang leela (courtyard theatre), draws its energies from tribal culture. One of the ironies of Manipuri theatre's post-union embrace of indigeneity, however, is that an old English play about Scotland has at least twice provided directors with a showcase for local tribal traditions.

In 1997, the Laboratory Theatre, under the direction of Lokendra Arambam, adapted a version of *Macbeth* called *Stage of Blood*. Performed on a boat in a Manipuri lake, it featured seven Witches, tribal male shamans who recited magical spells and fell into trances. The production attracted so much acclaim that the Indian government sent it to Britain to be performed on the Thames as part of the golden jubilee celebrations of Indian Independence—a double irony, given that the production's embrace of shamans stemmed in no small part from a discomfort with Manipur's absorption into India and that Manipur had joined the union two years after the date the jubilee commemorated. The director Ratan Thiyam produced another acclaimed adaptation of *Macbeth* in 2016 with the Chorus Repertory Theatre. It was shaped by indigenous cultural traditions that, although Thiyam has disavowed their connection to any specific Manipuri tribe, clearly derived from a non-Hindu, non-Christian, animist worldview. The Witches started off as tree stumps before morphing into tentacled prophets; in the performance I saw at the National School of Drama, they suggested to me the untimely power of a natural world that the rapacious Macbeth ignores at his peril.

In Kerala, despite a robust culture of rationalist skepticism that has accompanied many decades of Marxist rule, there is a strong tradition of sorcery embodied in a figure known as the kuttichathan or chathan. Supposedly a dark avatar of Vishnu, the chathan can either place or remove hurdles in human lives. To this day the chathan is paid money to protect business and love interests that, if he is not placated, he might otherwise blight. There have been many adaptations of Shakespeare in Kerala, and the spectre of the chathan has hung over them. Indeed, a local reimagining of *The Tempest* was called *Chathan Kattu* (Sorceror Play). While two recent reimaginings of the play in traditional kutiyattam and kathakali performance styles didn't dramatize the Witches, Jayaraj's acclaimed Malayalam film adaptation of *Macbeth*, *Veeram* (2016), presented them as sorcerers in the Kerala tradition. As a result the film traded in an untimeliness rather different from that of the Bengali and Manipuri Witches. Whereas the world of Bengali rupkatha has returned with untimely force from a supposedly discredited past, and the practices of Manipuri animism have offered an untimely interruption of the Indian state presence, the Kerala chathans are simply part of an untimely conglomeration in which, as one observer has noted, 'many centuries coexist'.

But what have Indian reimaginings of *Macbeth* done with the play's other thoroughly untimely character, the Porter? He has been by and large ignored. One notable exception is Rajat Kapoor's *What's Done is Done* (2014), a clown version of *Macbeth*. The production was memorable for having Lady Macbeth played by the three Witches. It also featured two Mexican clowns who served as a comic chorus reminiscent of the untimely Porter. One of them made King Duncan and the rest of the cast in Macbeth's castle pose for a photo, ordering them to 'say anachronism!' But the performance I saw also used the anachronistic power of the Mexican clowns to glance away from the medieval Scottish world to the contemporary political scene in India: one of the clowns, after a chilling scene of murder, remarked to the audience: 'you see how quickly you forgot murder on stage? This is how fascism works.'

The politically explosive anachronisms of Mexican clowns might seem some distance away from the untimely power of ancient traditions of Indian magic. Yet, as we have seen, *Macbeth* presents the wit of the Porter and the Witches as companions. One of the most extraordinary aspects of Vishal Bhardwaj's *Maqbool* (2003) is that it too conflates the Porter's black comedy and the Witches' black magic within a distinctive vision of masala time.

At first glance *Maqbool* is not a masala movie. It seems to belong instead to the genre of Indian parallel film, featuring actors—Naseeruddin Shah, Om Puri, Irrfan Khan, Tabu, Pankaj Kapoor—associated with that niche. Its opening scene, presenting an astrological chart shot in the night with eerie chiaroscuro plays of light and shadow, makes clear that Bhardwaj's cinematic vocabulary owes a large debt to Western film noir and horror. And his depiction of a mafia 'family' self-consciously glances at Francis Ford Coppola's *The Godfather* (1972).

Yet *Maqbool* is a parallel film that slides into masala. Abbaji (Pankaj Kapoor), the Bombay mafia don who doubles King Duncan even though he looks and sounds like Marlon Brando's Don Corleone morphed into a toad, has a business interest in commercial Hindi film and takes a particular shine to a Bollywood starlet. That interest begins to creep into the style of *Maqbool*. As the film progresses, it acquires elements of a commercial film that could have been bankrolled by Abbaji: musical numbers, a sentimental romance subplot involving the Fleance character Guddu and Abbaji's daughter Sameera, and a tale of forbidden love involving Maqbool (Irrfan Khan) and Nimmi (Tabu), the counterparts of Macbeth and Lady Macbeth. The film cannot avoid the masala multiplicity of its location, Bombay. And, as we will see, this multiplicity is rooted in a conception of masala time.

In fact *Maqbool* draws deep from the well of the Hindi gangster movie genre, which involves many masala elements. Crooked cops, dastardly dons and shocking shoot-outs notwithstanding, these gangster movies often dream of an inclusive pluralism in terms of religious community. At a time when Muslims have become increasingly absent from Hindi films, Bollywood gangster movies remain full of them, often in Bombay-located dramas that reproduce the distinctive linguistic and cultural mixtures of the city. Moreover, even as these films send an ideal of Muslim/Hindu solidarity literally underground, they do so in a way that does not straightforwardly demonize either Muslims or the ideal of cross-communal concord. If anything, as Shah Rukh Khan's recent film *Raees* (2017) shows, the figure of the underworld Muslim gangster can be a Robin Hood figure, modelling a hope for a more inclusive world that a corrupt establishment otherwise disallows.

In recent years gangster Shakespeare has become something of a subgenre in Indian cinema. Although these films' locations have shifted from Bombay, they draw on several elements of the Bollywood gangster movie. We've already glanced at the slew of masala gangster *Romeo and Juliet* adaptations: it's no accident that two of these, *Ishaqzaade* and *Arshinagar*, imagine Hindu-Muslim romance. *Zulfiqar* (2016), directed by Srijit Mukherji is a Bengali gangster adaptation of both *Julius Caesar* and *Antony and Cleopatra* that likewise imagines cross-communal solidarities and lovers. Mark Antony is played as two inseparable friends, one Muslim and one Christian. The Muslim don-cum-Caesar character, Zulfiqar Ahmed, is sexually involved with a Hindu moneylender. The Antony and Cleopatra relationship is also depicted as a cross-communal one, with the Muslim Markaz Ali (played by the Hindu Dev) falling for the Hindu Rani Talapatra (played by the Muslim Nusrat Jahan).

Maqbool is arguably the prototype for these later masala gangster Shakespeares. It presents us with a cross-communal world very much like that of *Zulfiqar*. At first it might seem that the film's gang is all-Muslim: we see assorted members in skullcaps, performing namaz, and attending an urs at the dargah accompanied by a qawwali soundtrack. Even the Lady Macbeth character Nimmi is a devout Muslim; the twist is that she is Abbaji's mistress, but falls into a secret affair with Maqbool. Yet it is only after a Mexican stand-off between two factions within the gang that we realize this 'Muslim' outfit also consists of Hindus. Abbaji's crime family is mixed, its kinships extending across communities. Maqbool's 'Kaka' is Hindu, and Kaka is in turn beholden to his Muslim Abbaji. Abbaji marries his daughter to the son of Kaka, and we see a mixed engagement ceremony with Muslim and Hindu paraphernalia. Abbaji also consorts with Hindu politicians, and becomes sexually involved with a Hindu filmstar. And Abbaji's men, particularly Maqbool, are also in league with two Hindu Brahmin cops, Inspector Panditji (Om Puri) and Inspector Purohit (Naseeruddin Shah). It is in this latter pair that we begin to see the workings of masala time in *Maqbool*.

These two Inspectors are Bhardwaj's version of the Witches. Like *Macbeth*, the film starts with a scene of prediction. We hear Panditji's and Purohit's voices as they shake down a member of a rival gang; but all we see is a patri, or horoscope chart, traced on the windscreen of a car. This chart becomes a crucial part of the story. Although Purohit asks 'kyaa likha hai Mumbai ke bhavishya mein (what is written in Mumbai's future)', he and Panditji attend primarily to Maqbool's future. Together, the Inspectors capture something of the doubleness of Shakespeare's Witches, but they lend this doubleness a recognizably Indian flavour.

They are not bearded hags, nor do they initially 'palter' with Maqbool in any obvious 'double sense': in fact their predictions are, at least initially, disappointingly straightforward. Yet they are shuddh Brahmins who eat meat, savouring the best kebabs in town and constructing their patris out of chicken bones. And as crooked cops working within Bombay's underworld, they are both in and out of the law.

Just as Macbeth receives three prophecies from the Witches, so does Panditji predict three things for Maqbool—'ishq aur (more love)', 'Bollywood', and ultimately a position as 'King of Kings'. Of course all three predictions come true: Maqbool will find love with Nimmi, career advancement managing Abbaji's film interests, and power through murdering and replacing his gang boss. But the predictions also introduce the elements of a masala film into *Maqbool*. These elements are the materials of Maqbool's future; yet they simultaneously mine Bollywood's past. 'Ishq aur'—as good a characterization of the logic of the Manmohan Desai formula 70s masala film as any—reframes the Macbeth-Lady Macbeth equation as a forbidden romance between Maqbool and Nimmi. 'Bollywood' permits the inclusion of an item number featuring an old-style vamp named Mohini. And 'King of Kings' is Panditji's English rendition of the Urdu word 'Shahenshah', a name that has become synonymous with Amitabh Bachchan since his star-turn, in 1988, in a film of the same name.

Maqbool's winking embrace of the old-style filmi masala that haunts its titular character's future repeats something of the logic of *Macbeth*. Shakespeare's titular character longs for a masculine singularity that is impossible in an irreducibly double world; similarly, *Maqbool* may speak the high language of arthouse noir cinema yet cannot escape the old masala mixtures of Bombay and Bollywood. Maqbool himself despises Bollywood, scowling about how it is full of 'ghatiya filme...ghatiya log (awful films... awful people)'. Yet he, and the film that shares his name, cannot escape the masala of this 'ghatiya' world. The inescapability of masala in a Bombay adaptation of *Macbeth* is hilariously illustrated by the scene in which Maqbool presides as the cook at the shaadi preparations for Guddu and Sameera, stirring a cauldron in an ironic evocation of the Witches. He directs the other cooks: 'acche se peesne ka... kyaa... itne se lehsan mein kyaa hone vala hai Melya... itna hi aur kato' (grind the spices well... what... we can't make do with such little garlic... you need to grind as much more). Bollywood masala, in culinary as well as cinematic form, prevails over the black and white of noir.

But the doubleness that haunts Maqbool—and *Maqbool*—goes well beyond this. It eventually takes the form of a radical uncertainty about lineage. Like Macbeth, Maqbool longs for a line that will extend into the future. Unlike Macbeth, his partner gets pregnant. But her child turns out to be of uncertain parentage: Nimmi has conceived it while sexually involved with both Abbaji and Maqbool. Her guilt about killing one of the possible fathers of her child drives her to madness and then death. This child—who will acquire two more parents when adopted at the film's end by Guddu and Sameera—embodies the 'both-and' logic of masala, with its five parents from mixed communities. The child is a counterpart to *Maqbool*: just as it cannot be given a single ancestry, so are the film's antecedents a mix of Shakespeare, arthouse cinema, film noir, Hollywood, and Bollywood.

It is telling that at the film's end the Inspectors' predictions have become as cryptically double as the mystery of Nimmi's child's paternity. In a counterpart to the riddle of Birnam Wood moving on Macbeth's castle, Inspector Panditji tells Maqbool that 'ab dariya khud chal ke tere ghar aaega Miyan to tu doobega (if the sea moves on its own and comes to your house, then Miyan you will drown)'. This prediction comes true when Maqbool is foiled by the sea police. But it is also emblematic of the Inspectors' commitment to a law beyond the law of the state or the law of the mafia. We could call it the law of cosmic masala, of balance between potentially rival elements. As their repeated catchphrase goes, 'shakti ka santulan bahut zaroori hai sansaar mein… aag ke liye paani ka dar banaa rehna chahiye (the balance of power is necessary in the world—fire needs to stay scared of water)'. Even as they lend tacit support to the 'aag' of Maqbool, they count on the 'paani' of his enemies to counterbalance his strength. This is a balance that the film quietly identifies not only with Maqbool and his rivals but also with what Panditji says is the real object of his patris—'Mumbai'. In *Maqbool*, this mixed city keeps providing its characters with venues in which the 'santulan' or balance to which Panditji refers is maintained through the frequently law-defying logic of 'both-and': Sufi dargahs where people of multiple faiths pray, shaadi halls frequented by families from different communities, kebab dhabas where Muslims and shuddh vegetarian Brahmins dine.

And Bollywood. In *Maqbool*, Bollywood is not just a masala style. It is also a synonym for the mixed world of Bombay and, in particular, its gangsters. The film repeatedly teases out links between Bollywood and the gangster world. Panditji says that Abbaji could have been an actor like Dilip Kumar; Kaka says that Nimmi should work with masala directors such as Karan Johar or Subhash Ghai. But in *Maqbool* the most significant connection between Bollywood and the criminal underworld rests in their shared embrace of masala mixtures. We see this most clearly when Mohini, Abbaji's starlet mistress, performs an item number at the engagement party for Guddu and Sameera. This Hindu–Muslim gangster jodi is matched by Mohini's inter-communal performance. Named for Vishnu's feminine avatar, Mohini performs a mujra—a dance traditionally performed in Mughal mehfils, combining elements of kathak with ghazals and thumris. Mohini's mujra also brings masala time into *Maqbool*. The dance is on the one hand a Bollywood form, not out of place in the nineties setting of the film. On the other, both the dance and the dancer's name offer reminders of older cultures of mixture in both Hindu and Indian Islamic traditions. Here the past powerfully haunts the present—a present that, outside the gangster world, has become altogether more singular.

It is hard not to see these untimely masala apparitions in relation to the time in which the film was made. In 2003, the smoke of the riots in Godhra still hung as heavily in the air as the smell of gunpowder had done in the first performance of *Macbeth* in 1606. And Godhra, for a Bombay audience at least, could not help but recall the communal riots in their own city a decade earlier following the demolition of the Babri Masjid by Hindu fundamentalists. The balance to which the Inspectors allude had been damaged, perhaps irrevocably, in Bombay. But untimely reminders of that balance are provided by the masala gangster underworld. Or, more accurately, they are provided by Bollywood fantasies of that world. In these fantasies, mixture is an asset rather than a provocation to violent dardnak kahaani. They are a reminder of what used to be recast as a hope for what can be.

The masala time of *Maqbool* is therefore a complicated affair. It operates at many levels, like a nested doll. It recalls but also exceeds the masala time of Indian *Macbeths* from Maharashtra and Kerala to Bengal and Manipur. But it is perhaps most evident, in typical Bhardwaj fashion, in the film's repeated black humour. The Inspectors are the film's Witches; but they are also versions of the Porter—drunken, pissing louts who laugh at those who seek to exercise absolute power and who interrupt Maqbool's dardnak kahaani with untimely comic routines. Baiting a member of a rival gang who has been taken into custody with the

promise of freedom if he rats on his bhais, they say: 'arre pi chikne pi…
mauj kar aaj teri 15 agast hai'. The English subtitles render this line as
'Drink up princess. Let it flow…tonight you've got freedom.' But the
line is more subtle: it means literally 'drink, fair boy, drink…have fun
because today is your 15 August'. To which the gangster blankly replies,
'navambar mein 15 agast kahaan se hoga saab (how will it be 15 August
in November, sahib)?' This cheeky anachronism makes reference to a
past event—the date of India's Independence—that erupts with untimely
power as a new future in the present. It is a riddling future too: the
gangster, like Macbeth or Hiranyakashipu, thinks he will be granted life
when in fact he will be murdered. But the irreverence with which the
Inspectors drag the past into the present and the future resembles less
the Witches than the Porter.

The Inspectors resemble the Porter as comic interlopers in an
otherwise intensely serious story. More importantly, they also recall the
untimely interruption of tyranny that he represents. In this guise they
are much closer to the 'both-and' world of Brahma's predictions to
Hiranyakashipu. And within that world, they swerve between the ancient
past of old traditions and a future that defies any individual's will to
singular power. In this we might spy something of the untimely, anti-
tyrannical spirit of Holi. Lawful and lawless, vegetarian and meat-eating,
inside and outside, modern and primitive, Bhardwaj's Witches-cum-
Inspectors-cum-Porters-cum-Brahmas embody masala time.

ACT FOUR SCENE THREE

'Marammat Mukaddar Ki Kar Do Maula'

Masala is not just an idea I discovered in India. A version of masala has travelled with me, in me, as me, all my life.

I have mentioned that I am a product of mixture. My father's line, despite its seeming rootedness in Britain, also includes Anglo–Irish and Huguenot migrants, as well as Direnzis from Italy who may have been Sephardic Jewish escapees of the Spanish Inquisition. And my mother traces her ancestry through generations of Ashkenazi Jewish migration, from Eastern European shtetls to cosmopolitan cities such as Vienna and Istanbul.

Mixture was part of my mother's life too. The storms of history had ripped her family apart in Germany and Poland, blowing her to Russia and Uzbekistan before dropping her in Palestine in 1946. She still speaks nostalgically about her time in a multicultural boarding school where her classmates were Palestinian Arabs as well as Jewish migrants. And then the storms of history blew again with the United Nations Partition Plan for Palestine, culminating in the formation of Israel in 1948. This Partition divided her from her Palestinian classmates, placing them on the different side of a border between the new Jewish state and its Arab neighbours. It also generated a historical amnesia that suddenly made enemies of Jews and Arabs, despite languages and histories that are more entangled than they are separate. One 'I' and one 'P', divided from each other by a traumatic Partition; perhaps I was fated to move to a part of India not far from Pakistan.

And perhaps because of my mother's experience in the Nazi Holocaust as well as Palestine, I was fated to embrace a certain set of political convictions. There's not much about me that is Jewish, at the level of belief or practice: I do not believe in God, I was never bar mitzvahed, and I attend Passover seders with a dread fear that I will be called upon to recite Hebrew blessings or parts of the Haggadah that I do not know. But I became a strong believer in the Jewish ideal of tikkun olam. This Hebrew phrase literally means 'repair of the world'. It used to represent, for ancient Jews, a call to reject idolatry; in recent centuries it has come to signify differently. The Siddur Sim Shalom, a

Jewish book of prayer, explains tikkun olam with the verse 'may citizens of all races and creeds forge a common bond in true harmony to banish all hatred and bigotry'. So tikkun olam is not simply an imperative to repair the lot of Jews so that 'hatred and bigotry' never happens again to us. It is a clarion call to insure that the majoritarian hatred that roiled Nazi Germany never again victimizes *anyone*.

For me, the ethical burden of tikkun olam demands the imaginative cross-communal solidarity to which the Mexican Zapatista revolutionary Subcomandante Marcos has given such beautiful expression:

> Marcos is gay in San Francisco, black in South Africa, an Asian in Europe, a Chicano in San Ysidro, an anarchist in Spain, a Palestinian in Israel, a Mayan Indian in the streets of San Cristobal,… a Jew in Germany, a Gypsy in Poland, a Kurd in Turkey, a Mohawk in Quebec, a pacifist in Bosnia, a single woman on the Metro at 10 p.m., a peasant without land, a gang member in the slums, an unemployed worker, an unhappy student and, of course, a Zapatista in the mountains.

Marcos asks that we think outside ourselves, invite others into our sense of who we are. Alas, tikkun olam seems to be increasingly mutating into something for Jews alone. Instead of Marcos's cross-communal solidarity with victims of bigotry and hate, 'repair of the world' has degenerated into the task of creating a greater Israel and, by means of illegal Jewish settlements on the West Bank, destroying the viability of any future Palestinian state.

But in 2003, I caught a strong whiff of Marcos's version of tikkun olam. And I caught it, of all places, in a street in Kerala.

Jew Street in Cochin—now known as Kochi—is the main thoroughfare of the ancient quarter known as Jew Town. It features a shop called Akbar Arts. Turn the corner, and you will pass the Sree Ganesha Café followed by the Lawrence Handicrafts store. And then, a few yards further, you will see the Paradesi synagogue. The name supposedly refers to the 'foreign' Jews who built it. But there is a lot else that is pardesi inside it. Look down, and you see white-and-blue Chinese tiles. Look up, and there are Belgian chandeliers. Stand at the front door, and look back down the street: Akbar, Sree Ganesha, and Lawrence. That's my kind of Jew Town: not majoritarian or pure, but nestling cheek by jowl with Muslim, Hindu, and Christian neighbours from whom it absorbs, and to whom it gives, the politics of the more-than-one, the more-than-me, the more-than-my-clan. This is tikkun olam I can believe in.

As I inhaled the mingled Malabar masala scents of Jew Street, where Jew, Christian, Hindu and Muslim have likewise mingled for centuries, I was reminded of Salman Rushdie's anti-hero Moraes Zogoiby in his extraordinary novel, *The Moor's Last Sigh* (1995). This Indian child of a Portuguese–Indian mother and a Jewish–Indian father, each with a splash of Moorish blood in their veins, is the 'high-born cross-breed male heir to the spice-trade-'n'-big-business crores of the da Gama-Zogoiby dynasty of Cochin'. As befits both his masala parentage and his family business, Moraes is born from 'Not only pepper, but also cardamoms, cashews, cinnamon, ginger, pistachios, cloves; and as well as spice 'n'nuts there were coffee beans, and the mighty tea leaf itself.' Here Rushdie uses Malabar masala as a metaphor for the rich cultural mixture of Cochin—a mixture the city shares, in his imagination, with modern Bombay and medieval Granada, both crucial locations in *The Moor's Last Sigh*.

But another masala city lurks in *The Moor's Last Sigh*. And that city is the Venice of Shakespeare's *Othello*. Indeed, the play's subtitle—*The Moor of Venice*—suggests something of Rushdie's thought experiment with masala identity. Shakespeare's Moor (the term is associated with both Muslims and Africans) belongs to white Christian Venice; as such, he is an exemplar of cultural mixture. Mixture is glimpsed also in Shakespeare's other Venetian play, *The Merchant of Venice*, whose alternate title for much of its production history was 'The Jew of Venice'. Taken together, the two plays and their migrant characters Othello and Shylock test the limits of what we might call masala identity: the possibility of being Moorish and Venetian, Jewish and Venetian, at the same time. In *The Merchant of Venice*, that possibility is warded off through enforced or elective Jewish conversion to the majority Christian community. But in *Othello*, masala identity is tragically strained to suicidal breaking point: when Othello kills himself at the play's end, he does so by telling a story about a patriotic Venetian slaying an evil Turk who had spoken rudely about his city. The poignant irony is that Othello, in his dramatic suicide, plays the parts of *both* the patriotic Venetian *and* the evil Turk. His masala identity is affirmed. But it is affirmed only as a deadly mix, where one part brutally rejects the other, killing it and dying too.

For Rushdie in *The Moor's Last Sigh*, the deadliness of Othello's masala identity has a chilling, tragic relevance to modern India. It is not just that Shakespeare's Moor is a victim of the villainous Iago's bigotry. It is that Othello himself also perpetuates that bigotry. The 'last sigh' of the novel's title refers to the mythic gasp of the final Moorish ruler in Spain, Sultan Boabdil, as he abandoned his gloriously multicultural Granada in the wake of the Christian Reconquista of 1492, ending with a sigh centuries of rich cultural dialogue between Jews, Muslims and Christians. But it also refers to Othello's last sigh as his patriotic Venetian avatar smites the evil Turk in himself. In Rushdie's nightmare vision of India, written in the wake of the demolition of the Babri Masjid in 1992 and the Hindu–Muslim Bombay riots of 1993, India has become a latter-day Othello, administering to its own rich mixtures a self-willed deathblow born of a lust for purity.

Cochin's Jew Street reverberates with many uncanny echoes of Shakespeare's Venice. Not just because of the rich legacies of Jewish and Muslim culture that are evident in the area. Nor just because of the similarities between Venice and Cochin as port cities, riddled with canals and multicultural traders. Even as modern Cochin seems to model a masala more-than-oneness, the pressures within it to purify and singularize identity are—as in Shakespeare's Venice—increasingly irresistible. The differences between my first visit to Cochin in July 2003 and my most recent one in September 2017 are revealing on this score.

In 2003, I first met Sara Cohen, the last living Jew in Jew Street. By that point most of Cochin's small but robust Jewish community had been persuaded post-Independence to move to Israel, on the utterly misguided assumption that religious identity must trump all other forms of cultural affiliation. Sara had resisted the tide: she was firmly a Jew of Cochin, content with her masala identity. In 2003 she was a still-sprightly 78, and I spent an afternoon with her in her apartment. We had been introduced by a mutual friend from the United States, who thought a Jew from one God's Own Country—New Zealand—might get along with a Jew from the other God's Own Country. And we did, as Sara was a very congenial host. But she was a little puzzled by my presumption of solidarity with her, as I spoke no Malayalam. Bored by my lack of conversational sparkle, she turned on her television and became lost in a Malayalam soap opera, *Sthree* (Woman). I couldn't understand the language, but I could follow its over-the-top action. I, too, became absorbed by what I saw.

Two Jews from different parts of the world bonded that day. And we bonded not over our Jewishness but, rather, over our shared absorption in the melodramatic masala tale of a hapless Malayali Hindu maiden tormented by wicked men. It could have been the tale of Desdemona's childhood maid Barbary—the shadowy figure who shares her name with the northwest coast of Africa, and who taught her young mistress a tragic song about the evils that men do to women. But as Sara and I shared cookies, watching *Sthree*, we also unwittingly acted different parts from *Othello*. Sara played Othello, a Pardesi of Venice. And I played Desdemona, absorbed by outlandish tales from a strange land. Part of me fell in love that day. Not with my seventy eight-year-old companion, sweet as she was, but with a vision of border-crossing possibility that I glimpsed in India's stunning pluralism.

Nearly fifteen years later I visited Jew Street again. Cochin has changed dramatically in the intervening time. The changes are partly for the good: there are now more cafes, the streets are cleaner, and the highly successful Kochi–Muziris Biennale has put more art in public spaces and more colour on the buildings. But it's hard not to feel that something has been lost too. Cochin's spice markets, though still active, are now becoming theme parks for tourists. And the transformation of the city's spicy masala outlets is a potent metaphor for the transformation of its cultural masala, at least the version that includes Jewish ingredients. Both types of masala are nowadays less part of the city's lived practices than they are exotic commodities for the titillation of tourists. Sara, now 93, had been turned into something of an exotic attraction herself; her once typical Malayali house has become a Jewish tourist shrine complete with wrought-iron window-grill Star of David, through which mostly Western visitors aim cameras to capture snaps of The Last Living Jew in Jew Street. She has also started wearing a kipa—a Jewish skullcap— as a badge of religious identity recognizable to foreigners, something I didn't see her do fifteen years ago when her sartorial preference was the standard-issue Malayali nightie.

This transformation is not as depressing as the supposedly 'comic' outcome of *The Merchant of Venice*. There Shylock, the Jew of Venice, is made to convert to Christianity; his daughter Jessica, having eloped with a Christian, is also absorbed into the majority community. But Sara's transformation does remind me a little of the end of *Othello*. Her wearing a kipa may not be the deadly tragedy of that play. But to make Jewishness the singular truth of her identity at the expense of the other masala ingredients in her mix—in other words, to repudiate how she is a Jew of Cochin who loves to watch Malayalam soap operas and to bake English cookies—is akin to Othello's deadly rejection of his own plurality.

Cochin's cultural masala has attracted the watchful interest of India's new political powers. At the time of my last visit in 2017, the central government had dispatched Amit Shah and Yogi Adityanath to Kerala—India's most committedly plural state, in which Hindus, Christians and Muslims each constitute around a third of the population—for a series of janrakshas. Their remit, to lecture Malayali Hindus against the danger of love jihad, was a saffronized version of Iago's warning to Desdemona's horrified father Brabantio: 'even now, now, very now, a black ram is tupping your white ewe' (1.1.88–9). But neither Brabantio nor Iago realize that, in the cultural mix of Venice, the ram is not definable just as black, nor the ewe as white. Identifications on the basis of colour alone—on the basis of any one 'core' identity—ignore the mixtures that constitute the Moor of Venice and his wife, the senator's daughter whose songs were taught to her in childhood by a woman named, and possibly from, Barbary. The Hindutva fight against love jihad takes aim not just at cross-communal desire. It also seeks to obliterate the possibility of mixture *within* each of us.

So, let the world know: I am a Jewish–Kiwi–Anglo–Irish love jihadi, partnered with a Malayali from a Hindu Nair family who probably has some Muslim Arab and Christian Portuguese and who-knows-what African ancestry. And my parents and their parents before them were love jihadis too, each of them marrying someone from another country and bequeathing mixture to their children.

As a love jihadi, let me say my love jihadi prayer: l'tikkun olam, l'tikkun Othello, l'tikkun Desdemona. L'tikkun tikkun. To the repair of the world, to the repair of Othello, to the repair of Desdemona. To the repair of repair.

This is not simply a Hebrew prayer. A version of it resonates in Urdu and Hindi in a beautiful song from the film *Delhi-6* (2009): 'marammat mukaddar ki kar do maula, mere maula (repair fate, oh master, my master).' And more: 'toot ke bikharna mujhko zaroor aata hai (I know very well how to scatter into pieces).' This scattering and shattering of the seemingly singular self is also an act of repair that acknowledges the plurality in all of us.

Because 'repair' is not just about making whole what has been broken. If we think that, then we need to repair the idea of repair. For me it is hard not to hear the 'pair' in 're-pair'. The modern word 'pair' refers to more than a couple; it derives from the Latin 'paria', from which we also get the word 'parity', meaning an equalization between different entities. To re-pair is to assert a parity between parts that might be different but work together, between parts that constitute a functioning more-than-oneness, between parts whose bond has been tragically broken. Broken within ourselves as much as with others.

Parity is not purity. May all mixtures be repaired, and respected, in their parts' parity. Our tragedy, in these days of purity, is that they are not.

ACT FOUR SCENE FOUR

Masala Castes (*Othello*)

Rohtak, Haryana, 2016. Pradeep and Seema are neighbours; the pair fall in love and secretly get married. They have known each other's families since they were children. But they decide not to tell anyone because, while Pradeep is a Brahmin, Seema is a 'chamar' or Dalit. Both fear retribution from family and community for their love. In January 2017, Pradeep finally informs his parents; to his relief, they raise no objection to the marriage, and tell Seema's parents of the match. They, too, seem surprisingly amenable, and promise to send Seema to Pradeep's house 'apne hisab se', when they reckon the time to be right. But the next day Seema's body is recovered, half-burnt, from a pyre in the Rohtak crematorium. Her father, mother, and brother are arrested and charged with Seema's murder.

This is no straightforward case of honour killing. Such murders are on the rise throughout India: 28 were reported in 2014, but a staggering 251 were registered in 2015, an increase of 792 per cent. The leap can be explained in part because the National Crime Records Bureau started collecting official data on honour killings only in 2014. And even these newer figures probably represent a mere fraction of the total number of murders prompted by a perceived loss of family and caste honour. Most are committed by members of high-caste families who, after discovering that their child, brother or sister is romantically involved with a Dalit, have either one or both killed in order to protect the supposed sanctity of family and caste. But what is striking in the Rohtak incident is that people from a community most abused by the caste system were, in this instance, its enforcers. In murdering her, Seema's family abided by the social imperative not to pollute Brahmin purity.

This is a tragedy of mixture—not just between the lovers, but within a single family. Seema's family occupied two positions at once: outside and inside the caste system, its victims and its protectors. Yet despite this doubleness—or maybe because of it—they could not accept the mixing of a Brahmin and a Dalit. Equally striking is how much Seema's murder was born of a deep horror of her desire. And this horror conspired to make the caste system momentarily invisible. The journalist Sagar, who wrote about the case in *The Caravan*, reported the head constable in Rohtak as saying, 'Biradari ki toh koi dikkat na thi. Inhone toh ye kaha hamari ladki corrupt thi, dekh na sake usko, gandi thi boley (There was no issue concerning caste. Seema's family said that she was corrupt, they could not bear to see her, she was dirty, they said).' When Sagar asked the constable what he meant by 'gandi', he replied, 'Chaal-chalan thik na tha uska, wo kahen (Her character was not correct, the family said).' Nothing to do with caste. Everything to do with unchaste women.

The constable's remark is illuminating. For the dardnak kahaani of caste often plays out most lethally at those moments when the system becomes invisible, obscured by a focus on 'not good' or 'dirty' or 'unchaste' individuals. At my university the parents of a prospective student once questioned me about the composition of our student body. When they heard that we admit students on scholarship, they wondered if the university was taking the 'right kind of children.' They said their child came from a 'good' school and a 'good' family. They worried too that their child wouldn't be able to eat 'good' food if students from different backgrounds were eating meals prepared in the same kitchen. Whatever 'good' might have meant here, it clearly had little to do with academic achievement, ethical integrity, or healthy nutrition. It was 'good' in the same way Seema's character was 'not good'. Behind that one simple word lurks an entire set of assumptions governing who we can eat with, study with, and fall in love with. And according to those assumptions, caste mixture is literally unspeakable.

The unspeakability of caste extends, sadly, to the Bollywood masala movie. For all its seeming inclusivity with respect to language, region and religious community, the Hindi film industry has consistently avoided stories that scrutinize the caste system or, horror of horrors, embrace caste mixture. One has to turn to regional cinemas outside Bollywood to find such tales. A notable instance is the Marathi movie *Sairat* (2016), directed by Nagraj Manjule. This sympathetically told love story features a boy from a fisherman's lower-caste family and a girl from a rich high-caste background; they elope, but are tracked down by the family of the girl and brutally murdered. *Sairat* is the biggest blockbuster in Marathi film history. It has been remade in Punjabi, Odiya, Kannada and Bengali; it has also been remade, by Karan Johar's production house, in a Hindi adaptation called *Dhadak* (2018). Yet this adaptation diluted the caste dimension, with Johar insisting on an 'upmarket milieu' designed to 'make it more *Romeo and Juliet* than a play on caste.'

Romeo and Juliet, with its two households alike in dignity, is for Indians a caste-invisible version of forbidden love. Not a single one of the many Bollywood *Romeo and Juliet*s makes caste the source of antagonism between their lovers' families. The Shakespeare play that has provoked Indian filmmakers to dream about inter-caste desire is, rather, *Othello*. This tragedy of masala identity about an outsider who is also an insider, who gets secretly married to someone from a different background and community, who murderously enforces a creed of purity of which he is nonetheless a victim, and who focuses myopically on his honour and its tainting by a woman's allegedly corrupt sexual character, bears an uncanny similarity to dardnak kahaanis of caste. The tragedy of Seema resonates in profound ways with the tragedy of Othello, the Moor of Venice.

◆

The subtitle of *Othello*—*The Moor of Venice*—is revealing. It suggests a tragedy of masala identity. Othello is two contradictory things at once: he is Moorish and he is Venetian, which is to say, African and European, Muslim and Christian. But *Macbeth* has taught us how, when confronted with doubleness, we crave singularity. And Othello's tragedy is he cannot allow his mixed identity to stand. He kills himself, acting by his own account as a loyal Venetian to destroy the evil 'turbaned Turk' (5.2.362) within him. Yet readers have understood Othello primarily as a Moor and only accidentally as a Venetian. They have also squabbled over what exactly his 'Moorishness' is, as if settling this question would also settle the question of Othello's identity. Does 'Moor' mean 'tawny-skinned' Moroccan or 'sub-Saharan' African? In short, Othello's identity has been singularized in terms of skin colour.

British and US film adaptations have increasingly regarded Othello as complexionally black. In the 1951 version, filmed partly on location in Morocco, Orson Welles played the Moor as a bronzed Berber. But Laurence Olivier's infamous 1965 film saw him done up in blackface, speaking in a quasi-Caribbean accent. The African–American actor Laurence Fishburne played the first 'authentically' black Othello onscreen in Oliver Parker's 1995 version. And in Tim Blake Nelson's 2001 high-school adaptation *O*, the Othello character was an African-American basketball player. Thanks in no small part to the US's vexed history of slavery and race conflict, Othello has become a synonym for 'black man who marries, and murders, white woman'. The disgraced black football star O. J. Simpson, notoriously accused of killing his white wife Nicole, was spoken of as a latter-day Othello. In the years after the O. J. scandal, I would often have to correct American students who referred uncritically to Othello as 'African–American'.

In India, however, Othello has been understood rather differently. Even though he and other characters repeatedly talk about his black complexion and 'sooty bosom' (1.2.71), Indian actors and directors have focused on non-racial aspects of Othello's character when adapting the play for performance on stage or screen. The enduring Indian legacy of the *Natya Shastra*—the ancient treatise on the performing arts—is that drama should explore rasa, or emotional flavour. As a result, *Othello* has often been legible to Indians more as a play about jealousy than about race. This is evident in adaptations ranging from stylized folk performances to melodramatic commercial films. A kathakali version of *Othello*, devised by Sadanam Balakrishnan in 1996 and staged throughout India, didn't present its titular character as racially different from the other characters. The production was, rather, interested in the rasa of jealousy that Othello embodies. Likewise, a recent Bengali film adaptation of *Othello* directed by Ranjan Ghosh, *Hrid Majharey* (2014), presents its story as 'a journey dotted by love, jealousy and destiny.' In this film, rasa and kismet eclipse Shakespeare's study of racial difference and tragic choices. *Hrid Majharey*'s maths-teacher Othello and its cardiologist Desdemona are not socially divided in any way, nor does their union attract any opposition. If the film's Othello has a divided self, it comes not from his experience of racial difference or migration but from a recognizably Indian split: he is a rationalist who is easily swayed by astrology, as we see when a Chinese female soothsayer in Kolkata predicts that love will be deadly for him.

To the extent that Othello and Desdemona's social difference has been represented on Indian screens, it is through the lens of caste rather than race or religion. One might expect a play whose titular character is a Christian convert of Moorish origin and violently opposes himself to the 'turban'd Turk' to lend itself to exploration of modern-day Indian Islamophobia. Yet something about this play conjures the spectre of caste. And caste mixture.

The Bengali film *Saptapadi* (1961), directed by Ajoy Kar, is less an adaptation of *Othello* than a colonial romantic drama that uses Shakespeare's play to help audiences interpret its two main characters.

The film has a happy ending, but it deeply mines the tragedy of *Othello*. *Saptapadi* tells of the vexed relation between Krishnendu (Uttam Kumar), a Bengali Hindu, and Rina Brown (Suchitra Sen), an Anglo-Indian Christian. Krishnendu's complexion is darker than Rina's—indeed, his name means dark moon—and she sneeringly calls him 'blackie'. Krishnendu and Rina perform in a student production of *Othello*, as a result of which they fall in love. Their complexional difference is underlined by the voiceovers for the two characters. Utpal Dutt, who also directed the play-within-a-film sequence following his own successful Bengali stage production of *Othello*, provided the voiceover for Krishnendu's Othello; the British actress Jennifer Kendal did the voiceover for Rina's Desdemona.

But this racial angle opens up to reveal a religious/caste subtext. Krishnendu's rigidly Hindu father is opposed to their union; Rina's English father is more accommodating, but demands that Krishnendu convert to Christianity before agreeing to their marriage. Meanwhile, Krishnendu's father persuades Rina to end the relationship. The twist comes when Rina finds out her biological mother is not dead as she had believed, but is rather the family's lower-caste cleaner, whom her father had sexually molested. The mixed identity that *Othello*'s subtitle associates with its Moor of Venice is therefore displaced onto its Desdemona. But the film ends happily by reuniting Krishnendu and a repentant Rina, who sees more sincerity in him than her father has shown. And so the scandal of caste mixture is transcended in a masala fantasy of communal inclusiveness. In this *Saptapadi* recalls the Indian *The Taming of the Shrews*: a foreign-adulterated woman submits to the authority of a decent Indian man. Caste and caste mixture, briefly invoked, fall away from view.

Caste is a more prominent concern in *Kaliyattam* (1997), directed by Jayaraj. Unlike *Saptapadi*, this Malayalam film adaptation of *Othello* matches Shakespeare's story very closely. Its Othello character comes from a stigmatized and dark-skinned community, but he possesses a skill that the dominant clans of his society admire. He marries a woman of fairer complexion from one of the most powerful clans. Yet after promoting someone else over his old sidekick, he is seduced into believing that his wife is unfaithful and murders her. His suspicions are proved groundless and, horrified by what he has done, he kills himself.

What lends originality to this reimagining of *Othello* is its immersion in a local tradition of folk performance. The tradition brings a caste dimension to *Kaliyattam* that cannot be happily transcended as it is in *Saptapadi*. The Othello character, Kannan Perumalayan, is a performer of theyyam, an ancient ritual form of worship from the northern Malabar Coast that features actor-dancers from the lower castes. Yet for the duration of the ritual, in which an actor first dances in human form and then reappears dressed and made up as a god, theyyam gives its lower-caste performer an unexpected if temporary power. He doesn't just act the part of a god; he is also worshipped as one by his higher-caste audience. But ultimately he must return to his socially inferior status. *Kaliyattam*'s director Jayaraj has said that he chose the theyyam setting for *Othello* because it captures the mixed identity of the Moor of Venice. The theyyam actor-dancer is both valorized and stigmatized, granted divine powers onstage even as he is at their receiving end offstage. This doubleness provides a powerful local context for Kannan Perumalayan's otherwise unconventional marriage to the fair upper-caste Thamara, the ease with which Perumalayan's fellow theyyam actor whom he has passed over for promotion preys on his fears about Thamara's love for him, and Perumalayan's final self-immolation in a ritual bonfire as a split act of holy sacrifice and self-loathing.

Kaliyattam reimagines Othello's masala identity in a more thoughtful way than any Western film adaptation I've seen. And its exploration of caste mixture is more rigorous and nuanced than the somewhat evasive treatment it receives in *Saptapadi*. Unlike the Bengali film, *Kaliyattam* doesn't view caste mixture as the scandalous product of a firangi's lustful behaviour. Rather it understands it as the inevitable outcome of a collision between cultural tradition and social structure. But *Kaliyattam* ultimately sees Perumalayan's masala identity as a self-cancelling proposition, cordoned off from the rest of the community in a space of sacred exception. Vishal Bhardwaj's film *Omkara* (2006), the middle instalment of his Shakespeare trilogy, likewise explores the play through the lens of caste mixture. Its extraordinary accomplishment is that it makes masala identity not the exception but the tragically disavowed reality of a caste-addled society.

◆

Omkara begins with two men speaking in the badlands of Uttar Pradesh. Their language is difficult for most urban Hindi-speaking viewers—let alone an English-speaking Kiwi—to grasp. The two speak in the rustic dialect known as Khariboli, or 'stiff speech', a somewhat pejorative term for the bhasha spoken in much of western Uttar Pradesh, the stomping grounds of Bhardwaj's childhood. Despite the 'stiff' or uncouth sounds that prompted urban speakers of Hindi to give it its name, Khariboli was once regarded as a high language, associated with the court culture of the Mughals. It was, from its inception, a masala tongue, combining elements of Braj Bhasha and Persian, vernacular and court dialects. Yet in this impure language, we hear the two men enact a drama of caste purity.

The first man wears a sehra or veil of flowers. A bridegroom en route to his wedding, he is counselled by the second, a lame man who is dressed less decorously and totes a rifle. Both are Brahmins: the bridegroom's surname is Tiwari, a name that translates as one versed in three vedas; the second man's surname is Tyagi, one of the highest Brahmin sub-castes. This Tyagi (Saif Ali Khan) informs the bridegroom Tiwari (Deepak Dobriyal), in a heavily accented Khariboli, that there has been a change of plans: 'Teri dulhan ko adhdha bamman thha ke le jaa riya hai (The half-Brahmin has taken your bride and is going).'

The bride-thief is the dark-complexioned Omkara Shukla (Ajay Devgn). But he is no pantomime villain. He is the bahubali or strongman of the local Brahmin crime boss, Bhaisaab (Naseeruddin Shah). The opening song presents Omkara as 'sabse bade ladaiya (the greatest warrior)', and his elopement with Tiwari's bride, the fair Dolly Mishra (Kareena Kapoor), receives Bhaisaab's blessing. Tyagi works under Omkara; indeed, he has engineered the bride-theft. But he refers to Omkara with a phrase that scornfully highlights his caste impurity: 'adhdha bamman' is Khariboli dialect for half-Brahmin. We find out more about the bahubali's mixed parentage when Dolly's father Raghunath Mishra, a Brahmin vakil or barrister, says (in more conventional Hindi) that 'bhool gaya ke tu bamman toh hai par aadha... aadha khoon toh tere badan mein us kanjari ka bhi hai (I had forgotten that you are only half-Brahmin—half of the blood in your body is also that whore's)'. As this makes clear, Mishra remembers Omkara's low-caste 'kanjari' mother only when the barrister's patriarchal authority has been disregarded by his daughter. The sun's corona—its flickering rim that makes it more than a pure disc—is visible only during an eclipse; likewise the scandal of caste mixture becomes visible only when Brahmin identity is eclipsed, in this case by the shadow of illicit female desire. And that illicit desire is both Omkara's 'kanjari' mother's and Raghunath's daughter's.

Initially Omkara speaks with confidence about his mixed caste, precisely because he is confident about Dolly's desire: 'hamaari jaat toh khoob pehchaani apne, vakil saab... par apni beti ke dil ki baat nai sun sake (you have recognized my caste well, barrister sir... but you couldn't listen to the matter of your daughter's heart).' Yet what Omkara presents as a relation between two consenting adults is then reframed by Dolly's father as a matter of scandal in the eyes of the entire community: 'puri biraadari mein naak kati so alag... aur phir kin haathon se apne phool ko us daitya ke haathon mein saunp doon... jaat ka bhi toh adhdha hai (not only did you insult me before the whole community... how then can I give you my flower when you are also a half-caste)?' Raghunath Mishra emphasizes how this community scandal involves more than Omkara insulting him. It also extends to the plucking of 'apne phool'—our own flower. Dolly's sexuality is owned by her father and community. And once plucked it threatens the social order: as Mishra says, 'jo apne baap ko thag sakti hai woh kisi aur ki sagi kya hogi (she who can trick her father, how can she be trusted by anyone else)?' These words resonate ominously through the film, especially for Omkara.

Bhaisaab needs Omkara as his strongman—just as the Duke of Venice needs Othello as his military general—and so the scandal that Dolly's father complains of is put aside. Indeed, the barrister himself redirects his critique of Omkara's caste doubleness by taking fuller aim at the doubleness of his daughter and all women: 'aurat ka triya charitra bhoolna mat (don't forget woman's two-facedness).' From this point on in the film, Omkara's caste is barely a topic of conversation. He may tell Dolly that 'doosri biraadari ki thi meri maa... is liye jaat ka adhdha kehte hain mujhe (my mother was from another community... so they call me a half caste).' But even here, his caste mixture is overshadowed by the apparition of the woman whose love crosses boundaries and disrupts order. This apparition dominates the rest of the film.

From the famous item numbers 'Beedi Jalai Le' and 'Namak Ishq Ka' to the plot resolution, the film and its characters are consumed with thoughts of the desiring woman. And in this patriarchal community such a woman automatically becomes 'triya charitra (two-faced)'. To guard against the possibility that Dolly might be unfaithful, Omkara gifts her a kamarbandh—a symbol of chastity. Yet the kamarbandh becomes a two-faced symbol once it reappears on the body of the courtesan, Billo (Bipasha Basu). All women in Omkara experience the 'triya charitra' fate of the kamarbandh. They are translated in the minds of men into sexually promiscuous deceivers. Tyagi says of his wife Indu (Konkona Sen Sharma) that he suspects her of cheating on him. Omkara, racked with doubt about Dolly and her supposed affair with his lieutenant Kesu Firangi (Vivek Oberoi), tells a chilling joke that cracks up all the other men in its casual misogyny: 'ek baar ek aadmi ki sadi hui (once there was a man who got married)', he says. The next line—'khatam' (the end)—is also the punchline to the joke, as if marriage spells the end of men's happiness. Then there is the television reality show 'Illicit Relations', which screens while Omkara broods jealously. The show tells a story of a man betrayed by a lecherous wife, who has sex with his brother. In *Omkara's* second half, then, female infidelity is a mass obsession for the male characters. Caste is not mentioned at all.

Does this mean caste drops out of view from the film entirely? And is Omkara's masala identity no longer an issue? To the contrary: there may be no mention of caste. But Bhardwaj hints at how caste mixture flickers behind the shadow of the deceptive woman. When Omkara tells Indu that he is haunted by the words of Dolly's father, she replies: 'triya charitra... hai na (double-faced... no)?'. Her referent is unclear—is she referring to Dolly or the hypocritical men who accuse women? But the context makes the meaning clear. She proceeds to say that 'jab granthon ne kalank ko hamaare manthe ki bindi bana diya hai, toh aapki kyaa galti hai Omi bhaiya (when the scriptures have placed taint like a bindi on our forehead, then what is your mistake Omi bhaiya)?' It is hard not to hear in 'granthon' or scriptures a reference to the *Manusmriti*. This sacred text stigmatizes women for their sexual desires: 'it is the nature of women to seduce men,' says one passage; 'women, true to their class character, are capable of leading men astray,' says another. It is no coincidence that the *Manusmriti* also prescribes the divisions of jaati or caste. It does so partly through a remark about the polluting powers of Dalit women that seems to have particular relevance to *Omkara*: 'When twice born [Brahmin] men in their folly marry low-caste Shudra women, they are responsible for the degradation of their whole family. Accordingly the children adopt all the demerits of the Shudra caste.' And it adds that 'if a woman enjoys sex with lower-caste men, she is to be punished'.

With Indu's remark Bhardwaj nudges his viewers towards an understanding of how the male characters' misogyny, as in the *Manusmriti*, is entangled in fears of caste mixture. Yet that entanglement is often disavowed. Just as the chief constable in Rohtak insisted that Seema's death had nothing to do with caste and everything to do with her bad character, so do the characters of *Omkara* displace the scandal of inter-caste love on to women's 'triya charitra'. Sadly, Omkara himself repeats the pattern with Dolly—as if the Brahmin in him believes that her free choice of a man with a lower-caste mother has polluted her, and that she should naturally gravitate to a shuddh Brahmin like Kesu. When he asks her, 'itni khoobsurat ho ke mujh jaise pe dil laga baithi (how can such a beauty fall for someone like me)?', we hear not modest gratitude but a self-loathing whose language hints at both her caste purity and its contamination. The Hindi 'mujhpe… pe dil laga baithi', translates literally as 'your heart sat on me', an image that puts Dolly on top of Omkara by making her love a literal 'crush' on him. The remark shades into doubt over the appropriateness of her desire, a doubt expressed by her own father.

As we have seen, Dolly's father objects to her relationship with the 'adhdha bamman' because it is a matter of shame for the entire Brahmin community: 'puri biraadari mein naak kati'. The English subtitle, and the translation in the official screenplay, render this as 'the whole community is slandering us'. But the Hindi is more complex. The phrase, 'naak kati', has multiple referents: it is the Brahmin community itself as much as Dolly's father who has been shamed. The phrase translates this communal shame into a graphic image of nose-cutting. We do not hear from Mishra again. But the image of the cut nose persists. Langda Tyagi, in what has now become a defining image from the movie (it is featured on posters as well as the cover of the screenplay), wears a plaster over a cut on his nose. Tyagi's injury recalls the iconic image of a nose-plastered Jack Nicholson in the Hollywood gangster movie *Chinatown* (1974). But Tyagi's plaster also evokes Mishra's 'puri biraadari mein naak kati'. By doing so it subliminally suggests the shame of the Brahmin community, dishonoured by Omkara's caste mixture, Dolly's unrestrained desire, and the pair's scandalous coupling. In other words, Tyagi's cut nose is not just a sign of individual gangster machismo. It is also, in the eyes of a Mishra or a Tiwari (who reminds Tyagi of his years of servitude to the 'adhdha bamman'), a licence to seek caste-based revenge. The lame Tyagi thus acts as a representative of the dishonoured bamman biradri.

We expect Tyagi, as the counterpart of Shakespeare's Iago, to be two-faced. Iago swears by Janus, the two-faced Roman god. But Tyagi's two-facedness is not a character attribute unique to him. It is entirely symptomatic of his community. Tyagi with his bandaged nose is just one instance of how shuddh Brahmin purity is a fantasy, superimposed on a culture of violent mixture. But this mixture is outsourced to 'dirty' women and, by implication, 'dirty' inter-caste desire.

◆

Kesu Firangi—by name both Indian and foreign—injects another kind of masala mixture into the film. A fan of American music, he teaches Dolly how to sing Stevie Wonder's cheesy song 'I Just Called to Say I Love You'. It is with musical sequences such as these that Bhardwaj most reminds us of the milieu of volatile mixture in which the Brahmin gangsters operate. He does so partly by using the masala convention of naach-gaana in unexpected ways: the film's two famous item numbers pictured on Bipasha Basu as Billo, 'Beedi Jalaile' and 'Namak Ishq Ka', both end in outbursts of Brahmin violence—the first a fight started by a drunk Kesu Firangi, the second a shootout between rival gangs. But Bhardwaj also finds subtle musical ways of highlighting the various mixtures concealed by Brahmin fantasies of purity. In particular, his compositions make inventive use of rhythm and cadence to subliminally suggest the shaping power of Omkara's caste mixture on Dolly's and his dardnak kahaani.

In this, Bhardwaj manages to channel something profound about Shakespeare's tragedy. We know that Shakespeare often uses lines of regular iambic pentameter—ten syllables consisting of five units of an unstressed syllable followed by a stressed syllable. But he is also fond of one particular subtle variation on the iambic meter. 'To BE/ or NOT/ to BE/, that IS/ the QUES/tion' (*Hamlet*, 3.1.58) is the most famous instance of this variation: against expectation, Shakespeare adds an extra unstressed syllable at the end of the Hamlet's line—the falling 'tion' of 'QUES-tion'—which creates a sense of doubt. (Try saying 'to be or not to be, that is the quest'—it sounds far more confident, because it ends with a stressed syllable.) The standard, somewhat sexist term for this eleven-syllable variation—the 'feminine ending'—implies that it represents a deviation, a falling off from an ideal of authoritative masculine prosody. I would prefer to call this variation the masala ending. Rather than acceding fully to the conventional rhythmic pattern, Shakespeare adds something else to it—something impure that shouldn't be there, something that flaunts the rules yet is given a home. This masala ending allows, too, for something of the melodramatic more-than-oneness of the masala movie: the upbeat pattern of the iamb is allowed to dip into something sad, doubtful, even tragic. Which is to say, the masala ending can provide a metrical reminder of mixture.

Shakespeare uses this trick repeatedly in *Othello* to convey the doubt the titular character feels about his wife. It is no surprise that, once Iago gets to work on Othello, the latter resorts to iambs with masala endings, aspiring to the force of certainty yet stumbling with that last extra syllable. For example, Othello tells Iago, 'i THINK/ that THOU/ art JUST/ and THINK/ thou ART/ not' (3.3.390). That falling 'not' represents Othello's condition at this point—a condition of excess and negation and mixed feelings. The use of masala endings here is not surprising, given the power of Iago's machinations. But if we listen closely to Othello's language earlier in the play, we can hear that, even before Iago has begun to destroy him, his lines subliminally voice doubt no matter how much he aspires to authority. When he is reunited with Desdemona in Cyprus after being divided from her at sea, he uses a series of regularly metric lines before trotting out a revealing instance of the masala ending:

> it GIVES/ me WON/der GREAT/ as MY/ conTENT
> to SEE/ you HERE/ be FORE/ me. O/ my SOUL's/ JOY
> if AF/ter EV/ery TEM/pest COME/ such CALM/ness
> (2.1.180-2)

This last line is revealing. Shakespeare could have easily made it regularly iambic by replacing 'calmness' with 'calm'. None of Othello's explicit meaning would have been sacrificed. But the mixed feelings conveyed by that extraneous, falling '-ness' would have been lost.

How might *Omkara* replicate the effect of the eleven-syllable line? Bhardwaj cannot use it, as it is a form completely foreign to Hindi cinema dialogue. But he can simulate something of the line's effect musically. Take the song 'O Saathi Re', which appears in the film's first half. It features Omkara and Dolly before he starts doubting her fidelity. Dolly and Omkara happily prance around their rustic house, overturning a barrow of red chillis—talk about masala!—as they make eyes at each other. Everything about the song's visuals indicate a couple happily in love. But at the level of sound, the song does something different. The melody plants a feeling of doubt with the ominous fall of its lyric from 'O Saathi' to 'Re'. If this was not Ajay Devgn and Kareena Kapoor but, rather, Anil Kapoor and Madhuri Dixit standing on a Swiss mountain in one of their late eighties movies, the melody would strive upwards. Instead, it performs the equivalent of diving off that mountain. As a result, the song sequence weds its visual depiction of domestic concord to a soundtrack that suggests discord.

'O Saathi Re"'s melodic fall works in concert with Gulzar's lyrics. These begin with the wish that the day not end—'din doobe naa'— but the falling 'naa' of that line forecasts the inevitable fall of day into darkness. The lyrics hope for endless sunlight but are haunted by shadow—'dhoop ke peeche daude, chaanv chhue naa (let us chase the sunlight, so no shadow falls on us)'. I would argue that the 'chaanv' or shadow is not just the shadow of Omkara's murderous suspicions. It is also the shadow of his caste mixture. The feared darkness of 'O Saathi Re' implicitly recalls the darkness that the film associates with Omkara's complexion—so different from Dolly's radiant fairness—which bears the lingering trace of his lower-caste mother. The lyrical adulteration of day by night, fairness by darkness, not only underscores the melodic fall of the song. It also illustrates the oscillation of light and shadow that trails Omkara and splits him throughout the movie.

With this split, Bhardwaj captures the tragedy of Othello's self-representation at the end of the play. The Moor of Venice's last sigh (as Salman Rushdie calls it) is not just a monologue expressing repentance for his murder of Desdemona. It is also a speech that performs the impossibility of his having a singular identity even as he longs to be solely Venetian. As we have seen, Othello tells a highly theatrical story about how once in Aleppo, he killed a Turk who spoke ill of Venice. And, enacting the story, he kills himself. The play splits the 'he' who kills and the 'himself' who is killed. This split identity, straddling the divide between Venetian and Turk, Christian and Muslim, is the crux of the play. It is the split we hear in *Othello*'s subtitle, *The Moor of Venice*. By contrast, the divided Othello compares Desdemona to a 'pearl...richer than all his tribe' (5.2.356–7) that he has cast away. The comparison is designed to value her supposedly pure singularity over his impure mixture. This is only one instance of how, throughout the play, Othello compulsively objectifies Desdemona as something white and inanimate—alabaster, a page from the Bible, a candle. She represents a fantasy of lifeless purity at odds with his masala reality.

The song 'Jag Ja Ri Gudiya' also suggests as much. It is first sung by Omkara when he and Dolly are at home. Here, the words 'jag ja ri gudiya (wake up, doll)' seem to be simply his sweet request to a 'doll' (appropriate for 'Dolly') to wake up and greet the day. But the song is then replayed after Omkara has murdered his supposedly 'triya charitra' wife by suffocating her with a pillow. Now the request that the 'gudiya' wake up becomes tragic—and sinister, because Dolly has been reduced to a lifeless 'doll', revealing the horrible literal reality that haunts what otherwise seems to be a term of endearment. She has, in short, become the inanimate pearl that Othello throws away. Interestingly, Gulzar's lyrics pick up on the image of the pearl. Dolly is described as 'os ke moti, motiyon sa mogra': 'os ke moti' are 'dewdrops', but the phrase literally means 'pearls of dew', an image that is supplemented by that of 'motiyon sa mogra', or 'jasmine pearls'. The line helps present Dolly as unsullied whiteness, a fantasy of Brahmin purity. Yet this line is curiously absent from the version sung after Dolly's murder—actualizing the casting away of the pearl in the text of *Othello*.

The visual setting of the two performances of 'Jag Ja Ri Gudiya' is striking. In both instances, the camera focuses on Omkara and Dolly's bed, which is also a swing. More than the kamarbandh, the swing enacts the back-and-forth movement by which the 'chaste' woman is transformed into a 'triya charitra.' But it does something else too. The final image of the film is of the dead Omkara, dressed in white, crumpled beneath the swing on which the suffocated Dolly's body lies as it rocks in and out of frame. Her red sari keeps moving over his bright white kurta, covering it in shade and then erasing it from view altogether, before swinging away to reveal it again. Omkara's masala identity can be glimpsed here, in a back-and-forth movement between light and darkness. Yet he is forever beneath Dolly, no matter whether he is clad in light or wreathed in shade. His masala caste identity is highlighted, then, in the lowlight of the film's final scene.

◆

I have deliberately dwelled at some length on *Omkara* before turning to the text of *Othello*. And that is because I think Bhardwaj's film allows us to grasp something very interesting about Shakespeare's play that might otherwise remain invisible to us. American readers have greatly influenced popular understandings of *Othello* by viewing it as a tale of race, a term that is absent from the play's vocabulary yet resonates powerfully with its presentation of difference and identity. But how might we in India, following the leads of *Saptapadi*, *Kaliyattam*, and particularly *Omkara*, understand *Othello* in terms of caste instead? Does it even make sense to do so, given that neither the word nor the concept were available to Shakespeare or his first audiences? Yet *Omkara* is such a devastatingly smart reading of the play that I have found it impossible not to view *Othello* differently in light of it.

The word 'caste'—that most poisonous of Indian concepts—in fact comes from a Latin word, 'castus', meaning pure or chaste. (Indeed, the word 'chaste' derives from it.) By the end of the fifteenth century 'castus' had evolved into the Portuguese 'casta', meaning breeding. This change speaks to the growing importance of bloodlines in Portugal after the Christian Reconquista, as a result of which the Moors and the Jews were driven out of the Iberian Peninsula. During the Inquisition, 'casta' became an important category by means of which to distinguish between those of 'pure' Christian breeding and those suspected of mixed origin, with some Moorish or Jewish blood. 'Casta' thus came to signify what we mean by pedigree. But it retained something of the 'chaste' sense of 'castus'. A pure 'casta' demanded sexual purity of its women, untainted by congress with men from outside the community.

The Portuguese 'casta' describes, then, what I call a breeding–chastity system. This system has certain overlaps with the system described by the Spanish term, 'raca', from which our word race is derived. The Spanish adopted 'raca' from the language of horse breeding to suggest the purity of Christian lines. But more than 'casta', 'raca' acquired a predominantly complexional dimension as it moved west from the Iberian Peninsula to the Spanish and English American colonies, where it became a lethally effective means of discriminating among white, black, and native 'races'. By contrast, 'casta' migrated east with the Portuguese to Goa in 1498. Delighted to find throughout India communities of locals who, like the colonists, distinguished themselves on the basis of pure bloodlines, the Portuguese named these communities 'castas'. 'Jaati' may be an invention of the *Manusmriti*. But 'caste' is a colonial term from which we still have to decolonize our imaginations as much as practices.

Yet 'casta' remains useful when understood in light of its semantic history. Above all, its twin associations with breeding and chastity help illuminate the intersection in *Omkara* of ideas of community purity and female sexuality. *Othello*, too, uncannily maps the intersectional terrain of casta that underlies both its Portuguese usage and its Indian afterlives. And that is because, in the England of 1604 when Shakespeare's company first staged the play, something resembling caste was already part of the local social landscape. Although the landed gentry no longer spoke French, they liked to derive their ancestry from Norman families who had come to England with William the Conqueror. The poorer classes tended to come from Germanic and Celtic stock. Shakespeare was born of the union between a yeoman-class father, whose surname derived from the old Germanic 'Schakken' (brandish) and 'Speer' (spear), and a gentry-class mother whose medieval ancestors adopted the French-sounding 'de Arden' as their family name. Shakespeare, possibly motivated by his mother's fears of ancestral French grandeur being sullied by her inter-class jodi, bought his family a coat of arms in 1596 to re-establish its gentlemanly credentials. There may be more of the mixed Shakespeare in the Moor of Venice than we realize.

In lines that seem to express Shakespeare's own desire for grand ancestry, Othello insists on his concealed high pedigree: 'Tis yet to know... I fetch my life and being/ From men of royal siege' (1.2.19, 21-22). The dominant meaning of 'casta', breeding, is apparent in this line. Elsewhere *Othello* explicitly uses 'breeding' as a synonym for pure pedigree. Cassio insists that his genteel 'courtesy'—a code of behaviour associated with the court—stems from his 'breeding' (2.1.101-2). And Othello petitions the Duke to allow Desdemona to accompany him to Cyprus, but on condition of 'such accommodation... / As levels with her breeding' (1.3.236-7). Here 'breeding' has many of the connotations of 'high caste'; Desdemona's bloodline demands specific accommodations, in terms of comfort, diet, and other domestic requirements.

But in *Othello*, 'breeding' as a noun signifying high pedigree bears the trace of the verb 'breed'. And Shakespeare often associates this verb with impure generation. Hamlet worries that 'the sun breeds maggots in a dead dog' (2.2.182); this disgusted image of mixing extends to his infamous question to Ophelia, 'why would you be a breeder of sinners?' (3.1.122-3). A similar anxiety attaches to the word 'breed' in *Othello*. The 'worms... that did breed the silk' of the handkerchief that Othello gives Desdemona may have been 'hallowed' (3.4.71). But the handkerchief, initially a sign of unsullied high 'breeding', comes to acquire dirty connotations, thanks to its associations with Desdemona's alleged infidelity. And when Emilia asks Desdemona whether 'affection' can 'breed' the impulse to be sexually promiscuous (4.3.96), we hear an anxiety reminiscent of *Omkara*: the spectre of unrestrained female 'breeding' or sexuality haunts the fantasy of pure 'breeding' or bloodline.

It is not only that a pure bloodline might one day sexually mix with a less pure one. Rather, the purity of a bloodline can be understood only in terms of its potential pollution. Desdemona's 'breeding' is always shadowed by the fear of her breeding promiscuously. 'Promiscuous', revealingly, comes from the Latin 'pro-' (toward) and 'miscere' (to mix). And so Iago is able to insinuate that a promiscuous will to mixture taints Desdemona's supposedly pure 'breeding'. As he tells her father, 'you'll have your daughter covered with a Barbary horse; you'll have your neighbours neigh to you; you'll have coursers for cousins and gennets for germans' (1.1.112–5). Purity can be understood only as always occupying a position of potential impurity.

Of course, Iago is a master of turning symbols of the high and pure into their vulgar opposites. He graphically reimagines Cassio's courteous gesture of kissing his fingers in the presence of women as a display of 'clyster-pipes' or enema tubes (2.1.176). He transforms the clean white handkerchief, displaced from Desdemona to Emilia to Iago to Cassio to Bianca, into a grimy symbol of spiralling sexual pollution. And he aspires to turn Desdemona's 'virtue into pitch' (2.3.334). That he is able to do so is not due to a unique skill in lying or manipulation. Iago recognizes something about the breeding–chastity system that, like the two-faced god Janus by whom he swears, is semantically and structurally unstable. Just as high breeding is haunted by impure sexual mixing, so too does the chaste always bear the trace of the unchaste. Othello underscores this when, in a fit of jealousy, he takes Desdemona's hand and pronounces it in need of a 'sequester from liberty' (3.4.38). The hand that Desdemona has given in marriage—which she presents as having 'felt no age or known no sorrow' (3.4.35)—is here transmuted by Othello into a groping, sweaty sexual organ. Again, this is less due to Iago's manipulation and more to do with a structural instability afflicting both the 'chaste' of Shakespearean English and the 'caste' of modern India.

Othello uses the word 'chaste' with startling regularity. For Othello, it is the supreme value that authorizes his murder of Desdemona. He says, standing beside her as she lies sleeping in the final act,

> It is the cause, it is the cause, my soul—
> Let me not name it to you, you chaste stars.
> It is the cause. Yet I'll not shed her blood,
> Nor scar that whiter skin of hers than snow,
> And smooth as monumental alabaster. (5.2.1–5)

Her promiscuity, he says, offends the 'chaste stars', and so she must be killed otherwise she will 'betray more men' (5.2.6). Chastity must be preserved from the impure promiscuity of desire. But Othello still views Desdemona's skin as 'white' and 'smooth…as alabaster', and so it must not be blemished or sullied. The domain of the chaste paradoxically expands here to include a woman whom he has accused of sexual impurity. This is but one example of the blurred line between the 'chaste' and the 'unchaste' that Iago turns to account: 'many worthy and even chaste dames thus,/ All guiltless, meet reproach' (4.1.43–4). In Othello's case, this blurring involves an obvious element of projection. He says of Desdemona that her 'name, that was as fresh/ As Dian's visage, is now begrimed and black/ As my own face' (3.3.392–3). Diana is the goddess of chastity. And what has polluted Desdemona's 'fresh' chastity? Othello's reference to his black face implicates him as the source of impurity. But his remark is haunted by a sense that what is at fault is *her* desire in choosing *him*. She herself has failed to respect the purity of her high 'breeding' and 'chastity', long before her alleged infidelity with Cassio.

And this self-loathing, of course, is what Iago plays on. It is not Desdemona's supposed affair with Cassio but, rather, her initial choice of Othello that is at fault. Soon after their marriage has been made public, Iago points out to Othello that it seems odd she should have chosen as she has:

> Ay, there's the point. As, to be bold with you,
> Not to affect many proposed matches
> Of her own clime, complexion, and degree,
> Whereto we see in all things nature tends.
> Foh, one may smell in such a will most rank,
> Foul disproportion, thoughts unnatural! (3.3.233–8)

Here we get the clearest articulation of the breeding-chastity system that undergirds the Portuguese notion of 'casta' and *Othello* alike. As in *Omkara*, and as in the *Manusmriti*, a breeding-chastity system flickers behind the shadow of the desiring woman. Again, it is not as if Iago has ingeniously invented this accusation to dupe a poor foreigner who knows little about the customs of Venice. He is playing on a set of assumptions that Othello has always implicitly shared. We have glimpsed this in his characterization of Desdemona listening to his tales: 'She'd come again, and with a greedy ear/ Devour up my discourse' (1.3.148–9).

In the breeding-chastity system, the woman is placed on a pedestal as the exemplar of the 'chaste'. But she also becomes suspect as soon as she starts desiring or, in Othello's language, devouring. Desire of the kind Desdemona displays, a voracious hunger for the exotic, is the dangerously impure force field within which Venetian social boundaries are crossed. But Desdemona's boundary-crossing desire also holds up a mirror to the mixture within Othello. He is not simply Christian, or of high breeding. He is an adulterated mix of Christian and Muslim, high and low, fair and black, Venetian and Moor. That mix becomes partly visible, like a flickering corona, when his aspirational purity is eclipsed by the presence of a voraciously devouring woman. And this is exactly how the Indian caste system works. It may be a textual error, but the Quarto edition is eerily prescient when it has Othello compare himself to 'the base Indian' (5.2.356). (The Folio edition's version of this line is 'the base Judean'.) This 'Indian' Othello cannot stand to witness the sullying of caste.

The fact is that mixture defines all these high-bred Venetians, no matter what fantasies of purity might bond them across their antagonisms. The Moor of Venice shares the stage with the man he abhors as the Florentine of Venice and the woman he demonizes as the 'cunning whore of Venice' (4.2.93). Cassio like Othello is mixed because of his foreign origin; Desdemona is mixed because of her desire for the foreign. Yet all these mixed characters claim high 'breeding' and 'chastity' to purify themselves. Look how Othello insists that 'the young affects in me [are] defunct' (1.3.262–3), or how Cassio honourably refuses Iago's provocations to sexual banter (2.3.23), or how Desdemona cannot imagine sexual interest in another during her scene with Emilia (4.3). All seek sanctuary under the cloak of the chaste. It falls on the play's most obvious incarnation of mixture, Othello, to purge mixture from the world of the play. But the way he does so only underlines how mixture is unavoidable and purity deadly: playing the Venetian to slay the foreigner in himself, he still embodies both, and by killing the one, he kills the other too. This is the dardnak kahaani of masala caste, where an 'impure' person most stigmatized by the breeding-chastity system ends up being that system's prime enforcer.

B. R. Ambedkar says in *Annihilation of Caste* that every Indian is 'commingled'. But whether we can live and love with our mixture remains to be seen. He also saw inter-caste marriage as the 'solvent' in which caste would be annihilated. Sadly, Omkara's and Othello's stories suggest otherwise. We who are mixed often desire nothing more than purity.

'Tujhko Pukaare Mera Pyaar'

In 2003, I saw Ram Gopal Varma's horror movie *Bhoot* (2003) in Delhi's
Pragati Maidan. It was a formula film, a knock-off of *Rosemary's Baby*
(1968) and other Hollywood horror flicks. In retrospect, the scariest
thing about the film was the smell of the venue. It was a hot summer
day, there was no air conditioning, and the cinema fans lazily recycled
the stench of overheated men's urinals. The film did little to make me
forget the bad smell. For *Bhoot* couldn't please palates like mine that
craved masala: the film had no interest in mixed languages, lovers, and
naach-gaana.

Talking with disappointed nose-clutching patrons during the interval,
I discovered that some of them felt they had been lured to the film
under false pretences. The title of *Bhoot* had evoked in them nostalgic
memories of a long tradition of Indian ghost movies at odds with Varma's
American-style flick. And this tradition was deeply masala. It had even
bred the unusual category of the 'bhoot song', the item number sung
by a ghost. A woman disappointed by Varma's film sang one such song
for me: 'Tujhko Pukaare Mera Pyaar', the Mohammed Rafi number
warbled by the Raaj Kumar character in *Neel Kamal* (1968). At that point,
it was as if another spectre had joined the conversation. The ghost of
masala bhoot movies had returned in the form of a music drenched in
longing. And that ghost began to haunt me. I found myself increasingly
drawn to Hindi bhoot movies from *Neel Kamal* to the Ramsay Brothers'
Purana Mandir (1984). The biggest surprise? They have given me a fresh
perspective on Shakespeare's most famous ghost story.

What is it about the bhoot movie that is masala? For one, it recognizes
a more-than-oneness that haunts the world we think of as rational.
Lurking beneath what seems explainable according to the laws of reason
and causality is another universe that is inexplicable. Or, if explicable,
only according to a different set of laws. As the lead character from
Hamlet says: 'there are more things in heaven and earth, Horatio,/ Than
are dreamt of in our philosophy' (1.5.168–9). But where the ghosts
of western tradition and Varma's movie tend to horrify, the bhoots of
masala cinema often provoke a different response. Bhoots tend to be

embraced rather than exorcized; they are reminders of a past that has been forgotten but whose unfinished business needs addressing in the present. Take the song 'Tujhko Pukaare Mera Pyaar'. Sung by a character as he is buried alive behind a wall, his ghostly words call ('pukaare') through the centuries to the current incarnation of his lover (Waheeda Rehman), forcing her to take action to free his soul from his prison. As this suggests, the bhoot of the masala film breaks down walls dividing time as much as space.

The character of the Ghost in *Hamlet* is more Bollywood bhoot than Hollywood spook, even though it inspires plenty of horror. It, too, calls from the past in the hope of restoring justice. And it breaks down walls between seemingly distinct categories: the Ghost is yet isn't, it is dead yet alive, it is from the past yet it haunts the present. In short, *Hamlet's* Ghost exemplifies a masala multiplicity that abides, in a riff on the play's most famous line, by the logic of 'to be AND not to be'. That is one of the reasons why Shakespeare's tragedy can seem uncannily Bollywood. And, conversely, why Bollywood bhoot movies can seem uncannily reminiscent of *Hamlet*. But does the condition of 'to be AND not to be' exemplify a cheerful masala inclusiveness? Or does it represent an impossibility, akin to the terrifying impossibility of matter and antimatter occupying the same space?

Many bhoot movies seem to embrace wall-breaking inclusiveness. Four years after seeing *Bhoot*, I saw *Om Shanti Om*, the masala Shah Rukh Khan movie that launched the career of Deepika Padukone. The film pays homage to the Hindi bhoot movie tradition. It is also a masala rerun of *Hamlet*. The main character, haunted by a ghost from the past who calls for justice, avenges the death of someone he loves. And he re-enacts this loved one's shocking murder in a play-within-a-play. Admittedly, the film's plot is *Hamlet* with a happy ending: the murderer is killed, the grateful ghost bids the hero a tearful farewell, and the film ends with the likelihood of a future romance between Shah Rukh and Deepika. As the film itself says, in a cheeky reflection on the masala formula, 'hamaari filmon ki tarah, hamaari zindagi mein bhi end tak sab kuchh theek hi ho jaata hai (in our films too, like in our life, everything is fine in the end)'. But the most masala aspect of *Om Shanti Om* isn't its happy ending. Rather, it is its sense of exuberant multiplicity. Shah Rukh Khan plays two roles (the two Oms of the title); Deepika Padukone, too, plays two roles; and in the film's titular item number, a never-ending procession of dancing Bollywood stars impossibly crowd into one sequence. Even Salman Khan and Shah Rukh Khan join together briefly in a naach-gaana frame.

But not all masala films celebrate the condition of 'to be AND not to be' as *Om Shanti Om* does. Some view it as a pretext for tragedy rather than festivity.

In 2012, while visiting New Zealand, I saw Karan Malhotra's *Agneepath* (2012). There had been a lot of chatter about the film before its release. I was wondering if it might mark a return to an older, masala Bollywood style: *Agneepath* is, after all, a remake of Mukul Anand's 1990 film of the same name, a highly stylized masala melodrama in which the hero suffers terribly, schemes patiently, and ultimately succeeds both in avenging the righteous and killing the bad guy. There may not have been an actual bhoot in this earlier film. But the words of the hero's dead father reverberate throughout the original *Agneepath* with the force of a bhoot's call to justice. And its hero, played by Amitabh Bachchan, is certainly haunted by that call.

The 2012 version of *Agneepath* is likewise a story of a loyal son seeking to honour the ghost of his dead father—not just in the film's onscreen narrative (starring Hrithik Roshan as Vijay), but also in its production history. Its producer, Karan Johar, revealed that he had long wished to do a remake of the original *Agneepath*, which had been produced by his late father Yash Johar. Though now regarded as a cult classic, the original had bombed on its initial release in 1990. Karan Johar described its failure as a major trauma that devastated his father both emotionally and financially. In commissioning Karan Malhotra to script and direct the remake, Johar sought to pay tribute to and do right by his late father. This is made clear by the homage in the opening credits, a caption saying 'we miss you' accompanying a ghostly photo of Yash Johar. Which is to say: Karan Johar has produced a film whose story of a son trying to salvage his dead father's lost honour mirrors the conditions of its production. The new *Agneepath*, then, is haunted by more than one daddy-bhoot.

Yet this conceals one important detail about *Agneepath*'s ghost-father/ son relations, in the remake as much as in the original. Although the hero Vijay claims to avenge his father, his seeming act of filial memory is really an act of forgetting. In both the 1990 and the 2012 versions, Vijay's father Deenanath is a Gandhian pacificist; after Deenanath has been falsely framed by the evil Kancha Cheena, and has been violently assaulted and hanged from a tree in the village of Mandwa, Vijay smoulders with a decades-long desire for righteous vengeance. But that desire means that, even as he insists on remembering his father, he forgets Deenanath's path of ahimsa and takes the opposite course—a course of violence learned in the Mumbai underworld.

A similar forgetting in the name of remembering afflicts the parallel story of the 2012 film's production. Even as Karan Johar paid tribute to the late Yash Johar with *Agneepath*, he produced a movie that differs greatly from his father's. The basic foundations of the story are the same. But the remake literally loses the plot once Vijay leaves Mandwa for Mumbai. In the original, Amitabh Bachchan's Vijay works for a quartet of crime bosses whom he knocks off, one by one; his sidekick is a Tamil nariyal paani-wallah and his love interest is a Christian nurse. All are missing from the new version, in which Hrithik Roshan's Vijay serves his underworld apprenticeship with an evil Muslim ganglord, Rauf Lala (Rishi Kapoor), and has a new love interest, Kaali Gawde (Priyanka Chopra). Whereas Amitabh's crusade for justice involved a masala coalition of North Indian and Tamil, Hindu and Christian, Hrithik's has become a battle between a Hindu hero and a Muslim villain. It also involves an altogether different scale of violence. The original Kancha Cheena was played by Danny Denzongpa as a somewhat effete, pipe-smoking villain; this time round, I was astonished to find that Sanjay Dutt's Kancha had morphed into an oversized ghoul—looking remarkably like *The Lord of the Rings'* Gollum if he'd spent two decades beefing up on a wrestler's diet and doing daily workouts at a gym next to a tattoo parlour. Because the new Vijay has to overcome a limb-tearing adversary who would give even the Incredible Hulk pause, the result is an exceedingly violent movie that dismembers as much as it remembers the original. If this is a masala film, it is a masala that is fighting violently against itself.

The effect of both Vijay's and Karan Johar's forgetting in the name of remembering is, uncannily, yet another Bollywood counterpart to *Hamlet*. Shakespeare's titular character also seeks to honour a beloved dead father and avenge him; but even as the father's ghost exhorts his son to remember his call, Hamlet keeps forgetting what he is meant to do. That is why he famously spends five acts dithering rather than avenging his father as the Ghost asks him to. (Kill Claudius? Sure! But first, let me torment my mother. And direct a play. And pretend to be mad. And say nasty things to Ophelia. And get exiled to England. And have my best friends killed. And hang out in a graveyard. And duel with Laertes. And... oh, what was it I was meant to do again?)

The original *Agneepath* parallels in another way this remembering that is also a forgetting of the father. Amitabh Bachchan's own father, Harivansh Rai Bachchan, wrote the poem that gave *Agneepath* its title. In the film, the poem is attributed to the father of Amitabh's character; Vijay dutifully memorizes it and recites it—'tu na mudega kabhi (you will never turn back)'—as he embarks on his path of vengeance. But he does so without ever fully comprehending what it means. The poem is an ode to virtuous perseverance, not to murderous violence. Vijay's forgetting of the poem in the name of remembering it is even more glaringly evident in the remake thanks to Hrithik Roshan's robotically brutal performance. His Vijay keeps reciting the words of the poem, but 'tu na mudega kabhi' means for him only that he will never turn his back on the task of inflicting maximum, bloody damage on his various enemies. At the film's end, after Roshan's Vijay has ruthlessly killed Lala, returned to Mandwa, executed Kancha Cheena following a particularly gruesome fight, and is dying in the arms of his estranged mother, he asks her: 'maine theek kiya (did I do the right thing)?' Rather than answer in the affirmative, she says simply that she hopes he will be reborn as her son in their next lives. Her non-committal response underlines the long distance Vijay has travelled from his father's non-violent path.

And so the 2012 *Agneepath* is, far more than its predecessor, a drama of mixture, even as its politics are less obviously masala. Vijay forgets his father's pacifist credo as he supposedly enacts it; Karan Johar forgets his father's film as he supposedly pays homage to it. We might glimpse here the younger Johar's personal psychodrama of needing both to honour his father and establish his independence from him. But the chord the new *Agneepath* struck with its audiences suggests that it had also tapped into a larger, national psychodrama of forgetting as remembering. Even as India's leaders continue to remember Gandhi as the 'rashtra pita' or father of the nation, they have moved away from his legacy under the pressures of globalization, urbanization, communalization, and a widening gap between rich and poor. In the process, just as Vijay violently deviates from the model of the Gandhian father he idolizes, so has India in the age of liberalization become increasingly estranged from the ideals of non-violence, secularism, and equal opportunity espoused by the man it continues to honour on its rupee notes and, more recently, as the mascot for the 'Swachh Bharat' campaign.

There may be no explicit bhoot in the 2012 *Agneepath*. But everywhere there are paternal ghosts. The voice of Vijay's father

Deenanath; the words of Harivansh Rai Bachchan; the ideal of Gandhi; the image of Yash Johar. All these ghosts haunt the film as spectral presences that are, like the Ghost of Hamlet's father in *Hamlet*, both revered and repudiated. This Bollywood counterpart to *Hamlet* could be described as a hot mess of warring desires: the desire to be the dutiful son is haunted by the desire not to be him. To be AND not to be. *Om Shanti Om* also gives us a fantasy of 'to be AND not to be': like the Ghost in *Hamlet* its ghost is and isn't, is dead and alive, is past and present. But whereas *Om Shanti Om* cheerfully celebrates this multiplicity, *Agneepath*'s version of 'to be AND not to be' is instead the foundation of an almost unbearable tragedy.

To be AND not to be: that is the question. This subtle yet significant deviation from Hamlet's famous question is something that was always already implicit in Shakespeare's play. In *Hamlet*, as we shall see, the multiplicity 'to be AND not to be' eclipses the singularity of 'to be OR not to be'. The masala bhoot movie has helped me recognize this dimension of Shakespeare's play. But does *Hamlet* embrace the celebratory AND of *Om Shanti Om* or is it racked by the agonizing AND of *Agneepath*? More specifically: what if this question is not an either/or choice, for the simple reason that *Hamlet* might both celebrate AND abhor the possibility of 'to be AND not to be'?

If ghosts are more-than-one, a masala sensibility might do more than just see *Hamlet*'s Ghost as plural. It might also conjure a plurality of ghosts: ghosts that we can celebrate, but also ghosts that can leave us despairing. And more ghosts besides. Perhaps, then, we should read *Hamlet* too as a masala study of many ghosts. But can we hear their diverse calls? Tujhko pukaare mera pyaar. Let us try to listen, then.

ACT FOUR SCENE SIX

Masala Ghosts (*Hamlet*)

A spectre is haunting the idea of India: Hamlet.

The broody prince's unanswered question, 'to be or not to be', has become a catchphrase in Indian politics. A study of the Tamil Tiger leader V. Prabhakaran complains that 'to be or not to be—Hamlet's confusion in decision making seems to be India's'. A book on the history of India's security policies slams the state for its vacillating 'to be or not to be attitude' in relation to theatres of conflict in Asia. A report that condemns the Indian state as terminally incapacitated by its economic inefficiency is titled 'State—To Be or Not to Be.' And as if to provide a corrective, or at least an indication of what good state leadership might entail, Nayantara Sahgal remarks in her biography of her uncle Jawarharlal Nehru that 'Nehru was no Hamlet and there was no 'to be or not to be' on the principle that Goa was Indian territory and belonged in the Union.'

To be or not to be may be the question. But to decide, one way or the other, must be the answer. Nehru decided 'to be' with respect to Goa's future in India. By contrast, Subhuti Anand Waight decided 'not to be' in his invitingly titled *When Shakespeare Lost the Plot: The Bard Stands on His Head, Hamlet Flies to India and Western Philosophy is Destroyed* (2014). Subhuti, a British-born disciple of Osho, writes not of Goa but of the advaitya philosophical tradition, which stresses that all being is an illusion; hence his Hamlet eventually chooses to embrace the 'Indian' conviction of the no-thing-ness of existence. Subhuti and Nehru may be poles apart, but they both see Hamlet's question as an invitation that demands a single decision, one in which an idea of India is at stake.

You might counter: why decide between seeming opposites, yaar? A masala sensibility would embrace instead the mixed possibility of 'to be and not to be'. And that possibility is embraced all over the subcontinent. Several years ago, I was looking for a turn-off from Delhi's Outer Ring Road. Not finding it, I stopped and asked a roadside policeman where it was. He pointed behind me, saying I had overshot the turn-off by five hundred metres, and told me to drive the wrong way down the road to take it. I looked at him nervously and stammered, but isn't that illegal? 'Thoda sa galat hai,' he replied. Only a little wrong. It is and isn't illegal.

'To be and not to be' is no doubt a practical necessity in an overcrowded nation with scant resources. It is the basis of jugaad, the patch-up job that both is and isn't a solution to an immediate problem. But in political discourse, the masala proposition of 'to be and not to be' sits uneasily with the idea of India. An area either is or isn't part of India: that's why Nehru didn't have, in Nayantara Sehgal's words, a 'to be or not to be' mindset in relation to Goa—or to Kashmir, his family's ancestral home. He regarded both as integral parts of the nation. Yet in very different ways, Goans and Kashmiris might feel that they are and are not Indian. Goa has accepted largely without protest its annexation by India in 1961, but many Goans retain a cheerful sense of their distinctiveness because of Goa's 400-year Portuguese colonial history independent of British India. In Kashmir, by contrast, 'to be and not to be' captures many of the painful dilemmas faced by the inhabitants of the Valley, who still await a plebiscite on their future amidst militant unrest and the imposition of the Armed Forces (Special Powers) Act (AFSPA). In Kashmir, 'to be and not to be' feels less like an inclusive answer and more like a painful question accompanying the interminable wait for self-determination.

Against the specifically Indian-and-not-Indian contexts of Goa and Kashmir, it is interesting to think about how *Hamlet* itself adjudicates the conundrum of 'to be and not to be'. As we will see, the play keeps returning to the problem of the ghost, the spectral apparition who is and isn't. But how are we to respond to the ghost's contradictory status, and what does this have to do with politics and the nation state? Does the 'to be and not to be' of the ghost invite, as it has done in Goa, a celebration of plural identities? Does it lead instead, as it has done in Kashmir, to a dardnak kahaani? Does it do both? Neither? Questions, and more questions. Masala questions. Questions of masala. Questions, too, of India.

◆

Few people would think of *Hamlet* as a masala play. Masala is mixture, seeking to blend incommensurable stylistic elements rather than conform to a single 'pure' genre such as tragedy, of which *Hamlet* is often considered exemplary. Masala is melodrama, requiring over-the-top displays of theatrical emotion rather than the deep psychological interiority we have come to associate with Shakespeare's play. Masala is about and for the masses, presuming a collectivity that binds people across social differences rather than focusing on the struggles of the privileged individual alone as *Hamlet* supposedly does. In modern film terms, *Hamlet*—and Hamlet—is surely more arthouse than masala. It is a deep psychological drama about a lone tragic hero, tackling issues that speak to a refined audience.

Yet on closer inspection, *Hamlet* is also the pinnacle of masala entertainment. And that is largely because of the ghostly 'to be and not to be' flavour of the play. It repeatedly mixes genres we think of as opposed. Scenes of philosophical weight are interrupted by the gaana (if not naach) of mad Ophelia and the irreverent gravediggers. The play's nest of poetry-spouting royals is mocked by the brash prose dialogue-baazi of lower-class characters. Hamlet may be the prince of broody procrastinators who delays his vengeance interminably; but one scene repackages him, in a possible memory of Shakespeare's revenge-play source, as an action hero who defeats a galleon of pirates and coolly transforms the device meant to kill him into a death sentence for his executioners. And this supposed tragedy features two explicit Clowns as well as other characters who channel the spirit of screwball comedy. Polonius may describe what sounds like a generic impossibility when he refers to the Players who visit Elsinore Castle as the best for 'tragical-comical-historical-pastoral' (2.2.381). But that generic more-than-oneness perfectly describes *Hamlet* too, a masala tragedy-that-is-and-isn't-tragic.

Why, then, do we think of *Hamlet* as a play that rises above masala? In no small part because its titular character dreams of purity—and many of us share that dream, especially now at this moment in India. Yet Hamlet's dream keeps shading into a nightmare of adulteration. He laments how those who are 'as pure as grace' are afflicted by a 'vicious mole' or the 'stamp of one defect', and 'take corruption/ From that particular fault' (1.4.18.17, 8, 15, 19–20). Later, he tells Ophelia, 'be thou as chaste as ice, as pure as snow, thou shalt not escape calumny' (3.1.136–7). By Hamlet's own admission, the purity he values cannot exist as it always already bears the trace of a corrupt more-than-oneness. And this corruption extends not just to purity in the abstract. It also includes the purity of the nation state. 'Something is rotten in the state of Denmark,' Marcellus says (1.4.67). Denmark is here both a political and an individual entity: the Ghost resembles 'the majesty of buried Denmark' (1.1.46), meaning Hamlet's father. We can see, then, how *Hamlet* is a play not just about an individual but also about a nation and its im/purity. Swachh Denmark? That is the question.

In Hamlet's view, the chief corrupting factor of individual and nation alike is 'matter'. The word 'matter' appears more often in *Hamlet*—twenty-five times—than in any other of Shakespeare's plays. It frequently features in the simple question: 'what's the matter?' Like 'to be or not to be', this question doesn't have one correct answer. What's 'matter' keeps shifting: it can be flesh, corruption, a pun on the Latin 'mater' or mother, human remains, dust. But broadly, matter is for Hamlet a force of adulteration. He tells the Ghost that he will commit the latter's plea for vengeance to his memory, 'unmixed with baser matter' (1.5.104). Yet his inability to execute the Ghost's command shows how the mixture he fears is unavoidable. We could say *Hamlet* is a play about purity brimming with impure matter. Anything that might allow us to claim what the play 'is'—individual saga, tragedy, defence of purity—gets ghosted by something else, some other matter that is and isn't quite there.

Revealingly, *Hamlet* starts with the question: 'Who's there?' (1.1.1). These two and a half words resonate through the play, never quite finding an answer because 'who's there' never fully *is* there. Or rather, 'who's there' is haunted by ghosts who aren't fully there. Though the question is asked of characters patrolling the battlements of Elsinore Castle, it is occasioned by the apparition of the Ghost. We don't quite know who or what the Ghost is. Hamlet cannot determine whether he is talking to 'a spirit of health or a goblin damned' (1.4.21). Although the apparition resembles his recently deceased father, the characters swing between using impersonal and personal pronouns 'Speak to it, Horatio.'/ 'Looks he not like the King?' (1.1.40–1). The Ghost is dead yet alive, is past yet present, is spirit yet wears the 'baser matter' of the dead King's armour and visor. (We think of ghosts as spirits, but so often it's their matter that haunts us.) The question of 'who's there' with respect to the Ghost, then, is impossible to answer. Because it/he is and isn't. It/ he is irreducibly impure.

Yet in the impure Ghost, Hamlet longs to find a past purity—his beloved father, an ideal of the nation. The absence of purity in Denmark initially drives him to righteous rage. His mother Gertrude, who has hastily married his Uncle Claudius after his father's death, tells him not to grieve excessively—'all that lives must die' (1.2.72)—and she asks him 'why it seems so particular with thee?' (1.2.75). He responds angrily to her question with yet another question:

> Seems, madam? Nay, it *is*. I know not 'seems'.
> 'Tis not alone my inky cloak, good-mother,
> Nor customary suits of solemn black,
> Nor windy suspiration of forced breath,
> No, nor the fruitful river in the eye,
> Nor the dejected haviour of the visage,
> Together with all forms, moods, shows of grief
> That can denote me truly. These indeed 'seem',
> For they are actions that a man might play;
> But I have that within which passeth show (1.2.76–85)

Hamlet tries to draw a sharp distinction between being and not being authentic. He insists his grief is real: it is not acted, unlike (or so he alleges) Gertrude's. Yet this either/or distinction becomes immediately problematic. Hamlet is a character in a play who hates the fact that he is in a play, 'Denmark the Fake', adulterated by the 'baser matter' of costumes ('inky cloaks' and 'customary suits'). Even as he aspires to three-dimensional psychological depth, his claim to pure interiority runs the risk of seeming like just another theatrical act, an act that tries to pass off the illusion that it is not an illusion. That risk is most fully realized when he commandeers a troupe of itinerant actors to 'catch the conscience of the King' (2.2.582) by staging a play within a play—the play of Gonzago, also known as the Mousetrap—that presents to Claudius and Gertrude the supposed truth of Hamlet's father's murder. 'Seems' has become here the inescapable medium of 'is'. Hamlet's either/ or distinction between the two, therefore, cannot help but dissolve into the impure masala reality of 'to be and not to be'. This shows how much the spirit (and matter) of the Ghost who is (and isn't) infects *Hamlet* (and Hamlet).

Ghosts proliferate in this masala entertainment whose lead character dreams of acting in an arthouse film called 'Being Purely Human'. (And no, this film doesn't star Salman Khan. At least not yet.) Three masala spectres haunt Hamlet after the early apparition of the Ghost. Each, like the Ghost, adulterates the Prince's dream of individual and national purity by mixing it with 'baser matter'. The first is the spectre of the sexually active mother whose flesh is and isn't her child's. The second is the spectre of the mind that has lost its mind and become mixed with the matter of madness. And the third is the spectre of human remains, commented on by lower-class clowns who laughingly recognize that all life, no matter how high and mighty, is mixed with the matter of death. All three spectres contribute to the perception that Hamlet inhabits a masala Denmark in which 'to be' is irreducibly mixed with 'not to be'.

These three masala spectres, like the bhoots of Hindi films, call for justice. But we tend to ignore their calls because they do not explicitly command Hamlet to seek justice in the way his father's Ghost does. Indeed, we measure Hamlet's tragedy in part by how far he strays from the directive to avenge his father's murder and thereby 'set right' the 'time that is out of joint' (1.5.190, 189). The Ghost has told Hamlet, speaking of Gertrude, 'leave her to Heaven' (1.5.86); but Hamlet's immediate response to the Ghost's command is 'O most pernicious woman!' (1.5.105) and he spends much of the play railing at her. It is, as if, by making himself the vessel for the command of the father-Ghost, Hamlet finds himself haunted also by the impure mother-spectre. When he promises the Ghost, 'thy commandment all alone shall live/ Within the book and volume of my brain,/ Unmixed with baser matter' (1.5.103–4), we can hear in this 'matter' an echo of the 'mater' or mother whose flesh is mixed with his. This spectral matter/mater is precisely what Hamlet's fantasy of unswerving allegiance to the father cannot shake off.

Hamlet's rage at his mother may seem excessive. But it is fully grounded in his rage at the fleshy matter she embodies and that he shares with her. When early on he wishes that his 'too, too sullied flesh would melt' (1.2.129), we hear the deep disgust he feels about his own 'baser matter'. He dreams of a retreat from matter—the matter of impurity, the matter of the flesh, the matter of the mother. But it's an impossible dream. Hamlet may insist on the purity of his namesake father, the 'sun' to whom he is son: he compares him to 'Hyperion' (1.2.140), a disembodied sun-god remote from the profane world of matter. But the comparison fails. The Ghost describes his earthly demise in terms that evoke the 'baser matter' of his flesh: the poison that the adulterous Claudius administered to him left his 'smooth body' coated in a 'tetter'—one of the symptoms of syphilis (1.5.73, 71). Soon after, Hamlet is imagining the 'sun breed[ing] maggots in a dead dog' (2.2.182), as if he now sees his father as irrevocably tainted by having been a sexual party to Hamlet's own maggot-like conception in Gertrude. Resorting to crass prose that taps the same vein of misogyny, he asks Ophelia—once idealized in his love poetry—'why would'st thou be a breeder of sinners?' (3.1.122–3). Hamlet's question emerges from his disgusted conviction that all sons (and suns) originate in women who contaminate the men they breed with, and then bequeath their sinful flesh to their offspring.

But if one strips away these layers of misogynist disgust, then the maternal haunting of male identity begins to acquire a masala dimension. Think of Amitabh Bachchan's and Shashi Kapoor's famous dialogue in *Deewaar* (1975). Bachchan's criminal character asks his righteous brother, played by Kapoor: 'aaj mere paas building hai, property hai, bank balance hai, bangla hai, gaadi hai, kya hai tumhaare paas (today I have buildings, property, bank balance, a bungalow, a car, what do you have)?' And Kapoor replies: 'mere paas maa hai (I have Ma).' This might seem to be an expression of filial devotion-cum-ownership. But the Hindi 'mere paas' is not quite the same as the English 'I have': it signifies intimate proximity rather than possession. 'Paas'—near—is the masala post-position par excellence, suggesting the closeness of different elements within the overcrowded plurality of India. The phrase 'mere paas maa hai' thus cuts two ways—it suggests an ethics of love grounded in deep closeness to another who is and isn't me, yet makes me. That is the ethics of masala, and the injunction of the maternal spectre.

But it also hints at a danger that comes from being *too* 'paas'. For Hamlet, the spectre of the breeding mother is too close for comfort. So when both the autonomous interiority of the son and the spirit of the sun-father become impossible to extricate from the 'baser matter' of the maternal flesh, another ghost begins to haunt him. Enter the spectre of the mad mind that has lost its mind. In Hamlet's madness, which is and is not an act, we again see the 'baser matter' of the body lurking. His language returns obsessively to thoughts of sex and sexual parts, as his graceless double entendres to Ophelia about 'lying in her lap' and speaking of 'country matters' (3.2.101, 105) make clear. Under the influence of this body-obsessed madness, Hamlet's conception of the human shifts from a pure, disembodied interiority to an impure masala mixture. 'What a piece of work is a man,' he ruminates; 'in apprehension how like a god—the beauty of the world, the paragon of animals! And yet to me what is this quintessence of dust?' (2.2.293–4, 296–8). 'Man' may be a singular 'piece of work'. But this work, Hamlet disgustedly recognizes, already entails a mixture of spirit and matter. The human is and is not god, is and is not dust.

Hamlet's madness leaves him flinching at the thought of mixture. By contrast, Ophelia's madness models another attitude. Her mad language, like Hamlet's, is highly sexual. But rather than expressing disgust at flesh, she sings about the hypocrisy of men who claim to have pure intentions:

> Young men will do't if they come to't.
> By Cock, they are to blame.
> Quoth she 'Before you tumbled me,
> You promised me to wed.'
> So would I 'a done, by yonder sun,
> An thou hadst not come to my bed. (4.5.59–64)

Ophelia, like mad Hamlet, may be mindlessly speaking her mind. But in that mindlessness, we can hear the truth of a past injustice. The injustice isn't that the song's 'she' has lost her chastity. The injustice is that the song's 'he'—who swears by the 'sun' to prove his investment in an ideal of high purity—rejects her after having sex with her. Ophelia's madness does not revile the 'baser matter' of the woman's body. In fact her song doesn't regard matter as base. What is base, or debasing, is the cavalier behaviour of the male who swears by the lofty singularity of the 'sun'. Purity, not impurity, is the issue here.

In the final act, the play's leading sun-bhakt encounters a third spectre of 'baser matter'. But this spectre now takes a radically different form. It comes in the shape of bones unearthed by two Clowns, gravediggers who mock the vain pretensions of humans. Yet in their mocking, they utter afresh the other spectres' calls not to spurn matter. The gravediggers remind Hamlet of the levelling effect of death on every human being. They know, too, that death is not the opposite of being but, rather, always intrinsic to it. After all, they have been digging graves since the moment Hamlet was born. Their understanding that death is less the end of life than a vital part of it also has a political dimension. It is the gravediggers who help Hamlet 'trace the noble dust of Alexander till he find it stopping a bunghole' (5.1.188-9): even the mightiest ruler cannot help but become, in death, 'baser matter' absorbed into a lively masala world composed of elements that were once part of living individuals.

This perception has been brewing in Hamlet for a while. After accidentally killing Polonius, he reflects on how we are all part of a larger ecology of feasting: worms devour dead humans, fish feed on worms, and beggars eat fish, which shows how a King can 'progress through the guts of a beggar' (4.3.30–1). This vision may recall the 'circle of life' from The Lion King (itself loosely based on Hamlet), but it adds to it an element of dark laughter. The view that we are interconnected biomass within a larger masala ecology of life-and-death haunts the rest of the play. From this point on there is no more talk from Hamlet of sun-kings and female breeders of sinners. He moves from idealization of his father and disgust at maternal entanglement to a seemingly Zen acceptance of the world's mixed matter.

'The readiness is all,' says the new Hamlet (5.2.160). But what this statement means is cryptic, and can be interpreted in two ways. First, Hamlet has finally asserted himself heroically as an 'I' who matters to the nation—'This is I, Hamlet the Dane,' he has just declared (5.1.241–2). So he now faces the inescapably mixed world, and his Ghost-given mission in it, with laudable equanimity. Or he has recognized that he is part of something bigger than him, and his 'I' doesn't matter. But once again, this is a false either/or choice. Because both paths engender a proliferation of ghostly contradictions. On the one hand, the Hamlet who asserts his 'I' will, minutes later, displace it in his memorably impossible utterance, 'I am dead, Horatio' (5.2.275). He is and isn't, and this spectral existence will continue in the posthumous stories about himself he asks Horatio to tell. Similarly, the resigned Hamlet who embraces the 'special providence in the fall of a sparrow' (5.2.157–8) morphs into his violent alter egomaniac Hamlet the avenger, who kills Claudius with glee at the play's end. Either way, the reading we may want of Hamlet—as a heroic nationalist individual, as anti-hierarchical self-denying sanyasi—is haunted by the spectre of something more. Who's there? Masala returns here not as a style of entertainment or a politics or a philosophy so much as an inescapable spectral reality, in which mixture can never be distilled conclusively into something singular.

This is not a masala of anything goes. It is rather a masala ghost justice: a justice of other possibilities—of the very possibility of otherness—at any moment of seeming finality. *Hamlet* models this justice most in its refusal to end. 'The rest is silence,' says Hamlet (5.2.300). But the rest is and isn't silent, thanks to Horatio and Fortinbras, who continue to speak. Other futures—individual and national—assert themselves. If the time is 'out of joint' or unhinged, this open-ended justice provides new hinges for new doors, through which new possibilities yet undreamed of may lie. The justice that masala promises doesn't lie in a predetermined programme. That would be to suggest that justice could be reduced to a singular outcome we can know in advance. Instead, masala justice consists in its ellipses, its inconclusive 'ands', its refusal of either/or. For in this time out of joint, 'who's there' is always ghosted by the matter of something more.

To be and not to be. That impure masala ghost is our fear. And our hope.

◆

Let's return to the Indian-and-not-Indian context with which we started. As we've seen, *Hamlet*'s 'to be and not to be' is a ghostly condition that models both a scary impurity and the promise of justice, the promise of impurity *as* justice. But how is it understood by those who see themselves as being and not being Indian? Do they experience this condition in fear or in hope? As dardnak kahaani or azaadi? As both? As neither? These are questions that bear on the very nature of masala. I suspect it is no accident that the masala movie's genealogy can in part be traced back to the theatrical practices of a marginal Indian-and-not-Indian community.

Like most Indians, Parsis are and aren't purely Indian. And in the nineteenth century, Parsi actors, writers and investors created a tradition of entertainment that exemplified their 'to be and not to be' position at the crossroads between India and Iran, Bombay and the British Raj, Gujarati and Marathi, Hindi and Urdu, Sanskrit and English. A hugely successful adaptation of *Hamlet* in the 1920s gives some indication of this cultural in-between-ness. A Parsi company with a Sanskrit name, Arya Sobdoh Natya, mounted an Urdu version of this English play about a Danish prince. And they made all its characters Muslim. *Khoon ka Khoon* (Blood for Blood) featured its director-creator, Sohrab Modi, in the Hamlet role, now renamed Jehangir—a Parsi as well as a Muslim name. The production's cultural mix was matched by its generic mix. Like most Parsi theatre adaptations of *Hamlet*, this version was not 'straight'. It embellished the play in ways designed to appeal to Bombay's multilingual, multicultural, multiclass audiences who wanted masala from their entertainment: song and dance, poetry and melodrama. And screwball comedy. In 2016, the elderly Parsi theatre veteran Sam Kerawala recalled a production from his childhood, *Hamlet No Omelette*, which had turned the play into a full-blown farce. Little wonder that Rajat Kapoor's farcical deconstruction of the play, *Hamlet the Clown Prince*, should find a ready audience in Bombay many decades later.

A measure of the popularity of these early masala entertainments is that some of the earliest Indian movies are filmed versions of Parsi theatre *Hamlets*. Mehdi Hasan Ahsan's storming melodramatic play, *Khoone-e-Nahak* (The Unjust Assassination), an Urdu sangeet natak adaptation of *Hamlet* first staged in 1889, was filmed and screened as a silent movie in 1928. And the filmed version of Sohrab Modi's *Khoon ka Khoon*, retitled *Hamlet-Khoon Ka Khoon* (1935), has the distinction of being the first 'talkie' Indian adaptation of Shakespeare. (The second was Modi's adaptation of *King John* in 1936.) *Hamlet-Khoon Ka Khoon* has not survived, but archival photographs and publicity indicate that the performance was highly Anglicized. A still shows the actors performing in Elizabethan costume under a proscenium arch with an image of Shakespeare at its apex; and the cast list indicates that the original names of Shakespeare's characters were retained. But the film also featured no fewer than seventeen songs in Urdu. This suggests again how *Hamlet-Khoon Ka Khoon*—as only suits its mixed title—was unapologetically foreign and Indian. Like its Parsi producers.

Another hybrid film adaptation indebted to the Parsi theatre appeared in 1954. Kishore Sahu's *Hamlet* (1954) was, like *Hamlet-Khoon Ka Khoon*, a filmed version of a stage production. This production aspired to even more Shakespearean authenticity than its predecessor: much of Sahu's performance in the title role seems to have been inspired by Sir Laurence Olivier's then-recent 1948 film of *Hamlet*. Yet Sahu's film also borrowed capaciously from the Parsi theatre, including (again) songs and poetic Urdu dialogues. Its final lines were a well-known couplet by the poet Zauq: 'Laayi hayat aaye, qaza le chali chale/ Apni khushi na aaye na apni khushi chale (Flung into life, by death sent away/ Unwillingly we come, and unwillingly we leave).' Though some have seen this couplet as an inspired substitute for Hamlet's 'readiness is all', it more accurately sums up the 'to be and not to be' mindset of the play and the Parsi theatre. Hamlet, stranded between life and death, is both coming and going. Or rather, is neither. And this in-between-ness describes the film too. Like its Parsi theatrical forebears, it is Indian and it is not. Yet the mood here isn't the celebratory 'to be and not to be' of Parsi theatre. It smacks, rather, of a disquieting neither-nor-ness.

Other conversations with *Hamlet* on the margins of India come closer to the neither-nor-ness of Zauq's couplet. Anjum Hasan conjures *Hamlet* in her haunting novel *Neti, Neti* (2009). Its main character, Sophie, keeps moving between Shillong and Bangalore. The former is her family home; the latter is the city where she has found work and independence. But she feels equally alienated in both Bangalore and her home in Meghalaya, to which her parents are migrants from Bengal and Bihar. Her scholarly father, Mr Das, dreams of translating *Hamlet* into Bengali and is perennially quoting from it. Sophie has, as a result, grown up with much of the play committed to memory even though she has never read Shakespeare. Her father's hope is that he will leverage his translation, once completed, into a professorship at a Bengali university. But he is mired in indecision, unable to finish the translation, leave his wife, or move forward. His condition mirrors his daughter's: Sophie, too, is stuck between Shillong and Bangalore, incapable of choosing between the two—hence the title *Neti, Neti*, Sanskrit for 'not this, not this' or 'neither this, neither that'. To be or not be northeastern, to be or not be Bengali, to be or not be modern, are decisions that the novel cannot make with finality. And that is why Mr Das's story is an ironic tragedy: he may not successfully translate the play *Hamlet*, but he fully becomes the character Hamlet, stuck between options and thus denying himself the happy ending he had hoped his translation would earn him. Mr Das and his daughter's 'neti neti' condition is a masala of negation, where the logic of either/or is rejected but the capacious possibility of both-and does not satisfy.

It is hard not to compare Hasan's masala of negation to the well-known, fascinating afterlife of *Hamlet* in another marginal region of the northeast: Mizoram. The play has something of a cult status there; although the state has no indigenous theatre tradition, a Mizo translation is performed repeatedly in halls and outdoor settings, its speeches broadcast on public speakers, sound recordings circulated on audio cassettes so that its text can be committed to memory, and catchphrases used in children's games. The adaptation's opening lines say that 'When Hamlet came to Mizoram he became a Mizo'. Yet its Hamlet is and isn't Mizo: he speaks the local language yet he wears western clothes. On the one hand, the Hamlet cult in Mizoram seems to embrace the kind of cultural syncretism we see in the Parsi theatre. But there is something of the logic of 'neti neti' about it too—not surprisingly, perhaps, in a region whose political and cultural identity has been a matter of some complication. Settled by tribal migrants from Burma in the 1500s, the area was annexed in the 1890s by the British, who went about converting the majority of the Mizo hill-dwellers to Christianity. They assigned part of its territory to Assam and part to Bengal; after Independence, Mizoram was given semi-autonomous status within Assam, experienced several decades of armed insurgency, and was then granted full statehood only in 1987.

The 'neti neti' ghosts of *Hamlet* seem to connect with Mizo audiences who feel themselves to be neither fully Indian nor fully foreign.

Hamlet has also been adapted in Goa both before and after its annexation by India. The tiatr form emerged in late nineteenth-century Goa as a Christian Konkani form of entertainment ('tiatr' is a corruption of the Portuguese 'teatro', or theatre); hybrid to the core, it combined English and Indian stories with music played on Portuguese instruments such as guitar and trumpet. One of the great tiatr exponents, Sebastiao Gabriel D'Souza (also known as Karachiwala), adapted *Hamlet* in the 1920s. Sadly, D'Souza's script hasn't survived. Given that tiatr entertainments customarily comment with satirical savagery on current events, the play almost certainly had a political dimension. But the politics of 'to be and not to be' are fully legible in a later Goan adaptation of *Hamlet*. The Konkani-language adaptation, *Soodh Zagor* (2015) by Shridhar Kamat Bambolkar, performs the Mousetrap—the play-within-a-play staged by Hamlet—in indigenous zagor style, at odds with the more realist flavour of the rest of the production. Zagor is a folk form associated with the Gawda tribal people of Goa, predating the Portuguese; its apparition in Bambolkar's play has a ghost-like power, returning from the past to help the Hamlet character resist his uncle—and an audience resist standard narratives of modern Goa and India. As a result the play is and isn't zagor; it is and isn't Goan; it is and isn't Indian. This is not quite the affirmative masala of the Parsi theatre, nor the 'neti neti' masala of Anjum Hasan. It is something different—something spectral.

In all these versions of *Hamlet*, 'to be and not to be' captures the liminality of peoples at diverse margins of India—Parsis, Assamese, Mizos, Goans. But what does the Indian state say back to them? Nehru, as we have seen, believed Goa 'to be' an intrinsic part of India. And he believed the same of Kashmir. How has this imperative 'to be' Indian shaped but also clashed with the spectral reality of those on the margins of India? Enter Vishal Bhardwaj and his film *Haider* (2014), the last instalment of his acclaimed Shakespeare trilogy. *Haider* is a meditation on the lived reality of 'to be and not to be' in Kashmir and, above all, the effects of the Indian army presence. In the process, it reflects profoundly on masala, both as a tool of Indian state power and as a Kashmiri political conundrum. And it unleashes a procession of masala ghosts.

◆

A spectre is haunting *Haider*: Salman Khan.

His ghost is unmistakable. The moves. The clothes. The mullet hairstyle. Salman Khan makes his first appearance in *Haider* in the shape of two video-shop clerks from Srinagar (Sumit Kaul and Rajat Bhagat) who are diehard Bhaijaan wannabes. The pair, who go by the names Salman and Salman, are *Haider*'s Rosencrantz and Guildenstern. But they are also more than that. At first they seem like harmless, comic buffoons. But Salman and Salman come to represent something more sinister, and not just because Pervez Lone (Lalit Parimoo)—the film's counterpart to Polonius—hires them to spy on and, ultimately, kill Haider. We could say the pair represent the doubleness of Bollywood in the Valley: masala cinema that offers Kashmiris fun entertainment but is also part of the machinery of Indian power.

That power is most apparent in an extraordinary scene. A line-up of detainees parade across the stage of a single-screen cinema that has been appropriated by the Indian army as an interrogation centre. Behind them, on the screen, a naach-gaana sequence from the masala film *Sangdil Sanam* (1994) plays, with Salman Khan mouthing the lyrics of 'One, Two, Three (Give Me a Kiss)' to Manisha Koirala. The scene stages the spectral presence in Kashmir not just of Salman but also of mainland India. This India may seem inclusive and diverse, making a hero of a Muslim. But its masala entertainments literally screen its actions in the Valley. A sangdil sanam (heartless lover) indeed. The heartlessness is underlined when we hear the two Salmans cheerfully belting out a song from Khan's film *Patthar Ke Phool* (1991) as they drive Haider off to be executed. But Salman and India are not the only spectres in these scenes. The detainees in the cinema hall too are ghosts: they have been 'disappeared', and so legally they are neti neti, neither alive nor dead. AFSPA gives the Indian army sweeping powers to detain without trial, Kashmiris suspected of militancy. And so Kashmir is a valley of ghosts on whom flicker the spectral images of Salman Khan as the face of Indian soft power.

This gives some idea of the complexity of *Haider*'s deep scrutiny of masala. It is the condition of an oppressed people; it is a tool of state control. The complexity extends to the film's treatment of *Hamlet*'s Ghost. Bhardwaj and his scriptwriter Basharat Peer have made the Ghost not one but two characters: Haider's father Dr Hilal Meer (Narendra Jha), who has been 'disappeared' for sheltering militants, and Roohdar (Irrfan Khan), his shadowy companion in the detention centre. Between them they mix 'jism aur rooh' (body and soul). Roohdar—literally giver of the soul—is doubly a ghost identity. He survives his extrajudicial killing and comes to deliver Hilal's message for vengeance to Haider (Shahid Kapoor). But Haider's uncle, Khurram (Kay Kay Menon) also claims Roohdar is a Pakistani double agent who has infiltrated Kashmir.

Roohdar's doubleness is symptomatic of the film's ghosts. All these ghosts inhabit the liminal space of 'to be and not to be'. The doctor who is 'zindagi ki taraf (on the side of life)' yet who reeks of 'maut ki boo (the smell of death)'. The dancing boy who jumps out of a truckload of corpses, screaming 'main zinda hoon! main zinda hoon (I am alive! I am alive)!' The gravediggers who dig their own graves. The disappeared men, neither alive nor dead, who leave behind 'aadhi beva (half widows)'. And, more generally, the status of Kashmir. 'To be and not to be' is the condition of a ghost people stranded between life and death, between Pakistan and India, between Islamabad and Islamabad (the other name for Anantnag, Haider's town in Kashmir). As Haider chants, along with family members of other men who have been 'disappeared', 'hum hain ki hum nahin (are we or aren't we)?'

Hamlet's 'to be or not to be' haunts this movie. The two Salmans winkingly refer to it when they debate, in English, about tailing Haider: 'to go or not to go?' they ask. But the film keeps returning to Hamlet's question and twisting it to the point of absurdity, refusing any answer and going beyond the masala affirmation of 'to be and not to be' or the negation of 'neti neti'. After meeting the shady Roohdar and learning from him of his father's death as well as Khurram's alleged role in it, and after Khurram has insisted that it was Roohdar himself who killed Dr Hilal Meer, Haider takes to 'to be or not to be' with a sledgehammer. Talking madly with Arshia, the Ophelia character (Shraddha Kapoor), Haider asks whether his uncle's explanation is a lie, which he follows with a slew of questions: 'Hai...ki hai nahin...? Bas yehi sawaal hai. Aur sawaal ka jawaab bhi sawaal hai (To be...or not to be...? That is the question. The answer to that is also a question)'. Here, the agonizing impossibility of 'to be and not to be' seems confined to Haider's individual situation. He goes on to ask, immediately after this, 'jaan loon ki jaan doon main rahoon...ki main nahin (should I take a life or should I give my life, should I remain... or shouldn't I)?' But these ruminations implicate not just Haider but also the larger polity.

Haider's scene of mad street-theatre at Lal Chowk beautifully illustrates the political implications of 'to be and not to be' within Kashmir. With a shaved head and a noose around his neck, he invokes the UN resolution No. 47 of 1948, the Geneva Convention, and Article 370 of the Indian Constitution, all of which insist on yet qualify independent Kashmir's right to exist. He asks: 'Hum hain ki hum nahin (Are we or aren't we)?'. This reworking of Hamlet's question expresses the agonized doubt not just of an individual but also of a people. As Haider goes on to elaborate, 'Hum hain toh kahaan hain aur nahi hain toh kahaan gaye (If we are, then where are we, and if we are not, then where did we go)'. And his mudslide of questions culminates not in an answer, but in another question, one that summarizes Kashmir's situation: 'Janaab... hum the bhi ki hum the hi nahin (Sir...did we ever exist or not)?'.

Bhardwaj and Peer certainly take the side of Kashmir, and to that extent sympathize with its agonizing limbo of 'to be and not to be'. But they also take the side of the more-than-one: they don't assume Kashmir to be singular. There are many ghosts that haunt the Kashmir of this film. And in these ghosts we can glimpse many Kashmirs. The Pandit exodus of the 1990s is mentioned. But this is no whataboutery designed to make us choose between Hindus and Muslims. *Haider* instead prods us to recognize the Valley's countless violently suppressed stories.

And it does so by converting the spectres of 'baser matter' from *Hamlet* into reminders of 'disappeared' Kashmiri histories. When Arshia goes mad after the death of her father, she sings in Kashmiri—almost the only time we hear the language in the film. The inclusion of Arshia's song doesn't just add local linguistic colour. She sings the words of Habba Khatoon (1554–1609), the semi-mythic figure also known in Kashmir as Zoon and Bulbul-e-Kashmir. A poet and ascetic, Habba Khatoon had been married to the Kashmiri king Yusuf Shah Chak; when Akbar invaded in the 1580s, the story goes, Yusuf was exiled and the couple were separated, prompting Habba Khatoon to write a series of haunting love poems. Her poems have acquired a legendary status in Kashmiri oral tradition, speaking not just to her own but also Kashmir's heartbreak. They make a fitting soundtrack for the heartbroken Arshia. But they also speak to the ongoing traumatic history of Kashmir's people in relation to the state.

Other ghosts of Kashmiri-Indian history haunt the film. In the item number 'Bulbul-e-Bismil'—*Haider*'s ingenious equivalent of the Mousetrap play-within-a-play—Bhardwaj does a version of what *Soodh Zagor*, the Goan *Hamlet*, did. He uses a local theatrical form of Kashmiri performance, with puppets, to protest the Kashmiri agents of India. The lyrics tell of two bulbuls (nightingales) ravaged by a predatory baaz (hawk). This is Haider's story of Khurram interfering in Hilal and Ghazala's relationship. But it is also the story of the unrest in the Valley: the army operation that results in Dr Hilal Meer's capture is called 'Operation Bulbul'—an eerie echo of Habba Khatoon's Urdu name—and it seeks to wipe out militancy. Yet the song is more than just a protest against the state. It again pluralizes Kashmir: Bhardwaj's set is constructed on the ruins of the ancient Hindu Martand Sun Temple, built in the eighth century and destroyed in the fifteenth. Like Arshia's song by the 'Bulbul-e-Kashmir', 'Bulbul-e-Bismil' commemorates the ghosts of suppressed Kashmiri histories.

The spectres of the past keep pluralizing the Kashmir we see in this film. And again the script draws ingeniously on the 'baser matter' of *Hamlet* to produce this effect. As Haider chats with the gravedigger's son, he tells him about the bones they are digging up: 'Chahe Sikandar ho ya Akbar, Hitler ho ya Gandhi... aakhir mein mitti hi banta hai (Whether it is Alexander or Akbar, Hitler or Gandhi...finally everything turns to dirt)'. The reference to Sikandar (Alexander) turning to dirt seems to come straight from *Hamlet*. But the spectre of the graveyard bones leads less to a recognition of death in life, as it does in *Hamlet*. Instead it references, again, the history of violence in the region. After Porus lost the battle of Hydaspes in 326 BCE, King Abisares of Kashmir submitted to the Greek conqueror Alexander the Great, commonly known as Sikandar. Haider's reference to Sikandar—and to Akbar—again serves as a reminder, not so much of the fall of the powerful, as of Kashmir's 'disappeared' histories.

In terms of plot, *Haider* deviates from its Shakespeare source play more than the other two films in Bhardwaj's trilogy. That is partly due to the influence of his co-scriptwriter, Basharat Peer, whose 2010 memoir, *Curfewed Night,* outlines with chilling power the trauma of growing up in Kashmir at a time of violent militancy. Much of the memoir finds its way into the film's first half, which provides a back story about Haider's family history. Indeed, Peer himself makes a cameo in the film as a Kashmiri who cannot enter his house unless he is ordered to, accustomed as he is to having his life utterly controlled by the Indian Army and its special powers. It is only in the film's second half that the story of *Hamlet* clicks into shape. But there is a great deal from *Hamlet* that the film channels in its first half. In particular, it embraces the masala justice of the more-than-one.

Much has been made of the Oedipal drama of Haider's relationship with his mother, Ghazala (Tabu). In fact the film dispenses with Hamlet's obsession with maternal flesh and his resulting disgust with women: Haider doesn't have hang-ups about originating in the body of a woman, nor is he horrified by the thought of sex with Arshia. But the film picks up on the play's sense of toxic proximity between son and mother. That toxic proximity is largely displaced, however, into Haider's relation to Kashmir and its militancy, from which his mother wants to distance him. Ghazala stands in for both the place of Haider's birth and his painful exile from it. But so does Dr Hilal Meer, whose disappearance leaves Haider longing for a lost connection to Kashmir as much as to his father. As a result, the Oedipal drama of *Haider* is played out largely at the level not of the individual but of the political. And this drama instills in Haider a ghostly sense of presence and absence, of being and not being.

Haider rejects 'to be and not to be' as an unbearable condition. But it also embraces the ghostliness of 'to be and not to be' as a means of undermining the tyranny of either/or. On the surface, the film gives Haider an either/or choice between his father and mother. This is in some ways a psychological choice with roots in the Freudian family narrative: we are told that, when Haider was young, he was tremendously jealous of his father and used to say, 'bada hokar mauje se nikah karoonga (when I grow up I will marry mummy)'. But now that he is older, and has supposedly grown out of his Oedipal phase, he seems instead to embrace his father. Beneath this straightforward mother/father choice lies another. His father may say, in response to Ghazala, that he provides medical treatment to the militants because he is on the side of life. But if Roohdar's story is right, Haider's father ultimately advocates for intaqaam (revenge). Against this, Ghazala has taken the path of her father-in-law, Dr Hussain Meer, who says in a flashback that 'yaad rakhna, intaqaam se sirf intaqaam paida hota hai' (remember, revenge only begets revenge). Ghazala, too, thinks nothing will come of revenge and the escalation of violence, and so she has sent Haider out of the Valley to be educated in India.

At the end of the film, Ghazala's and Dr Hilal Meer's two positions compete in Haider's mind as he contemplates whether or not to kill Khurram. It seems as if he takes his mother's side, because he chooses to spare his uncle. But the matter is appreciably more complex. His mother has mortally wounded Khurram in the qabristaan (cemetery), ripping off his legs by detonating a suicide bomber's vest that Roohdar has given her. So her position is hardly one of non-violence. Nor is Haider's when he chooses not to kill Khurram: after all, leaving his mutilated uncle alive is arguably a nastier form of intaqaam than killing him. Neither the father's nor the mother's position is singular or clear; nor is Haider's. And nor is Bhardwaj and Peer's. The script of *Haider* offers two possible endings: in the first, Haider stumbles and falls, suggesting his death; in the second, he is received by Roohdar, suggesting his conversion to militancy. But the film has a third ending, in which Haider keeps walking, ghost-like, into an uncertain future. Clearly there is something about this story that stands in the way of decisive finality.

But that is symptomatic, also, of the 'to be and not to be' history of Kashmir. Bhardwaj has added appreciative comments in the closing credits about the bravery of the Indian Army in Kashmir during the recent floods. Despite these there is no doubt that *Haider* is a film deeply critical of the Indian military presence. What is striking is that Bhardwaj and Peer don't see the correct response to the situation in terms of an either/or choice between militancy or Gandhian ahimsa. Instead they allow a ghostly masala of multiple possibilities to offer—if not a solution to the problem—then at least a refusal of any singular story of Kashmir. Because it is the murderous will to singularity that has produced the tragedy of the Valley.

ACT FIVE
toofaans

CHORUS

The firangi and the desi twins have each weathered their fair share of toofaans or tempests. These are often experienced as catastrophic endings. We say that a storm lashes, as if it were a mad whip-cracking maniac intent on inflicting maximum pain. But what happens when an angry toofaan ebbs? As we survey the wreckage left in its wake, we can't know for sure what the future holds. And so the aftermath of a tempest can be a time of horror too. Horror over what has been brought to an end; horror, too, over what more suffering may come.

But the twins know from their own poetic traditions that even a lashing downpour—whether the cruelest of Chaucer's April showers or the wildest of Kalidasa's uttara meghduta—can create as much as it can destroy. It can generate the world afresh even as it devastates much of what we hold dear. And that 'we' is important. It is not a royal 'we' but a masala collectivity, one that a storm can bring into clear focus. An individual might see a tempest simply as a reflection of his or her unique misfortune. Yet the truth is that any storm is part of a larger ecology in which we're all implicated. No matter how indifferent we may be to that ecology, a toofaan is equally indifferent to whether we are rich or poor, Brahmin or Dalit, Hindu or Muslim, man or woman. Storms may spell the end of masala, smashing it into bits. But they can also occasion it.

The twins understand this. They understand that in a fierce toofaan—a toofaan so strong that it ruptures even the insulated comforts of the privileged—we are all in it together, for better and for ill. And in the stormiest of times, the hope for a brave new world persists. But what that world may be, we can't tell. Yet.

ACT FIVE SCENE ONE

'Aaj Mausam Bada Beimaan Hai'

In May 2018, I suddenly lost my house—the house in which I wrote most of this book. The night after my landlady informed me that, due to her marital problems, I would have to vacate the premises within two weeks, a massive storm struck Delhi. Lightning lit up the whole sky, bathing the forest next to our house in flashes of garish yellow. During each flash I could see the forest's branches, lashed by the wind and rain, waving frantically as if in helpless despair. The vision left me feeling as if the forest and I had been cast in some badly adapted version of *King Lear*. Like that play's titular character, I had lost my home and was in a storm. I wasn't outdoors, exposed to the elements as Shakespeare's mad king is. But I certainly experienced the storm, and those frantically waving branches, as expressing the thunder in my own helpless heart. And Mohammed Rafi's song from the Dharmendra film *Loafer* (1973), 'Aaj Mausam Bada Beimaan Hai (Today the Weather is Very Fickle)', began playing in my head:

> aaj mausam bada beimaan hai…
> aane wala koi toofaan hai
>
> (today, the weather is very fickle…
> some storm is on its way)

Of course, my response to the storm was an example of that species of individualist megalomania called the Pathetic Fallacy: the idea that inanimate objects express what I'm feeling. But my reaction to the storm was influenced by more than mere narcissistic projection. It didn't help that the loss of our house happened just two days before my elderly parents in New Zealand were due to move into an assisted living facility. My mother's dementia had left her memory dimmed, my father's macular degeneration had left him blind, and their combined frailty meant they had no choice but to give up their house. That's why *King Lear*, a tragedy that features scenes of old-age madness and blindness as well as the trauma of losing one's home, was already very much in my mind. The loss of my own house, and the storm that accompanied it, was emotionally tied up for me with an ominous sense of radical generational shift, of the peeling away of a layer of parental protection that, even many thousands of miles away, I had carried with me all my life like a quilt.

What a difference from nearly twenty years earlier when I encountered my first Bollywood storm in *Lagaan*. That toofaan was not the corollary of a desperate heart. Instead, it was a welcome reassurance to an entire community that included Hindu, Muslim, Sikh, and Dalit. It was a reassurance that a long season of misery was now over, that life would be regenerated for all the villagers of Champaner, thanks to the coming of the monsoon. The rain started to fall after Aamir Khan hit the winning six in their daring match against the English team—as if the rain-gods themselves had approved the Indian victory that would relieve the villagers of the burdens of triple taxation and debt. The monsoon would also strike away the burdens of drought and famine. And so the entire community danced for sheer joy in the downpour, and we with them.

I already had a sense that this was a standard masala movie routine. Just before I first visited India and was swept away by *Lagaan*, I had seen *Monsoon Wedding* (2001), Mira Nair's tribute to Delhi and the masala movies of her teenage years. It includes a version of Rafi's song too. And it also features a wonderfully memorable closing sequence. As the monsoon rains drench a upper middle-class Punjabi shaadi that had threatened to fall apart because of sundry family tensions and scandals, all the characters—men and women, rich and poor, Hindu and non-Hindu—come together to dance for joy in the downpour. Clichéd as the sequence was, there was something deeply affecting about it too. The 'Wedding' of the title is in fact a double one: the wealthy Anglophone bride and groom are matched by a poor Hindi-speaking couple, the clownish wedding planner Dubey (Vijay Raaz) and the Christian maidservant Alice (Tillotama Shome). When the rich patriarch Lalit Verma (Naseeruddin Shah) invites Dubey and Alice to join him in dancing, there is a split second of hesitation from Dubey—and then he, followed by Alice, join their employer with gusto. Of course the vigour of their dance cannot erase the jagged edges of class and religious difference. But something about it also dares dream of a world in which those edges are dulled.

The fact that Rafi's song appears in *Monsoon Wedding* is important. It is a reminder of the pain as well as the joy of the monsoon. The final dance wouldn't have moved me so much weren't it for the pain—individual, but also collective—that the film allows into view before the shaadi. The pain of the rich Hindu bride's agony at the prospect of arranged marriage; the pain of the bride's sister's sexual abuse and its cover-up; the pain of Partition that had left the Verma family penniless; the pain of the wedding planner's humiliations; the pain of his poor Christian bride's poverty and loneliness. Rafi's 'Aaj Mausam Bada Beimaan Hai' somehow became the soundtrack for all this pain, even as the 'toofaan' of which he sings is miraculously transfigured with the final sequence into an occasion for joyous solidarity across difference. And that, in a nutshell, is the logic of the masala movie monsoon. Pain and joy, rich and poor, Hindu and non-Hindu all come together under the large shaadi tent of masala. And there is room for all of them to dance, separately and together.

Of course this utopian fantasy is easy to criticize. Not least because it is out and out fantasy. The most common objection to the masala movie is that it is utterly escapist: its shining, smiling India, dancing in the rain, is a universe away from the horrific realities of caste, communal violence, patriarchy and poverty. But this objection is based on the faulty assumption that fantasy is as distant from reality as rich are from poor, Hindus from Muslims, and Brahmins from Dalits. What I find most compelling about the masala movie is that it takes fantasy seriously as a part of real life. Not just because it understands that the reality of the world is steeped in fantasy. But also, more generally, because it recognizes that fantasy is the real fabric out of which our longing for a better world is fashioned. Dreams are not just an escape from the horrors of waking Indian life. They are also the medium in which alternatives to it are crafted. In all its escapist unreality, the beating heart of the masala movie is immersed in the traumatic realities of the world. We have seen this repeatedly: the masala musical expressions of longing that we have heard from Gulzar to Bhardwaj spring from historical traumas of partition, displacement, and disappearance. These practitioners of masala do not stick their fingers in their ears and pretend that trauma doesn't exist. For them, it is the wellspring of desire for a different, better world.

The monsoon of Hindi cinema is therefore a particularly illustrative instance of the complex politics of masala. It is inclusive not just in terms of community, or in generic mixture—a plot element and an occasion for naach-gaana. It is inclusive also because it is located simultaneously in reality and fantasy, pain and joy. And that simultaneity is what makes the masala monsoon a collective experience. By recognizing the diversity of experiences it engenders and invites under its big tent, it dares to imagine the power of joyous solidarity in a time of painful crisis. When we make a rainstorm mean *either* pain *or* joy but not both, we not only perform the dardnak kahaani of singularization. We also become susceptible to the individualizing impulse of the Pathetic Fallacy. That, in retrospect, is what happened the night I lost my house. I made the storm entirely my own, and so for me it belonged to the same order of things as the house I had thought of as my own. But the fact is neither were my own: others could lay claim to them too. 'My' home was also the home of another, someone in need. And I didn't give a thought to the other people who were caught in the midst of 'my' storm, who were more exposed to it than I was, whose own homes were in jeopardy and even destroyed because of it.

King Lear is instructive on this score. We may think of it as a play about an old man who loses everything. His loss of home, property, clothes, family and servants is an upper middle-class Indian's nightmare of the complete loss of identity. But it is also so much more than that. We could call *King Lear* a tragedy of de-individualization. It is about de-individualization in the double sense that it is concerned not just with how the individual falls apart but also with how one might move from an individual to a collective consciousness. The irony is that, as Lear tragically loses all the appurtenances of individual power, he moves from hierarchical selfishness to caring for others. This arrogant old man who had once viewed the people he reigned over as insignificant ant-like creatures separated from him by a lofty distance suddenly begins to see his former subjects as close-up equals.

The storm on the heath—which rages through much of the play's third act—is crucial to this movement. Initially, Lear views the storm simply through the lens of his own personal grief. He sees its lashes as reminders of his supposedly cruel daughters who owe him no paternal allegiance: 'Nor rain, wind, nor thunder are my daughters:/ I tax not you, you elements, with unkindness;/ …then let fall/ Your horrible pleasure' (3.2.14–15, 17–18). In narcissistic fashion, the storm is an extension of 'the tempest in my mind' (3.4.15). But the storm also gets Lear outside himself. For the first time he notices the physical needs of his Fool: he says to him as the storm rages around them, 'Come on now, my boy: how dost, my boy? Art cold?/ I am cold myself' (3.2.66–7). And he adds: 'Where is this straw, my fellow?' (3.2.67). The word 'fellow' is

JONATHAN GIL HARRIS

striking here: it acknowledges the Fool not as a possession but as an equal, also afflicted by the storm.

Even more, the storm helps Lear begin to realize his intimate connection to a collectivity much larger than him. He says:

Poor naked wretches, whereso'er you are,
That bide the pelting of this pitiless storm,
How shall your houseless heads and unfed sides,
Your loop'd and window'd raggedness, defend you
From seasons such as these? O, I have ta'en
Too little care of this! (3.4.29–34)

Of course, this moment of illumination doesn't radically change things. It still falls within the purview of a feudal sense of responsibility to one's vassals and a self-sentimentalizing patriarchy. It remains motivated by a deep, misogynist antipathy to the daughters who have turned him out of their homes, and whose perspective is never taken into account. Nor is there any talk here of how to change the material conditions that produce poverty and homelessness—Lear imagines only taking care of those who experience hardship. For him, paternalistic feudalism is not the problem: indeed, a gentler, kinder version of it is offered here as the solution.

The politics of masala is in some ways similar. When a masala movie invites the marginal and neglected into its big tent, it can easily seem like an act of patriarchal feudal largesse like Lear's. The oppressive class system that allows a Lalit Verma to profit and an Alice to languish goes unquestioned: it is swept under the carpet—even justified—by Verma Sahib's gesture of benevolent inclusion. It is a fair criticism to say that the inclusiveness of masala can collude with unjust structures of power. But in the midst of a tempest, the criticism also runs the risk of being lazily cynical. When the alternatives are the craven selfishness of solipsistic individualism, the lumpen aggression of fascistic uniformity, or the violent mob rage of communal violence, feudal largesse can at least provide a welcome shelter. A shelter in which to regather, recoup, and imagine other, new possibilities.

I eventually found another house, of course. And my parents settled into their new assisted living community quite comfortably. Not just because we grimly persevered and rose to the challenges of the day. Things worked out largely because of others who pitched in with their kindness, connecting us with friends, associates, contacts who were willing to help us out. Because the masala monsoon is not just an onscreen fantasy. As Lear discovers, it can also animate our interactions with others in a time of crisis. Off-screen as well as on, a storm can be an occasion for regeneration as much as destruction. The real tragedy is not that the storm destroys. It is that we avert our gaze from the million and one storms that are raging all around us. And that's because we think that they have nothing to do with us.

If anything is sapping the power of masala as a lived reality in India, it is this frightening skill we have developed of looking away. When Muslims are lynched on suspicion of eating beef, and we say—nothing to do with me; when Dalit girls and boys are killed for loving Brahmins, and we say—why worry about that when it doesn't involve me; when civilian Kashmiris are blinded by pellet guns, and we say—it's not my business; then we need to ask, at what cost do we cordon ourselves off from these atrocities? If the storms of *King Lear* and *Monsoon Wedding* tell us anything, it is that we are never just atomized individuals. We are all interconnected.

So if aaj mausam bada beimaan hai, then how can I look away from my storm-stricken fellows?

ACT FIVE SCENE TWO

Masala Storms (*King Lear* and *The Tempest*)

In March of 2015, I attended a talk by the Pakistani writer Intizar Hussain at the India International Centre in Delhi. The occasion was the Jashn-e-Rekhta festival, an annual celebration of Urdu language and culture. It was an unseasonably cold and wet day: we got soaked in a cloudburst as we arrived at the venue. The rain fell from an outlier front of the same storm system that had been lashing Kashmir that week. The Jhelum River, swollen by the deadly combination of heavy rains and spring snowmelt from the Himalayas, was flowing well above the danger mark. For the second time in seven months following the horrific floods of September 2014, Srinagar was facing the prospect of going under water.

Against this stormy backdrop, Hussain told us an Urdu fairy tale—a fairy tale with links to a storm. He was ninety-two years old and moving with difficulty. But his voice sounded strangely young as he narrated the tale, which he had first heard from his nani-amma (maternal grandmother) in the 1920s when he was a child living in the Bulandshahar district of Uttar Pradesh. The story was about an elderly zamindar who decided to bequeath his estate to whichever of his three daughters most loved him. The first two daughters pronounced their love in florid but hollow terms. But the third, who truly loved her father, told the zamindar simply that 'main tumhe iss tareekhe se chahti hoon jaise namak chahte hain (I love you as much as I love salt)'. For her unvarnished honesty, she was banished. The zamindar realized his folly only when he too was banished by his 'loving' daughters. The young Hussain had believed the tale to be his nani-amma's invention until, at Aligarh Muslim University, he read Shakespeare and realized that this Urdu fairy tale was also an English tragedy. It was, of course, a version of *King Lear*.

As Hussain retold the story of the zamindar and his three daughters, I found myself thinking about the obscure threads linking the Jashn-e-Rekhta festival, the tale, and the weather devastating Kashmir. The festival was a celebration of a powerful lived experience of masala. The poet-lyricist Javed Akhtar had pointed out in an earlier session that Urdu is a masala language, combining elements of Braj Bhasha, Punjabi, Persian,

229

Arabic, Turkic, even Italian: it is a 'rekhta', a mixture, testimony to the extraordinary cultural and linguistic diversity of South Asia. Hussain's tale of the zamindar was another instance of this rekhta—a reminder that any tale is, in his words, an 'awaara' (traveller), disdaining borders of geography, politics and religion. Like Urdu itself, the deliciously masala tale of the zamindar is both Indian and foreign. Yet the tale is the bearer of a less palatable truth. Neither the storm of *King Lear* nor the heavy rainfall in Kashmir are simply acts of nature. Both are deluges caused in no small part by humans.

Monsoon showers may make for scenes of joy in Bollywood. But off-screen, monsoons are fast becoming anything but occasions for collective celebration. Too often they don't arrive when they should. Farmers' crops are being destroyed by droughts when the monsoon rains don't come; they are destroyed also when the rains do come because they fall with a fury previously unknown. Here in Delhi, rainstorms are increasingly happening at unseasonable times, accompanied by apocalyptic dust storms that scoop up the desert sand of Rajasthan and dump it on the city with a ferocity that can destroy entire colonies. It is almost always the poor who are most traumatically affected by storms. Just ask the villagers in Kashmir who lost their houses in the devastating flashfloods and landslides of 2014 and 2015. Or the basti-dwellers in Bombay whose settlements were destroyed in the unprecedented downpours of 2005 and 2017. Or the small farmers in Tamil Nadu, impoverished by the loss of crops due to the torrential rainstorms and floods of 2015. Or the villagers of Kerala, their lifeworlds drowned by the apocalyptic monsoon floods of 2018.

The horror is that these 'natural' apocalypses aren't just acts of nature. As Amitav Ghosh puts it in *The Great Derangement,* his study of climate change, the stormy weather of recent years is the 'mysterious work of our own hands returning to haunt us in unthinkable shapes and forms'. What we call 'progress'—especially the progress promised by industries that produce massive amounts of greenhouse gases as they encourage us to consume ever more things we don't really need—is having a devastating effect on our environment and the weather. The toxic smog choking the city where I live is the product of such 'progress': more cars on the roads are belching more fumes, more construction is tossing up more dust, and burn-off from new, highly profitable rice paddies is dispatching thick plumes of smoke across the region. In the 1930s, amidst the high wind of Nazism, the German–Jewish cultural critic Walter Benjamin had a nightmare vision of the Angel of History being blown backwards into the future by a catastrophic storm. This storm, he says, 'is what we call progress'. But progress nowadays isn't only creating metaphorical storms. It's also contributing to real ones.

Just over 400 years ago, in a series of plays written in the waning years of his career, Shakespeare repeatedly staged devastating storms that Benjamin would have recognized. These storms weren't caused by climate change. But Shakespeare had come to understand that the environment around him was changing radically because of human behaviour. *King Lear* and *The Tempest* glance at huge changes specific to Shakespeare's moment: the demise of feudalism and the rise of capitalism and colonialism. They also speak to our modern moment here in India, as creaky old social institutions are smashed by the high winds of development and fundamentalism. We are progressing towards a future that we can't quite imagine. The outlook is stormy, in every sense of that word. What can Shakespeare's two tempest-ridden plays tell us about the future? And what might they tell us about the future of masala?

♦

King Lear and *The Tempest* are rarely lumped together. The first is Shakespeare's bleakest tragedy; the second is a romance with a happy ending. Yet they are uncannily similar stories of cranky old patriarchs who theatrically give up their power, young daughters who stand to inherit their fathers' legacies, and rebel bastards who threaten to shatter them. This family narrative is in each case punctuated by a fierce storm that does double duty as plot device and metaphor for massive generational change. Same story, different endings: but when we read tragedy and romance together, we can begin to see the radical ambivalence of the masala storm.

And 'see' is the right word, for *King Lear* is a deeply image-driven play. Lear dividing up his kingdom on a map; Lear's courtier Kent placed in the stocks; the blinding of Gloucester; blind Gloucester jumping from what he thinks is a precipice; Lear carrying his dead daughter Cordelia onto the stage: this is a play that bombards its spectators with memorable visual tableaus. But perhaps the signature image of the play is of the mad Lear in the storm, railing at the elements:

> Blow, winds, and crack your cheeks! rage! blow!
> You cataracts and hurricanoes, spout

Till you have drenched our steeples, drowned the cocks!
You sulphurous and thought-executing fires,
Vaunt-couriers to oak-cleaving thunderbolts,
Singe my white head! And thou, all-shaking thunder,
Smite flat the thick rotundity o' the world! (3.2.1–7)

The storm, which takes up the better part of the third act, is an astounding meteorological event. But it is an astounding theatrical event too: when the play was first staged in 1606, it would have required an unusual assortment of special effects to produce its 'sulphurous and thought-executing fires'. Shakespeare's company may well have dipped into the stock of sulphur-scented squibs it had amassed for the Witches' spectacular opening scene in *Macbeth*, staged earlier the same year.

But unlike the thunder and lightning of *Macbeth*, *King Lear*'s storm is also a metaphor for generational change. This change has been brewing since the beginning of the play. When the Duke of Gloucester's bastard son Edmund vows that 'Thou, nature, art my goddess' and rejects the 'plague of custom' (1.2.1, 3), he embraces a view of nature as an amoral, constantly transforming state in which power comes from brute strength rather than inheritance. This view also unleashes a tempest in the old feudal order, sundering the hierarchical bonds between father and son, master and servant, king and subject. This order is already teetering due to its inherent iniquities, evident in Lear's feckless treatment of his three daughters. He gives away his kingdom to the two daughters he thinks love him most, with scant regard for their true feelings, their abilities to govern or the fate of those they will rule. And his idiocy continues with his assumption that Goneril and Regan, the daughters he has rewarded for their ripe professions of love, will finance his extravagant lifestyle, including his large fleet of servants. The daughters refuse to comply. They cut his entitlements and demand that he let go of his retinue; soon he is left alone, with only his Fool and loyal follower Kent as company. The storm on the heath might seem less a sudden change of weather, then, than the metaphorical consummation of the old order's collapse.

This collapse has a larger historical resonance. *King Lear* may be set in a distant, pre-Christian past; but it engages deeply felt realities of Shakespeare's time. Edmund's critique of the 'plague of custom' is of a piece with the new sensibility that accompanied the sudden growth of London and the rise of the urban mercantile class, a transformation that progressively swept aside the customs of the feudal-aristocratic society of medieval England. These old customs are embodied in the play by Lear: he believes that royal power must manifest itself in displays of superfluous wealth, including large numbers of servants. His feudal attitude is immediately familiar to any Indian. Even when Lear seems to undergo a radical awakening in the storm and acknowledges the lives and needs of the poor, he never sees an actual beggar—and nor do the audience. Instead he clings to an outmoded feudal view of the universe. In his view, the poor should stay poor and not ask for redress; they are simply to be provided for by munificent kings. By contrast, his daughters Goneril and Regan subscribe to a new capitalist ethos of cost-cutting rationality, one that refuses excess and also values individual self-interest at the expense of the social collective, let alone the needs of the poor. They may be dead by the play's end. But the ethos they represent will long outlive them.

King Lear's characters are propelled irresistibly into a future to which their backs are turned. This future is understood largely in the negative—as the absence of the old feudal order. Gloucester says that 'Love cools, friendship falls off, brothers divide; in cities, mutinies; in countries, discord; in palaces, treason; and the bond crack'd 'twixt son and father' (1.2.99–101). He is describing here a decaying ancien régime, but he is also sketching an unclear future opened up by its collapse. As such the future is understood not for itself but, rather, as the negation of the past. We see this negation with Lear's extraordinary response to his youngest daughter Cordelia's unexpected death: 'Thou'lt come no more?/ Never, never, never, never, never' (5.3.309–10). That 'never' is picked up in Albany's last words, which address the time to come by glancing back to the absence of the older generation: 'we that are young/ Shall never see so much, nor live so long' (5.3.324–5). Now that the storm of progress has struck, the play's characters cannot see the future; they can only see the ruins of the old order. This predicament is most powerfully illustrated by the spectacle of Edgar guiding his father Gloucester, blinded by Lear's daughter and son-in-law, to the edge of an imagined precipice from which he hopes to commit suicide. Here we see a ruined representative of the old order peering into the dark void of a future in which he literally sees nothing.

Perhaps this is one of the reasons why the word 'nothing'—which appears thirty-one times in the play, more than in any other of Shakespeare's works—resonates so loudly in King Lear. When the old order is shown to be bankrupt, both that order and what will replace it become, in the wise words of Lear's Fool, a zero, an 'O without a figure' (1.4.168). That 'O' is echoed in Lear's 'O, I have ta'en/ Too little care of this!' (3.4.35–6), his admission that he has been blind to the sufferings of others. It is a blindness to the future as much as the past. And Gloucester's blindness is the condition not just of a wronged man but of the entire play, standing at the edge of a precipice—let's call this precipice the dawn of capitalism and the ideology of individualism—and unable to see whether jumping off it will result in salvation or total disaster.

This inability was no doubt shared by Shakespeare and his theatre company. They embodied the contradictions of a society undergoing huge upheaval as its old feudal forms crumbled in the face of new realities. On the one hand, the very name of the King's Men advertised a feudal relation to their patron. They were King James's servants, and received livery—a uniform of service—from him, the traditional obligation of a feudal lord to his vassals. On the other hand, the King's Men were a joint-stock company engaged in a commercial enterprise, seeking to reap profit from the sale of their labour in their public playhouses. Shakespeare's company therefore had one foot in the old feudal world and the other in a new capitalist universe. Their craft of playing reflected that contradiction: it was a means to honour their patron, the king; it was also a route to personal profit. This contradiction is apparent in *King Lear*. Lear is a great believer in performing his feudal power through grand spectacles and gestures. By contrast, Edmund the bastard more instrumentally plays parts for his private gain. The theatre of old is literally bankrupt; the new theatre is dangerously manipulative.

Written five years after *King Lear*, just as an ageing Shakespeare was about to retire from the London theatre and return to his family in Stratford, *The Tempest* presents another storm-swept version of the earlier play's double theatricality. But it conflates both types of theatre in the person of its lead character, Prospero, the Duke-turned-magician. He is torn between old and new orders, between performing his royal authority and manipulating appearances for profit. The play's tempest is therefore as much embodied in him as it is a grand spectacle for the audience. But the tempest differs from *King Lear*'s storm also because the play is a romance. And a romance, at least in Shakespeare's hands, not only demands a happy ending. It also requires that the lead character get back something he has lost. If the tragic vision of *King Lear* anticipates

Walter Benjamin by seeing a storm as the ruination of a past that will forever be lost, then the romance vision of *The Tempest* regards a storm as an opportunity to regain the past.

The play starts with the unforgettable stage direction, '*A tempestuous noise of thunder and lightning is heard*' (1.1.0). This is quickly followed by another, '*Enter Mariners, wet*' (1.1.45). The stage briefly becomes a ship at sea, sinking in a storm. And with it sinks an entire social order and the hierarchical bonds that forge it: son (Ferdinand) is divided from father (King Alonzo), fool (Trinculo) from king. But this storm is different from *King Lear*'s. It is explicitly shown to be not an act of God but, rather, the work of Prospero. He creates the tempest, with the help of his spirit servant Ariel, as part of a scheme to bring his enemies to the island to avenge a past wrong they have done to him. But Prospero's storm is more than a device in a revenge plot. It also acquires something of the metaphorical character of *King Lear*'s storm as a symbol of change. It is not for nothing that the word 'tempest' derives from the Latin *tempus*, meaning time. The tempest represents a turbulence in time as much as space. It blows the unfinished business of the past into the present in order to create a brand new future, or what Prospero's daughter Miranda famously calls a 'brave new world' (5.1.186).

At first, the tempest seems to challenge the feudal order in the manner of *King Lear*'s storm. The Boatswain refuses to kowtow to the aristocrats on board his storm-stricken ship, roaring at them to pull their weight or get beneath the deck. This is but one in a series of subversions of order that the tempest seems to unleash. But the order that it sweeps aside is not quite the feudal order of *King Lear*. Rather, *The Tempest*'s order is a *perversion* of feudal rule: Prospero, we soon discover, was unseated as Duke some years earlier by his brother Antonio with the connivance of Alonzo, the King of Naples, both of whom are on the ship. The tempest will end Antonio's illegitimate rule and restore Prospero to his 'rightful' position as Duke. So when his daughter Miranda meets Prospero's brother and associates and says of them, 'oh brave new world, with such people in it' (5.1.186–7), the irony is that this 'new world' is really the old world of aristocratic Europe. The future amounts to a repossession of the past.

In fact the characters in *The Tempest* keep dreaming of repossessing lost pasts as a way of countering the storm of change. Prospero wants his Dukedom back. Ariel wants his freedom back. Alonzo wants his son back. Caliban wants his island back. Miranda wants her pre-exile childhood back. Prospero's old counsellor Gonzalo wants the ancient Golden Age back. And all—except Gonzalo—recover what they have lost. These magical conjurations of the past as the post-tempest future avoid the horrifying prospect of 'nothing' that pervades *King Lear*. They replace stormy nothingness with the consoling fantasy of return to an original state of perfection, in which every paradise lost is regained as surely as the Boatswain has his tempest-tossed ship returned to him magically intact. In this, *The Tempest*'s 'new world' is much more like the Hindutva dream of a glorious future achieved through the recovery of an idealized, singular past.

But Miranda's 'brave new world' points to another storm. The rise of colonialism in the so-called 'new world' of the Americas, and the exploitation of its resources, was one of the engines of the new European capitalist machine. Just as the character of the bastard in *King Lear* suggests an emerging capitalist disposition, so, too, does the bastard in *The Tempest* evoke a related new world. Caliban is a native inhabitant of the island who toils as Prospero's slave. As such, he not only recalls contemporary accounts of the American 'new world' (his name seems to be loosely derived from 'Caribbean', and he swears by 'Setebos', a name Shakespeare found in European travel writing about Patagonia in South America). Caliban also represents a new economy: he is a reminder of early European capitalism's dependence on slave labour. On the island, Prospero is not just a feudal patriarch but also a plantation owner, profiting from Caliban's forced work. That's why Miranda's 'brave new world' is in fact double faced. Even as she evokes what seems like a single entity, the phrase points both to the past and the future, to European feudalism and American colonialism.

Lurking in *The Tempest*, then, is a misgiving that its 'brave new world' may not really be the old feudal Europe after all. I am talking here not just about the phrase's gesture to the 'new world' of the Americas. I am referring also to the new commercial world of instrumentalist profit-seeking in which Shakespeare's theatre was implicated. Prospero serves up illusion after illusion for profit: these are investments from which he will reap the dividend of a future in which he regains his past. His illusions involve not only spectacular theatre but also what we might call pre-modern social media. Ariel, Prospero's spirit servant, is a creature of the ether who acts as a long-distance mouthpiece for his master. He often does so virtually, accosting Prospero's adversaries in invisible form. Let's call him a spirit troll disseminating fake news. Ariel's messages manipulate Prospero's targets, whipping up outrage, fear, and panic.

We can glimpse in Prospero's self-serving manipulation of image and ether a hint of the new capitalist world. And *The Tempest* seems to know this about itself, and understands how its own theatrical medium is complicit with this world. Even as Prospero's theatrical magic results in the restoration of the feudal order, *The Tempest* also presents that magic as a dangerous, stormy power that must be given up. Prospero admits that, with his dark arts,

> I have bedimmed
> The noontide sun, called forth the mutinous winds,
> And 'twixt the green sea and the azured vault
> Set roaring war: to the dread rattling thunder
> Have I given fire and rifted Jove's stout oak
> With his own bolt; the strong-based promontory
> Have I made shake and by the spurs plucked up
> The pine and cedar: graves at my command
> Have waked their sleepers, oped, and let 'em forth
> By my so potent art. (5.1.41–50)

Prospero's magic is a 'potent art' that doesn't just create tempests. It creates tempests against 'Jove'. With this speech he blurs into his nemesis, Caliban's mother Sycorax—the dead Algerian witch whom he condemns for using magic against the order of nature. No wonder he says of Caliban, 'this thing of darkness I/ acknowledge mine' (5.1.278-9). Prospero fleetingly acknowledges here that he is a white European magician who is indistinguishable from a black African witch. Fascinatingly, Shakespeare stole the words of Prospero's speech about his magic from Medea, the dark Asian witch in Ovid's *Metamorphoses*. This man who seeks to repossess a pure past turns out to be the quintessence of a border-crossing, masala impurity.

And that is why, immediately after owning up to the storms he has unleashed against the hierarchical order he wishes to restore, Prospero says: 'But this rough magic/ I here abjure' (5.1.50–1). By renouncing his magical powers, his return to old Europe is supposedly secured. Yet there is a lingering sense that this happy outcome is a capital dividend secured by his shrewd investment in 'rough magic.' The well-laid plot that supposedly restores the old order is, in fact, the essence of the new world that will destroy it. No matter how much feudal Prospero may try to repudiate the profit-driven regimes of colonialism and commercial illusion-manipulation, the genie of capitalism is now out of the lamp. The tempest he has unleashed is not over.

◆

How have these two plays about social change become part of recent conversations about India, a deeply feudal land buffeted by hurricanes of development? Interestingly, Indian reimaginings of each play are often haunted by the ghost of the other play. Versions of *The Tempest*, even as they imagine a return to the past, have echoed *King Lear* by noting the devastations of tradition unleashed by the storm of progress. And reworkings of *King Lear*, imagining the demise of an old order, have been in thrall to a *Tempest*-style fantasy of repossessing it. The result is what we might call a generic masala: reimaginings of Shakespeare's storm plays have often incorporated elements of both tragedy and romance. This generic masala is apparent in four recent conversations with *King Lear* and *The Tempest*—a graphic novel, a play, and two films.

The Return, a yet-to-be published graphic novel by Chandigarh artist-writer Purvai Aranya, reimagines *The Tempest* in a village in the Indian jungle. Its Prospero, Prashant, is a university-educated Naxalite; its Caliban and Ariel, Kamlesh and Atram, are tribals who have worked in Prashant's house and been raised alongside Prashant's daughter, Meera. *The Return* begins with an image of a boat buffeted by what looks like a massive sea storm. Subsequent frames reveal that it is actually a paper boat bobbing in a stream, a toy in one of Meera's forest games. This 'tempest' comes across first as a savage monsoon squall and then as child's play. But the perspectival change the images demand of us is mirrored by another: the idealism that had long ago led Prashant to take up armed struggle in the forest has waned. He longs to return to the comforts of his old urban life; this pitches him into battle with Kamlesh, who feels betrayed by him. Beyond this storm are others: the 'vortex' that swirls in Atram, who is torn between anger at his treatment by Prashant and a longing for peace; the whirlwind of political conflict between the Indian state and the local rebels; and, above all, the tempest of economic development, as a result of which traditional tribal culture has been shattered. *The Return*'s opening image of a water storm thus becomes a powerful point of entry into many other metaphorical Indian tempests. These tempests have the force of the storm of progress that sweeps through *King Lear*, smashing everything into nothingness. The romance of Prashant's return to his city life is juxtaposed with the tragedy of the ravaged forest community he leaves behind.

The sea-storm of *The Tempest* has also spoken with particular force to Tamilians. That is because their lives are defined by water, its lack, and its excess—'dried up wells, extinct aquifers, giant tidal waves, clogged rivers, to the recent floods,' as the theatre director Samyuktha P. C. has put it. Her 2016 Tamil-language reimagining of the play with the theatre group Crea-Shakthi responded to the floods of the previous year. Prospero became Parasparam, a Chennai landowner who drowns his city against the objections of his daughter, as vengeance for past wrongs by corrupt politicians. Highlighting tensions between old and new, magic and science, and romance and tragedy, the production suggested that Parasparam's tempest has its origin in generational conflict. This conflict is not only between father and daughter but also, at a larger level, between feudalism and economic progress. Parasparam's tempest was therefore much more than just a dramatization of Tamil Nadu's 2015 floods. It was also, *King Lear*-like, the outcome of storms of historical change battering a rapidly modernizing India.

These two conversations with *The Tempest* both register the destructive impact of development on India. For Aranya and Samyuktha alike, development has unleashed a tempest that is shattering old social bonds, whether in tribal communities or cities. As a result, their reimaginings of Shakespeare's romance are suffused with the sense of nothingness that pervades *King Lear*. Conversely, *The Tempest*'s dream of repossessing the past haunts Indian film reimaginings of the tragedy. It is striking that *King Lear* has been adapted at least twice to tell the story of a once great actor whose craft has been superseded by self-interested commercialism. As a result, each film's 'Lear' channels something of the highly theatrical Prospero. In *The Tempest*'s epilogue, Prospero addresses the audience not just as a duke who has given up magic, but also as an actor-playwright who is abjuring theatre: 'release me from my bands/ With the help of your good hands' (5.Epilogue.9–10). But that double renunciation is necessary for a two-fold return to the past—Prospero to his dukedom in Milan, and Shakespeare to his family in Stratford. Indian film *King Lear*s likewise abjure theatre; yet they also reclaim it as a bulwark against the threat of nothingness.

The Marathi film *Natsamrat* (2016)—based on the acclaimed 1970 play of the same name by Kusumagraj—is a tragedy about a retired stage actor, Ganpat (Nana Patekar), who loses everything in a storm by placing too much trust in his treacherous, grasping children. Yet the film's ending, in which Ganpat returns to a playhouse surrounded by memories of his great performances from days gone by, is more *Tempest* than *King Lear*. Ganpat again becomes his past characters: 'mee aahe Prataprao. Mee Othello (I am Prataprao. I am Othello).' His last words are 'do you understand... that this is what theatre is all about? To fulfil one's longing.' The man who has had to give up theatre joyously regains it. Tragic nothingness shades into the 'fulfilment' of romance.

The twinning of *King Lear*'s tragic storm of nothingness and *The Tempest*'s romantic storm of repossession is even more explicit in Bengali director Rituparno Ghosh's English-language film *The Last Lear* (2007). Harish Mishra (Amitabh Bachchan), also known as Harry, is a stage actor from Kolkata who has devoted his life to performing Shakespeare. He has retired because of a tempest of change: classical theatre is becoming obsolete due to the rise of commercial cinema. Yet Harry is prevailed upon by a director, Siddharth (Arjun Rampal), to star in his film, *The Mask*. *The Last Lear* starts with the opening night of *The Mask*; Harry isn't present because, we learn, he has fallen into a coma. His co-star Shabnam (Preity Zinta) also skips the opening to visit Harry, and she speaks with his wife, Vandana (Shefali Shah), and his nurse, Ivy (Divya Dutta). In flashback, we learn what has put Harry in a coma. He has been persuaded to do the movie because he respects Siddharth's knowledge of Shakespeare. Initially dismissive of Shabnam's commercial acting career, Harry has paternally bonded with her on the set, getting her to perform Cordelia's reunion scene with Lear. But he is critically injured when he insists on performing a stunt for the film that requires him to dive off a Himalayan cliff.

So far so Lear. But *The Last Lear* is more than an adaptation of *King Lear*. It is also, like *Shakespeare Wallah*, a film that reflects self-consciously on Shakespeare's status in a new India. Both *The Last Lear* and *Shakespeare Wallah* see Shakespeare as a bastion of supposedly pure art laid to siege by the storm of commercialization. Ghosh came up with the story for his film after seeing Utpal Dutt's play, *Aajker Shahjahan* (Today's Shah Jahan, 1971), which is also about a stage actor whose art has been rendered obsolete in the new age of cinema. This actor is not an aficionado of Shakespeare, but of Bengali theatre. Yet Dutt's play chimes with the tragic sensibility of *King Lear*. Rituparno Ghosh, who gave Dutt joint billing as co-scriptwriter for *The Last Lear* despite his death fourteen years earlier, makes explicit the Shakespearean subtext of *Aajker Shahjahan*: he teases out its echoes of *King Lear* by crafting a story of a cantankerous old man, his vexed relations with three younger women, and a jump from a precipice.

But Ghosh's understanding of the storm of historical change is very different from Dutt's. *Aajker Shahjahan* values the impure forms and languages of an older Bengali theatre that—like the Calcutta playhouse of Saikat Majumdar's *The Firebird*—combines elements of local and foreign drama. By contrast, *The Last Lear* is a deracinated English-language film that genuflects at the altar of a singular Shakespeare-devta. This devta is the antithesis of masala: he is Thomas Macaulay's Shakespeare, the repository of high art rather than mixture. In *The Last Lear's* romance of a golden age of theatrical purity assaulted by a corrupt, fallen age of commercialism, we can see how the film channels less *King Lear* than *The Tempest*.

Indeed, *The Last Lear* refers repeatedly to *The Tempest*. When Siddharth is trying to persuade Harry to sign up for *The Mask*, he impresses the actor by correctly identifying Harry's quotations of Ariel from the second scene of the play. Siddharth then cannily mentions Harry's past performances of Prospero:

SIDDHARTH: But I've always heard your best performances were in *The Tempest*, as Prospero.
HARRY: Which Prospero? Bombay, Madras, Calcutta? Act Five? Act Two? Which?

And then, to show off his acting chops, Harry performs Prospero's 'rough magic' speech. It is a bizarre sequence, made all the more bizarre by Bachchan's delivery: he doesn't so much speak the lines as bark them. This is the performance of an undirected ham. Yet Ghosh wants us to think the performance has a magical power. Seconds before Harry begins the speech, the sun is shining through the windows of his Kolkata apartment. Once he starts, the light changes: Harry is now lit in an eerie green, and the soundtrack becomes stormy. The sequence, which disrupts the realism of the film, evokes the storm of change that has forced Harry to abjure the 'magic' of theatre and reduced his great art, Lear-like, to nothing.

Yet this is a strangely masala episode. Ghosh has reproduced the cinematic syntax of the masala movie item number, where a fantasy scene of naach-gaana showcases a star performer. There may be no naach in

Harry's 'rough magic' sequence—unless the sight of Bachchan wearing a bad wig and flailing in a robe counts as dancing—and Shakespeare's iambic gaana has been superseded by Bachchan's staccato shouting. But the sequence underlines, and pays homage to, Bachchan's star status. This is a symptomatic paradox of an English-language film that deplores the eclipse of theatrical art by commercial film yet has cast leading Bollywood actors—Bachchan, Zinta, Rampal—in its main parts. They may act differently from how they do in Hindi masala movies. But the film still trades on their star power.

That power lends an extra dimension to Bachchan's performance of Harry's performance of Prospero. We are first invited to understand Prospero's abjuring 'rough magic' as a counterpart to Harry's giving up acting. But the speech isn't just the utterance of a Lear fading into insignificance amidst the storm of progress. It is equally the outburst of a Prospero who gives up darkness to repossess something pure. The sequence prods the audience to realize that this is no longer Harry Mishra but Amitabh Bachchan, Hindi cinema icon, speaking. And the 'rough magic' he abjures is not acting but his own Bollywood career. For the film seeks not just to capitalize on Bachchan's film-star power but also to rebrand it by having him endorse 'classical' Shakespeare over contemporary entertainment. In other words, the film inhabits the darkness of Bollywood commercialism to conjure up a pure Shakespeare, just as *The Tempest* resorts to the darkness of colonialist capitalism to conjure up feudalism. *The Last Lear*'s romance of return takes the form of what we might call Englutva—a species of Anglophone fundamentalism whose sacred scripture is the works of Shakespeare. In its piety, Englutva utterly erases the impure, masala qualities of Shakespeare's drama.

Several conclusions can be drawn from these four Indian mash-ups of *The Tempest* and *King Lear*. First, Shakespeare's two storm plays loom large in the imaginations of Indian writers, artists, and directors. Moreover, their storms serve a powerful function as metaphors for the turbulent transformations wrought in modern India by development and commercialization. Yet the consequences of these transformations are open to a wide array of interpretations. The devastation of *King Lear*'s post-storm landscape is echoed in reimaginings of *The Tempest* like Aranya's or Samyuktha's. But *Natsamrat* and *The Last Lear* dream of returning to a golden age in ways that are more redolent of *The Tempest*. This suggests something of the current allure of imagined Indian pasts as a corrective to the storms of progress.

For all their generic masala, their mixing of tragedy and romance, what gets erased in *Natsamrat* and *The Last Lear* is the genuinely radical masala potential of Shakespeare's storm plays. *King Lear* hints at how, in a storm and its aftermath, every human being—whether rich or poor—is part of a larger, interconnected environment that includes a multiplicity of non-human elements too. Let's call this interconnection masala ecology. A version of masala ecology can be glimpsed also in Caliban's assurance to two frightened Europeans, Stephano and Trinculo, that 'the isle is full of noises,/ Sounds and sweet airs that give delight and hurt not' (3.2.130–1). The Europeans take the sounds as proof that they are surrounded by demons that need to be driven out. Caliban understands the sounds as emanating from a collectivity of spirit and animal beings who share the island, in fair as much as stormy weather. He is capable of living with, and in, difference. But an unholy pairing of capitalist individualism and fundamentalist nostalgia is making Indians repudiate masala ecology and seek solace instead in dangerous dreams of purification. A storm is brewing in India. And masala's future is in question.

◆

Preti Taneja's brilliant and brutal novel, *We That Are Young* (2017), dares to dream of masala ecology. It does so through a reimagining of *King Lear* set in Delhi, Punjab and Kashmir. And fascinatingly, this reimagining is again touched by *The Tempest*. Narrated by counterparts to the five next-generation children in *King Lear*—Lear's three daughters and Gloucester's two sons—the novel presents a chilling portrait of the economic, religious and political storms that are transforming India from a land of many voices into a totalitarian dystopia. Crucially, these metaphorical storms are also helping to create real ones.

At the novel's centre is a horrific toofaan. The storm's ground zero is a basti near Amritsar, where Devraj Bapuji—the former maharajah of (the fictional) Napurthala and CEO of the Company, India's wealthiest industrial organization—takes shelter after he has fled the posh hotel in which his daughters Gargi and Radha are staying. He has earlier handed over the management of the Company to them in exchange for their professions of deep love. Bapuji continues to swan around the country with his Hundred, a retinue of corporate male lackeys, making increasingly mad yet popular speeches about how his daughters are ruining Company and country. Yet he still expects Gargi and Radha to extend him and his flunkies every courtesy. When he descends on the Company's Amritsar hotel, his daughters raise questions about his behaviour, and he storms off into the night. He strays into the Dhimbala basti adjoining the hotel, accompanied only by his elderly mother, Nanu, who is given to speaking in cryptic parables and verses. When the toofaan hits, it causes untold devastation to the slum. First it cakes the basti in sand, and then it drowns its nine circles—an echo of Dante's vision of Hell—in an apocalyptic flood. Countless slum dwellers drown. But somehow Bapuji and Nanu survive.

Bapuji is discovered in the storm by Jeet, the missing son of the Company's managing director, Ranjit Singh. Jeet is a closeted homosexual with spiritual yearnings. Fingered for illicit trade in valuable old Indian artworks, he has been encouraged to skip town by his scheming bastard half-brother, Jivan. Jeet too has found refuge in the Dhimbala basti. There he has masqueraded, despite his Sikh background, as a holy Hindu renunciate. After he has tended to the storm-drenched Bapuji, he joins him as a speaker in public morchas against corruption. Bapuji, inspired by his experience in the basti, has refashioned himself as an advocate for the aam aadmi against the corruption of industrialists. It is literally the aadmi, not the aurat, he champions: Bapuji's anti-corruption campaign is waged explicitly against the corruption of his daughters in particular and women in general. This misogyny is cheered on by crowds all over India, and applauded by the equally misogynist Jeet. Playing Ramdev Baba to Bapuji's Anna Hazare, Jeet becomes an increasingly full-throated advocate for a muscular, nationalist Hindutva. After the storm, he returns to the Dhimbala basti; he organizes the male residents into cadres, dividing them by 'caste and sect', and encourages them 'to compete in Yoga positions and to sing the national anthem before doing eka hasta bhujasana in the dirt'. Jeet's return to the basti is the prologue to his eventual takeover of the Company following the deaths of Bapuji and his three daughters. Jeet by name, jeet (victory) by nature. But it isn't just his own jeet: it is the jeet of a new generation of Indians, defined by a cynical marriage of convenience between crony capitalism and religious fundamentalism.

We That Are Young's storm serves several functions. It is a critical turning point in Bapuji's and Jeet's stories, pushing each down the path of populist spiritual-political activism. This activism seems to follow the model of the original 'Bapu', Gandhi. Like the Mahatma, Bapuji speaks to adoring audiences across the nation and threatens fasts to the death to achieve his political aims. But the storm isn't just a plot point. As in *King Lear*, it is also a metaphor for the devastating economic and social developments that are convulsing India. And the storm is more than a metaphor. *We That Are Young* goes beyond Shakespeare's play by underscoring Amitav Ghosh's insistence that bad weather is the 'mysterious work of our own hands returning to haunt us in unthinkable shapes and forms'. The metaphorical storm of economic development is responsible not just for the mountains of trash that we see in the Dhimbala basti. It has also created the atmospheric conditions for the horrific tempest that strikes it. Masala ecology knows that the more we try to harness nature's resources, the more nature will push back against us. Those resources aren't simply there for the taking.

Jeet's credo suggests otherwise. It entails a volatile mix of nationalism, Hindutva, and voracious material greed. As he says, in a nightmare passage that follows the storm,

> We that believe in India shining… We that believe we are better than all others. We that are the youngest, the fastest, the democracy, the economy, the future technology of the world, the global Super Power coming soon to a cinema near you, we, hum panch, that are the five cousins of the five great rivers, everybody our brother-sister-lover, we that are divine: the echo of the ancient heroes of the old times, we that fight, we that love, we that are hungry, so, so hungry, we that are young! We that are jigging on the brink of ruin; we that are washed in the filth of corruption; chal, so what? Aise hi hota hai: we that are a force of all that is natural—slow—death to Muslims, gays, chhi-chhi women in their skin-tights, hai! We that sit picnicking on the edge of our crumbling civilization… we that are the future of this planet, we that begin with this beloved India, will endure, yes, it all belongs to us, and we will eat it all. All of it is ours, we that are India and no longer slaves. We that are young!

This is the novel's true storm: Jeet's all-consuming path, which valorizes masculinist capitalism even as it claims to resurrect 'tradition', which creates real storms because of its utter disregard for the environment, which destroys masala by backing the I over the more-than-one.

The storm in the basti literalizes this destruction of masala. In spite of its hell-like qualities, Dhimbala is also as close as *We That Are Young* comes to imagining a masala community. The novel's other locations are all bubble worlds of bhadrata or class privilege: a wealthy Delhi farmhouse, an air-conditioned Delhi office, the swank bedrooms and bars of Company hotels. The basti is a stinking open-air alternative to these claustrophobic spaces of privilege. Its circles are populated by an assortment of Muslims and Christians as well as Hindus. During the storm, they help each other—and Bapuji, Nanu and Jeet—with scant regard for anyone's class, caste, or religious community. But under Jeet's influence in the storm's aftermath, the slum's masala mixture is spatially subdivided and ideologically purified. Militant Hinduism and aspirational consumerism are the only games left in town.

Nevertheless, pluralism remains the irreducible foundation of *We That Are Young*. It's crucial that the pronoun of the novel's title is 'we.' In Jeet's nightmare of India, the pronoun acquires something of the chilling fascist uniformity of the royal 'we'. But throughout the novel, 'we' is irreducibly plural. *We That Are Young*'s five narrators each have distinctive voices: Jivan, the Harvard-educated prodigal bastard son of Ranjit Singh, speaks an American English; Gargi, the workaholic Delhi University commerce graduate, speaks a corporate English; Radha, the pretty party girl, speaks a high-class Delhi English; Sita, the Cambridge-educated eco-feminist, speaks a very proper English; and Jeet, the aspirational guru, speaks an English filled with chaste Sanskrit and Napurthali. Yet these aren't five singular linguistic tracks. All the narrators' voices are mixed, as each speaks large amounts of untranslated Hindi. And these voices are displaced in turn by very different ones from the working and slum classes. *We That Are Young*, however, chronicles the historical tempest that works to replace many voices with one. Jeet's victory represents the temporary triumph of a certain kind of Indian voice, one that aspires to singularity. But it cannot shake off mixture.

In this sense, Jeet is not just a closeted homosexual. He is more precisely a closeted pluralist. He is a secular Sikh but masquerades as a Hindu ascetic. He loves Urdu poetry but calls for a Sanskritized Ram Rashtra. His best friend is Gargi but he loathes women. He loves his Kashmiri boyfriend but he takes over a Company that exploits the Valley and its people. To this extent, he is less Edgar than he is Prospero. Like Prospero, he is dispatched into exile for a supposedly shameful act in a past that we do not see. Like Prospero, he longs to regain his former power. Like Prospero, or like Amitabh-Bachan-as-Harry-as-Prospero, he fully embodies the multiplicity of masala even as he repudiates it.

But Jeet isn't the novel's only Prospero. The name of the Company invokes, through its echo of the East India Company, a history of colonialism. And, as in *The Tempest*, the history of colonialism is linked to a theatricality that combines feudal spectacles of power with profit-driven manipulations of illusions. The very word 'Company' suggests a theatre as much as a business. And Bapuji is both a feudal player and a capitalist actor. Bapuji is given to theatrical displays of his feudal might: he wears diamonds on his bandhgala, even in the basti, as he performs his outrage on behalf of the aam aadmi. But he is also involved in a longer-term, more calculating theatre for profit directed against the daughters he feels have wronged him. The distinctive fusion of feudal patriarchy and capitalist profiteering that we witness in vengeful Bapuji—a typically Indian phenomenon—makes him a Prospero as much as a Lear. His mixed feudal-capitalist power, like Prospero's, is partly dependent on the manipulation of information in the ether. One of the most ingenious presences in Taneja's novel is a shadowy Twitter handle, @MrGee, which disseminates dubious news about Bapuji and the Company. This handle is arguably the Ariel of *We That Are Young*. Like Shakespeare's spirit, @MrGee's posts occasionally question the patriarch's acts—but, by and large, fall in line with them.

But who is the novel's Caliban? The slum-boy Samir, who shows Jeet every inch of the basti just as Caliban shows Prospero every inch of the island? The Company worker who is beaten to within an inch of his life by Bapuji? The Kashmiris who are at the receiving end of the Company's neo-colonial designs in the Valley? I was able to pose the question of who the novel's Caliban is to Preti Taneja. She gave me an interesting answer: she said that she herself is its Caliban. For Caliban says to Prospero, 'You taught me language, and my profit on't is I know how to curse' (1.2.366–67). Born in Britain to an immigrant Punjabi mother, Taneja has taken the English and Shakespeare of her mother's adopted island and wickedly hybridized both, giving us a novel written in a Hindi-haunted English that tells us a *Tempest*-haunted tale of *King Lear*. The novel could be renamed *We That Are More-Than-One*. Its India is masala still, but battered by the storms of progress. Battered, too, by the very real storms that these metaphorical tempests are spawning.

◆

I finished this chapter on a June afternoon in Delhi. As I typed its last words, the bright sunlight imperceptibly began to dim. Suddenly the sky turned a reddish brown, then pitch black. It was only 5.30 p.m., but it was darker than midnight. A colossal dust-storm, carrying more of the Thar Desert than I'd like to imagine, had completely blackened the sky. Huge gusts battered the trees outside; two groaned and fell with a hideous, tearing crash. As I peered out the window, I saw the corrugated iron walls of a building site unfasten themselves and lurch into the sky, pursued by a flock of flapping plastic bags. I was reminded of a haunting line in Taneja's novel, an epigrammatic statement with the imagistic precision of a haiku: 'everywhere the wind catches filth and whirls it upwards, strange plastic birds taking flight'. These plastic birds are not an act of God. They are the detritus of industry, the detritus of a nation experiencing metastatic growth, the detritus of a seemingly unstoppable orgy of me-first-ness that is drying up rivers, felling forests, and driving ever more parched topsoil and construction dust into the air. And this storm isn't abating.

ACT FIVE SCENE THREE

Exit MASALA (*Manet PERICLES*)

A storm is brewing in Indian film conversations with Shakespeare. One of the storm's harbingers is *The Hungry* (2017), directed by Bornila Chatterjee. This film reimagines a play I never thought I would see on Indian screens: Shakespeare's earliest tragedy, *Titus Andronicus*. Chatterjee has adapted this shockingly violent revenge play about rape, mutilation and cannibalism by moving it from its classical Roman setting and relocating it to a modern Punjabi shaadi. The main character is no longer the Titus Andronicus counterpart—renamed here Tathagat Ahuja (Naseeruddin Shah)—but his nemesis Tulsi Joshi (Tisca Chopra), based on Shakespeare's Tamora, the wicked Queen of the Goths. In Chatterjee's reworking, Shakespeare's tale about the wrongs done to the Andronicus family by Tamora and her villainous Moorish lover Aaron is transformed into a story of women wronged by greedy, violent men.

The Hungry is in many ways a powerful film. But it is not masala Shakespeare. The style of this 'Indian' film is anything but Indian; the Punjabi wedding setting notwithstanding, it has very little that belongs to the grammar of the masala movie. There is no naach-gaana, no high sentimentalism leavened by comedy, no partition busting, no interest in class or community mixture. Even though it channels *Monsoon Wedding*, in which Naseeruddin Shah likewise appears as the family patriarch in a story about a large wedding roiled by scandal, it does not take on board Nair's interest in diverse classes and religious communities. *The Hungry* dabbles in touches of local colour such as the haldi paste applied to bride and groom at the shaadi, or an Iqbal poem recited by Naseeruddin Shah's character (the only acknowledgement of Indian Muslims in a story that consists entirely of Hindu characters). But just as the dialogue drops snatches of Hindi into what is mostly an English script, so are these touches of local colour rare sprinklings of Indian content upon what is otherwise a predominantly Western cinematic canvas. Although Naseeruddin Shah's character insists that 'hum log zameen se ugein hain (we have sprung from the soil)', the dark soil of this movie is coloured the shade of Western film noir and horror. Likewise, even as *The Hungry* depicts a Punjabi wedding, its musical soundtrack consists of a European orchestra playing demented chamber music.

The absence of a masala sensibility from *The Hungry* is no surprise. Bornila Chatterjee was trained at film school in New York and imbibed there the idioms of Hollywood and European arthouse cinema alike. Masala movies can involve no end of blood and guts (think of the abundant blood of *Goliyon Ki Rasleela Ram-Leela*). But masala violence is often of a highly stylized, operatic kind that alternates between laughable dhishoom fights and aesthetically appealing daubs of crimson on its beaten heroes. *The Hungry*, by contrast, presents us with scenes from the 'gross-out' syntax of Western horror: Loveleen, Tathagat Ahuja's daughter, is gruesomely disfigured by Chirag—her tongue ripped out, her face pounded to pulp; Chirag is in turn hung up by Tathagat Ahuja in his kitchen and turned into a shaadi meal, with bones reminiscent of Ridley Scott's *Alien* (1979) decorating the banquet.

But what most makes *The Hungry* an instance of non-masala Shakespeare is its production background and release platform. The film was commissioned and bankrolled by a British company, Film London, as a commemoration of Shakespeare's four-hundredth death anniversary. And, after screening in several global film festivals (Toronto, London, Rome), *The Hungry* went straight to view-on-demand (VOD) on Amazon Prime. That platform—doubtless part of Film London's pre-production creative and marketing strategy—has had a huge effect on the form of Chatterjee's film.

Speaking of the virtues of the new view-on-demand platforms, Chatterjee has told an interviewer that:

> In theory, I love the experience of watching film in a theatre but, in practice, it usually amounts to bad sound and/or bad projection and/or fellow audience members who are doing a whole bunch of things—talking, laughing, texting, eating, breathing—just way too loudly for me. With VOD I get to control the environment in which I watch content and I love that. More importantly, I have 24/7 access to a whole bunch of content that I would never have the chance to see otherwise. I am a fan.

Chatterjee repeats a claim commonly heard in Anglophone India. VOD entertainment, it is argued, has enabled a content revolution that is providing Indian viewers with better stories and more choices. But what gets forgotten in the fetishization of innovative content is the radical transformation of cinematic form—not just the form of a film's style but also the form of its consumption. *The Hungry* reflects the conditions of VOD film viewing: it presumes a private, elite viewership—we could, inspired by its musical soundtrack, call this viewership a chamber movie audience. The film is set almost entirely indoors, in darkened rooms that are surprisingly empty, despite the shaadi setting. This is the opposite of the crowded masala movie frame, which even when already full—like an overloaded Haryanvi scooter rickshaw or a crammed train carrying more passengers on its roof—always finds room for one more actor, one more dancer, one more junior artiste. *The Hungry*'s sparsely populated frame replaces the masala ethos of the more-than-one with the VOD aesthetic of 'you-are-the-one', catering to the private, individual consumer uninterrupted (in Chatterjee's words) by 'fellow audience members who are doing a whole bunch of things'.

This new aesthetic is best illustrated by a quick comparison of the last scenes of *Titus Andronicus* and *The Hungry*. Shakespeare's play concludes with a gruesome banquet at which Titus (wearing the garb of a cook) serves Tamora, the Roman Emperor Saturninus, his family, and the Goth army a shocking feast as revenge for the rape of his daughter Lavinia by Tamora's two sons, Demetrius and Chiron. The sons, savagely slaughtered and baked into a meat pie, are fed not just to Tamora but also to all the diners. The stage direction spells out how huge the dinner party is: '*The Company sits at the table.*' The word 'Company' indicates that the entire cast are seated onstage, making the banquet a collective ritual feast. Romans and Goths, patricians and plebeians break bread. And bones. For all the sickening gruesomeness of the gathering, Shakespeare's 'Company' represents a comradely plurality that reflects a sense of its mixed audience too.

In *The Hungry*, Tathagat Ahuja serves only the married couple—Tulsi and her groom, his coke-addled son, Sunny. There is no sense of a community coming together, which makes for an odd resolution to a Punjabi wedding. Tathagat kills his son, but is then killed himself, leaving Tulsi alive, alone at the table. This is, the film seems to say, a gender empowering moment where the wronged woman survives the man who has done so much damage to her (he has had one of her sons killed two years previously, and the other cooked into the wedding banquet). But it is hard not to see Tulsi, solitary and triumphant, less as a wronged woman than an onscreen version of Chatterjee's ideal VOD viewer who gets 'to control the environment' in splendid isolation.

The Hungry is representative of the new media of Indian entertainment.

I am not just speaking of VOD and online viewing platforms such as Amazon Prime and Netflix. It is part of a more wholesale fragmentation of viewers into niche groups. Increasingly audiences are cut off from other viewers, especially if they are from different classes, castes, religions, and linguistic communities. And this homogenization of niche audiences fosters an intolerance for social mixture: what else does Chatterjee's eye-rolling objection to venues full of 'talking, laughing, texting, eating, breathing' refer to? With cultural, political and market forces increasingly denying film-makers the means to assemble such diverse viewerships, the masala movie as we know it is withering on the vine.

What does this mean for masala Shakespeare? I would like to think that something of the masala ethos will survive in Indian conversations with Shakespeare. The country is too diverse for it not to. But it will most likely survive more outside the cinema than in it. In particular, I am hopeful that masala will continue to find a home in theatre. Masala Shakespeare is already thriving in new dramatic entertainments that draw on Indian folk forms of entertainment. We can see it in the extraordinary success of *Piya Behrupiya*. And we can see it in smaller-scale attempts by theatre groups to reimagine Shakespeare in Indian contexts. A storm is brewing, but masala isn't going away.

◆

In 2014, shortly after I moved to Delhi, I was elected President of the Shakespeare Society of India. I was an 'Indian' of only a few months standing, so it was hard not to feel a little like a cultural impostor. But for someone who had in his childhood never felt quite Jewish or Kiwi enough, the experience of failing to coincide with my supposed identity was by now deeply familiar and even vaguely comforting. Besides, one of the joys of the Shakespeare Society of India was how ardently it embraced Shakespeare in many accents and tongues. There was no English purism here, nor no deracinated globalism.

If Bornila Chatterjee's *The Hungry* represented a non-masala response to the four-hundred year anniversary of Shakespeare's death, the Shakespeare Society of India's 2016 conference, *Shakespeare's Ashes*, was in some ways *The Hungry*'s polar opposite. The conference show-stopper was an unusual theatrical performance, *Chahat ki Dastaan* (Story of Desire), in which Indian actors, dancers, poets, and scholars presented twenty-two of Shakespeare's Sonnets translated into eleven Indian languages and forms—Urdu qawwali, Malayalam mohiniattam,

Tamil bharatanatyam, Khasi folk song, Kashmiri shayari, Punjabi naatak, Hindustani ghazal, English slam poetry, Chhattisgarhi nacha, Hinglish monologue, and Bengali baul. This was no mere multilingual gimmick. *Chahat ki Dastaan* succeeded in doing something both completely Shakespearean and entirely Indian. And that is because the poetry of each repeatedly swerves across boundaries, refusing the straitjacket of one track—or one language. The performer-creators celebrated, individually and collectively, how Shakespeare and India alike are comprised of mixtures that result in unexpected confluences and conversations.

Chahat ki Dastaan was a counterpoint to one of the most successful annual events organized by the Shakespeare Society of India: the National Drama Competition, which stages short half-hour adaptations of Shakespeare by college troupes from across the country. In recent years, the best adaptations have been not in English but in mixed Indian tongues. A significant contributing factor to this linguistic diversification has been the growing involvement of student actors from non-English or mixed-language backgrounds. The competition's most consistently brilliant performances have been a sequence of Urdu-Hindustani re-imaginings of Shakespeare created by students from Zakir Husain College in Delhi. Written by Danishmand Khan and featuring two unusually talented actors in Zeeshan Khan and Arham Sayeed Quadri, the Zakir Husain College re-imaginings of Shakespeare have drawn inspiration equally from north Indian history, Vishal Bhardwaj's films, and Urdu poetry. Their contribution to the 2015 competition, *Zafar*, was an inspired adaptation of *Julius Caesar*. It relocated Shakespeare's Roman play to a medieval Mughal court; but it also drew on Faiz Ahmed Faiz's poetry, set to music, to provide a drama of political intrigue born not of period nostalgia but conversation with the present. Similarly, their contribution to the 2016 competition—*Raana*, an adaptation of *Richard the Third* filled with music as well as Urdu shayari and Hindi prose—again featured Zeeshan Khan in the lead role, playing a charismatic nineteenth-century Indian strongman reminiscent not just of Shakespeare's famous crookback king but also certain contemporary political figures. The two plays underscored for me how much masala Shakespeare is more than a genre of entertainment. It is also a sensibility born of conversation across supposed differences—Hindu and Muslim, Hindi and Urdu, Hindustani and English, India and Shakespeare, present and past. Inspired by the Zakir Husain College students' example, I was determined to explore the possibilities of masala Shakespeare with my own students at Ashoka University.

In 2018, an Ashoka University colleague and I worked with a group of six students on an adaptation of Shakespeare's romance *Pericles*. The group had already 'adapted' Shakespeare's lost play, *Cardenio*, the previous year, working with his ostensible source—an episode in Miguel Cervantes's *Don Quixote*—and a likely eighteenth-century rewrite by Lewis Theobald called *Double Falsehood*. But their reimagining of *Pericles* was a more direct conversation with a text by Shakespeare.

Pericles, Prince of Tyre is arguably the most masala entertainment in the Shakespearean canon. It is a generic khichdi, veering between tragedy and comedy, fight sequences and scenes of sentimental reunion, spectacle and song. It is even of mixed authorship, as Shakespeare co-wrote it in 1607 with a junior playwright named George Wilkins. It features royalty, jousting knights, a goddess, and a large assortment of low types—fishermen, sailors, pirates, and bawds. Its action ricochets between Europe, Asia, and Africa. It lurches abruptly from one time to another, covering decades in its two-hour traffic onstage. It is patched up from multiple sources, drawing on a medieval adaptation of an old tale, *Apollonius of Tyre*, a recent novella, *The Pattern of Painful Adventures*, and Philip Sidney's *Arcadia*, from which it has plucked a new name for its titular character. It alternates between soaring poetry and dull prose. And it takes the author of its medieval source, Sir John Gower, and makes him the narrator, creating a masala onion of sorts in which the play effectively functions as a story within a play. All these mixed elements attracted the ire of Aristotelian-minded critics; the Victorian scholar Edward Dowden lamented that *Pericles* 'entirely lacks unity of action'. But its mixtures made it a hit with its earliest audiences, who flocked to it in huge numbers.

It was most likely *Pericles*'s masala qualities that also made it very popular, in adapted naach-gaana form, among pre-Independence Indian audiences. A Gujarati version by Dosabhai Framji Randhelia, *Daad-e-Dariya urf Khusro na Khavind Khuda* (Salute of the Seas, or, The Almighty is Khusro's Protector), was performed in the late nineteenth century. Karimuddin Murad Barelvi wrote a liberally reimagined Urdu version called *Badshah Khudadad* (King Khudadad, i.e. Gift of God) for the Parsi theatre in 1890. Another version called simply *Khudadad*, by Jahangir Pestonjee Khambatta, was staged in 1898; it was transformed into a film version of the same name in 1935. And in 1891, a Malayalam adaptation—*Pariklesharajavinte Katha* (Pericles's Life Story)—was written by P. Velu. Clearly, something about the mixed worlds of *Pericles* spoke to the mixed Indian audiences in the Parsi and Malayalam theatres. But something else in the play may have attracted the attention of its nineteenth-century Indian adaptors. Like so many of Shakespeare's later plays, *Pericles* is storm-ridden. What makes it different from *King Lear* or *The Tempest* is that it features more than one storm. Even its weather, then, features the more-than-oneness of masala.

There are two physical storms in *Pericles*. The first shipwrecks Pericles on the shores of Pentapolis, where he meets the woman he will marry, Thaisa. The second strikes as Pericles travels back to Tyre with Thaisa; she seems to die while giving birth to their daughter, Marina, and her body is cast overboard. Both these storms, in typical Shakespearean fashion, are endings that are also beginnings. And these physical storms are accompanied by a sequence of other turbulences in the social order.

These storms in certain ways resemble those of *King Lear* and *The Tempest*. They threaten in tragic fashion to smash everything into oblivion: Pericles is, after the second storm, a broken shell of a man. They also hold out the promise of regaining what has been lost: he is eventually reunited with both Marina and Thaisa. But there is a third outcome of the storms, one that is perhaps more significant in this context. The world of mixture that *Pericles* embodies manages to survive each *toofaan*.

The students who adapted *Pericles* underscored for me the indestructibility of masala. On the one hand, all six of them are children of the VOD era. They have come of age watching films on their laptops courtesy of Netflix and Amazon Prime. They are more fluent in what is current in Hollywood and US TV than I am. On the other hand, they have a keen sense of the infinite variety, and divergence between, different cultural styles of performance. Some of them have been trained in bharatanatyam, Hindustani and Carnatic classical music, even in Bollywood dance. Just as they swerve between English and their local bhashas, so, too, do they swerve between different modes of entertainment. Mixture is the irreducible building block of their sense of self and of the world in which they live. This was apparent in their reimagining of *Pericles*. They named it *Hera-Phericles*, a cross-lingual wordplay that evokes the title of a Hindi movie franchise, *Hera Pheri* (Crooked Designs, 2000).

The students' greatest innovation was to dispense with a single stage. Intrigued by the episodic nature of *Pericles*, they wanted to convey something of the play's restless movement, its refusal to stay grounded. They wanted the audience to experience movement not just in what they saw but also in their own embodied response to the performance.

So they hit upon the idea of staging the play entirely on the perimeter of the theatre, creating multiple performance spaces against its four walls. The audience, rather than sitting and facing in one direction for the duration of the performance, would have to keep moving as the action moved, led by Gower (Purvai Aranya) as a sutradhar figure.

The audience's physical movement was mirrored by the production's formal shape-shifting. Each of the theatre's four walls was reserved for a different style of performance from a different part of the subcontinent, bringing with it a different linguistic landscape. The first wall featured a television screen on which a sequence in the style of a Bombay soap opera played. Here the audience were introduced to members of Pericles's sanyukt parivaar, presided over by a Dadi (Ira Sen), who alternated between English and Bambaiyya Hindi. The second wall was the scene of a highly stylized Tamil therukkuttu dance, performed by Pericles (Anirudh Saigal) and a woman warrior (Sreya Muthukumar), and accompanied by a mridangam player (Goutam Piduri). The third wall featured an Urdu thumri and kathak dance, performed by Pericles's daughter (Sreya Muthukumar) and watched by Thaisa (Udeshi Basu). The fourth wall was where Gower delivered her English epilogue, but also interrupted it to question characters on the other walls. Storms punctuated the scenes enacted against the various walls, seeming to wipe clean the slate each time in order to usher in a new style of performance. But these storms could not wipe away the mixtures that each style embodied.

Hera-Phericles is a thoughtful meditation on how mixture survives the storms of change. It is an allegory too for the survival of masala. The students' performance offers a reminder that the masala politics of the mixed crowd, and the more-than-oneness of India, lives on in various venues—the university, but also the bazaar, the train, the dhaba, the cricket match. These venues may be shrinking in number and influence as India's middle classes increasingly congregate in walled off, air-conditioned spaces such as multiplexes, malls, and airport terminals. And yet, as the old adage goes: pessimism of the intellect, optimism of the will. No matter how much the new technologically-driven VOD platforms and the politically-driven segregation of communities may divide us from each other, the sheer pressure of population in a country as diverse and overcrowded as India means we will still have to come face to face with people who are not like us, and make our peace with living alongside them. The question is whether we have the will, in a time of growing fundamentalism in the political sphere and increasing consumer atomization in the economic sphere, to respect the ethics of mixture in our art as much as our lived lives.

◆

In the future the desi may well do without the firangi. We await our new Kalidasa, our new Khusro, our new Kshetrayya. But when she comes, she will not speak to us in Sanskrit or Urdu, or English or Hindi, or Tamil or Kashmiri, or even Bengali. She will no doubt speak in some blended tongue that we cannot yet predict. And she will do so in a mixed medium that we cannot yet imagine, conversing with a mixed audience whose mode of association and spaces of assembly we cannot yet conceive. It will be a masala to come. The storms of so-called progress may shatter masala Shakespeare and much of what it stands for. But no storm can rid us of mixture. After all, in a mixed country in a mixed world, there can be no end to masala.

Hum toh aise hi honge, bhaiyon aur behenon. Aur actually hum toh always aise hi the.

ACKNOWLEDGEMENTS

As only befits a homage to pluralism and the more-than-one, this book has been the product of conversations with hundreds of people over many years. More voices than I can possibly name have offered suggestions, counter-views and tight slap-cum-corrections that have guided me in some way. But it would be remiss of me not to thank the following people in particular:

Poonam Saxena, who many years ago gave me space in the *Hindustan Times* to publish an article about *Lagaan* that ended up being the seed of this book, and who always instinctively understood my argument about why masala is so important to the idea of India.

Namrata Joshi, who a few years later gave me a chance to apply my argument about masala to Shakespeare in an article for *Outlook*.

Monojit Majumdar, who invited me to write in the *Indian Express* about the anti-Romeo squads and unwittingly coaxed what had been a series of articles into becoming a book.

Aparna Sen, Basharat Peer, Preti Taneja, Saikat Majumdar, Tim Supple, and Vishal Bhardwaj, who all took time to talk with me at length about their various creative visions of Shakespeare.

My fellow executive board members of the Shakespeare Society of India while I was its unlikely president—Supriya Chaudhuri, Harriet Raghunathan, Jobim Thomas, Anavisha Banerjee, Vikram Chopra, Payal Nagpal, and Anannya Dasgupta—who gave me wonderful Shakespeare colleagues and a venue in which to present early versions of my argument.

My hero, Ranjit Hoskote, one of the most brilliant thinkers of transcultural mixing and confluence, who backed this project from the beginning and invited me to speak about it in Bombay.

My Goan friends Luis Francisco Dias, Vivek Menezes, Frederick Noronha and Rafael Fernandes, who did able detective work on my behalf at a critical juncture.

Countless friends, students and family who helped me with the various languages in which Indian conversations with Shakespeare have been conducted: chief among them Sambuddha and Nivedita Sen as well as Supriya and Sukanta Chaudhuri (Bengali), Chandan Gowda (Kannada), Goutam Piduri (Telugu), Darshana Devarajan (Tamil), Indira Menon (Malayalam), Ishanika Sharma and Anupama Chandra (Hindi), Dan Husain (Urdu), and Vibha Kamat (Marathi).

Thea Buckley, who helped me with *Macbeth* in Kerala and facilitated my participation in the 2016 conference in London about Indian Shakespeare on Screen.

My dear Ashoka University colleagues and fellow Bollywood enthusiasts Rita Kothari and Abir Bazaz, who read the manuscript, directed me to some fascinating source materials, and corrected some of my missteps.

My colleagues in Philosophy, Performing Arts, and Political Science—Alex Watson, Justin McCarthy, and Ali Khan Mahmudabad—who educated me about shunyata, frame stories, therukkuttu and cross-gendering, and the possibilities of the daayraa, proving in the process the virtues of transdisciplinary liberal arts education in India.

My dear friend Nasreen Munni Kabir, who knows more about Bollywood than Bollywood itself does, who provided beautiful archival images when I needed them and put me in touch with many people who could help me on the rare occasions she couldn't, and who has left a larger footprint on this book than nearly anyone.

Atul Kumar, Gulzar, Mehelli Modi, Purvai Aranya, Sharat Katariya and Vishal Bhardwaj, as well as Alliance Media and Entertainment Pvt Ltd, Click to Cherish Photography, Hyphen Films, Minerva Movietone, the National Film Archive of India, Rajshri Productions, Shemaroo Entertainment Ltd, VB Films and Yash Raj Films, for permissions to use images; and Devansh Agarwal, Vijay Kumar, Poonam Surjiani Makecha and Prakash Magdum for their help in sourcing stills.

My brilliant research assistants, Rishabh Raghavan (who tracked down many instances of the figure of the roadside Romeo), Ayesha Verma (who educated me about Utpal Dutt's work and Bengali Shakespeare), Shaurya Oberoi (who translated *Piya Behrupiya* for me), and Goutam Piduri and Ishanika Sharma (who performed double toil and trouble over the last lap, particularly with images and the essay on further reading).

My Ashoka University students, particularly the undergraduates who took my seminars on Spectres of Hamlet in Spring of 2017 and Masala Shakespeare in Spring of 2018, the Young India Fellow postgraduates who took my classes on Shakespeare and the World from June 2012 to November 2017, as well as the six students—Anirudh Saigal, Goutam Piduri, Ira Sen, Purvai Aranya, Sreya Muthukumar and Udeshi Basu—who worked with me on creative re-imaginings of *Cardenio* and *Pericles*.

Cyrus Patell and Katherine Williams Schaap at New York University Abu Dhabi, who for four years have given me and my students a creative as well as intellectual home at the annual NYUAD Global Shakespeares Festival.

My wonderful editor, David Davidar, who embraced me and a book of mine for a second time at Aleph, my brilliant copy-editor, Pujitha Krishnan Fernandes, who once again has been a model of attentive reading and helpful guidance, and her meticulous colleague, Roshan Kumar Mogali, whose keen eye has saved me from many an embarrassment.

My professors Michael Neill, Alan Sinfield and Jonathan Dollimore, who taught me how to read Shakespeare many years ago in New Zealand and the United Kingdom.

My thespian guides Bruce De Grut, Susie Lamb, Linda Cartwright, Raymond Hawthorne and Michael Hurst, who inspired me to listen to Shakespeare long ago in New Zealand.

My parents Norman and Stella, who fostered in me a love of theatre from a very early age.

And the master-mistress of my passion, meri jaan Madhavi, who has inspired my love of India and Bollywood, who is the best reader of Shakespeare I know, and without whom not a word of this could be:

Kisi ki muskurahaton pe ho nisar,
Kisi ka dard mil sake toh le udhaar,
Kisi ke waaste ho tere dil mein pyaar,
Jeena isi ka naam hai.

FURTHER READING

This book owes numerous debts to the ideas of others. Some readers will detect in its general themes—particularly its explorations of the more-than-one, mixture, and multilingualism—the influence of the French theorist Jacques Derrida and the Russian critic Mikhail Bakhtin. Derrida's incredibly difficult but hauntingly beautiful study, *Specters of Marx: The State of the Debt, the Work of Mourning and the New International* (New York: Routledge, 1994), is not just a compelling rereading of Marx after the fall of the Berlin Wall; it is also a mesmerizing attempt to think through the politics of the plus d'un, a French phrase that means both the more-than-one and the less-than-one. It is additionally—and unexpectedly—a sublime reading of *Hamlet* and how it continues to haunt Western understandings of the political. Derrida's ideas have, in ways both obvious and oblique, shaped my own. Bakhtin's influence has been no less significant. His theory of 'heteroglossia', the many voices that pluralize what seems to be a single language, underwrites all of *Masala Shakespeare*. If readers want to explore Bakhtin's theory in more detail, they are recommended to look at Michael Holquist (ed.), *The Dialogic Imagination: Four Essays*, (Austin, Texas: University of Texas Press, 1981).

My thinking about Shakespeare has been influenced in no small way by my teachers—chief among them, Michael Neill at the University of Auckland and Alan Sinfield and Jonathan Dollimore at the University of Sussex. All of them infused in me a deep conviction that the best readings of Shakespeare manage not so much to get the plays 'right' as activate other voices in them. Michael Neill's work on New Zealand adaptations of Shakespeare—for instance, his essay on a Samoan-themed reworking of *Romeo and Juliet*—has been exemplary for me. So, too, has Jonathan Dollimore and Alan Sinfield's insistence that Shakespeare be read from the vantage point of the present and its political imperatives: see their influential collection, *Political Shakespeare: New Essays in Cultural Materialism* (Manchester: Manchester University Press, 1984). Stephen Greenblatt, too, has shaped my thinking about Shakespeare's love of mixture; his book *Shakespeare's Freedom* (Chicago: University of Chicago Press, 2010) not only chronicles Shakespeare's repeated fetishization of adulteration, stains and spots, but also sees in his plays a persistent refusal of absolutism. Greenblatt develops these themes in his meditation on Shakespeare and tyranny, *Tyrant: Shakespeare on Politics* (New York: Norton,

2018). The book is decidedly American in more ways than one, not least in its emphasis on individual liberty rather than the collective; but in its oblique resistance to the rising authoritarianism of Greenblatt's America it is a cousin once removed of *Masala Shakespeare.*

But Indian voices have played an even stronger shaping role in my thinking about masala. Chief among these, as many readers will have gathered, is Salman Rushdie, whose novels—particularly *Midnight's Children* (London: Jonathan Cape, 1981) and *The Moor's Last Sigh* (London: Random House, 1995)—constitute an extended meditation on the ideas of masala and hybridity as foundational to the idea of India. Another teacher of mine at Sussex, Homi K. Bhabha, has theorized mixture in ways that resonate profoundly with Rushdie's novels; his essay 'Of Mimicry and Man: The Ambivalence of Colonial Discourse', published in *October* 28 (1984), pp. 125–33, is rightly regarded as a classic theorization of hybridity. But unlike Bhabha, I see Indian hybridity only secondarily as a product of colonialism and more primarily as intrinsic to a centuries-long history of trans-cultural and trans-lingual encounter. Ania Loomba's inspired essay on Indian Othellos—'"Local-manufacture made-in-India Othello fellows": Issues of race, hybridity and location in post-colonial Shakespeares', in Loomba and Martin Orkin (eds.), *Post-Colonial Shakespeares* (New York: Routledge, 1998), pp. 143–63—was what got me thinking about how subcontinental conversations with Shakespeare are often much more about local hybrid traditions than they are about reimagining Shakespeare's texts.

There is now a very rich body of scholarly work on Indian versions of Shakespeare, onscreen and off. Chief among these is Poonam Trivedi and Dennis Bartholomeusz (eds.), *India's Shakespeare: Translation, Interpretation and Performance* (Delhi: Pearson, 2005). The contributions by Poonam Trivedi on 'Folk Shakespeare' and by Rajiva Verma on 'Shakespeare in Hindi Cinema' have been particularly helpful for me while writing this book. Also helpful have been Shormishtha Panja and Babli Moitra Saraf (eds.), *Performing Shakespeare in India: Exploring Indianness, Literatures and Cultures* (Delhi: Sage, 2016) and Craig Dionne and Parmita Kapadia (eds.), *Bollywood Shakespeares* (New York and London: Palgrave Macmillan, 2014). Poonam Trivedi and Paromita Chakravarti's eagerly awaited volume, *Shakespeare and Indian Cinemas* (New York and London: Routledge, 2018), was published only after this book went to press.

All references to Shakespeare's plays and poems throughout this book are to the text of Stephen Greenblatt, Walter Cohen, Jean E. Howard, and Katharine Eisaman Maus (eds.), *The Norton Shakespeare: Based on the Oxford Edition*, second edition (New York: Norton, 2008).

My more local debts, act by act, are signalled in the notes that follow.

Act One: Khaandaans

The quote from Manmohan Desai is taken from Philip Simpson, Andrew Utterson, and Karen J. Shepherdson (eds.), *Film Theory: Critical Concepts in Media and Cultural Studies* (New York and London: Routledge, 1993), p. 368. All quotes from *Shakespeare Wallah* are from the film version, whose script departs somewhat from the screenplay published in the *Savages/Shakespeare Wallah* (New York: Grove Press, 1973).

The assumption that *Hamlet* was performed on board an East India Company ship in 1607 is an old chestnut of Shakespearean lore. But it has been firmly rebutted by Bernice Kliman in her essay, 'At Sea about *Hamlet* at Sea: A Detective Story', *Shakespeare Quarterly* 62 (2011), pp. 180–204. The *Julius Caesar* speech recited by Comrade Pillai's son appears in Arundhati Roy's *The God of Small Things* (New York: Random House, 1997), p. 274; the play features frequently in the novel as a point of reference. For Pranab Mukherjee's quote from *Hamlet*, see 'I must be cruel only to be kind: FM quotes Shakespeare', *India Infoline (*16 March 2012), https://www.indiainfoline.com/article/news-top-story/i-must-be-cruel-only-to-be-kind-fm-quotes-shakespeare-113103100602_1.html; for Smriti Irani's quote from *Macbeth*, see 'Smriti Irani in Rajya Sabha: I Don't Use My Officers For Political Gains', *India Today* (25 February 2016), https://www.indiatoday.in/india/story/smriti-irani-in-rajya-sabha-i-dont-use-my-officers-for-political-gains-310613-2016-02-25; for Sitaram Yechury's quote from *Macbeth*, see 'Truth, Hype and the Gujarat Development Model', *Hindustan Times* (8 October 2013), https://www.hindustantimes.com/columns/truth-hype-and-the-gujarat-development-model/story-qOE3MhOsKHQtolX9YLxGKN.html.   I have used the relevant text of Thomas Macaulay's *Minute on Education,* from paragraph 10, available at http://www.columbia.edu/itc/mealac/pritchett/00generallinks/macaulay/txt_minute_education_1835.html. Premchand's comments on masala are from his 'Upanyas Rachna' in *Madhuri* (October 1922), p. 354; Francesca Orsini discusses Premchand's fiction, including these remarks, in her introduction to *The Oxford India Premchand* (Oxford: Oxford University Press, 2004). The quote from Bhoja of Dhar is sourced from Sheldon Pollock, 'The Alternative Classicism of Classical India', *Seminar* 671 (2015), pp. 1–9.

Samuel Johnson's disdain for the quibble is sourced from his 'Preface to Shakespeare' (1765), paragraph 44. Philip Sidney's remarks about mingled drama can be found in *An Apology for Poetry or A Defence of Poesie* (1595). Thomas Rymer's comments on *Othello* are from 'A Short View of Tragedy' (1693). And Edward Ravenscroft's 'rubbishing' of *Titus Andronicus* is from 'Preface to Titus Andronicus' (1686).

There is a wide range of commentary on mistaken identities in *The Comedy of Errors.* Barbara Freedman's 'Reading Errantly: Misrecognition and the Uncanny', in *Staging the Gaze: Postmodernism, Psychoanalysis, and Shakespearean Comedy* (Ithaca, NY: Cornell University Press, 1991), focuses on how the uncanny doubling of the twins dashes our attempts to find 'meaning' in the play. The play's theme of misrecognition is explored in relation to Indian cinema and Gulzar's *Angoor* in Richard Allen's 'Comedies of Errors: Shakespeare, Indian Cinema, and the Poetics of Mistaken Identity', in *Bollywood Shakespeares*, eds. Craig Dionne and Parmita Kapadia (New York and London: Palgrave Macmillan, 2014). Information on Shakespeare in the Parsi Theatre can be found in *India's Shakespeare: Translation, Interpretation and Performance*, eds. Poonam Trivedi and Dennis Bartholomeusz (Delhi: Pearson, 2005). On the early history of Bengali adaptations of Shakespeare, see the introduction to Shormishtha Panja and Babli Moitra Saraf (eds.), *Performing Shakespeare in India: Exploring Indianness, Literatures and Cultures* (Delhi: Sage, 2016). Utpal Dutt's book on Shakespeare is *Shakespearer Samaj Chetana* (Kolkata, M. C. Sarkar & Sons, 1972).

Gulzar's poem is quoted from his remarkable book, *Footprints on Zero Line: Writings on the Partition*, trans. Rakhshanda Jalil (New Delhi: Harper Collins, 2017). The story of Karam Singhji and Fazlji appears in his subsequent book about Partition, *Two* (Delhi: Harper Collins, 2017).

Act Two: Jugalbandis

On the Vishva Hindu Parishad's (and Bajrang Dal's) objections to *Bajrangi Bhaijaan*'s title, see 'Salman Khan's "Bajrangi Bhaijaan" faces trouble over its title', *Indian Express* (3 July 2015), https://indianexpress.com/article/entertainment/bollywood/salman-khans-bajrangi-bhaijaan-faces-trouble-over-its-title. Kabir Khan writes about his childhood experience playing Hanuman in a Ramleela play in 'Ramayana Special: This god is yours, this god is mine', *Indian Express* (10 November 2015), https://

indianexpress.com/article/lifestyle/art-and-culture/ramayana-special-this-god-is-yours-this-god-is-mine/.

Readers interested in learning more about the music of Shakespeare's lines—in particular, how and why he uses rhythm in the way he does—will find there is a virtual planet's worth of material on the topic of prosody, including the effects of poetic metre. A good starting point is Timothy Steele, *All the Fun's in How You Say a Thing: An Explanation of Meter and Versification* (Athens: Ohio University Press, 1999). More advanced studies of Shakespeare's prosody include George T. Wright, *Shakespeare's Metrical Art* (Berkeley: University of California Press, 1988), and Russ McDonald, *Shakespeare and the Arts of Language* (Oxford: Oxford University Press, 2001).

My summary of Indian theatrical conversations with *A Midsummer Night's Dream* is indebted to Sukanta Chaudhuri's superb introduction to his edition of the play, *A Midsummer Night's Dream: Arden Third Series* (London: Bloomsbury, 2017). The description of the Bengali playhouse set can be found in Saikat Majumdar's *The Firebird* (Delhi: Hachette India, 2015), p. 164. The review of *Chaitali Raater Swapno* appeared in *The Statesman* (9 December 1964). My comments about Habib Tanvir owe a debt to Jyotsna G. Singh's unpublished paper, 'Travelling Shakespeares in India: the Genesis of Habib Tanvir's *A Midsummer Night's Dream*'; the quote from Habib Tanvir is from 'Translating Spirit of a Poetic Comedy', *Economic Times* (8 March 1994).

Ramanujan's essay on the many Ramayanas, 'Three Hundred Ramayanas: Five Examples and Three Thoughts on Translation', is anthologized in Paula Richman (ed.), *Many Ramayanas: The Diversity of a Narrative Tradition in South Asia* (Oakland: University of California Press, 1991). For the quote from the Shiv Sena district head on Nawazuddin Siddiqui's desire to perform in his town's Ramleela play, see 'Nawazuddin Siddiqui pulls out of Ramleela event after Shiv Sena protests', *Hindustan Times* (7 October 2016), https://www.hindustantimes.com/bollywood/nawazuddin-siddiqui-pulls-out-of-ramleela-event-after-shiv-sena-protests/story-J7IhaXawaXY1UOmnIGqBWO.html. All the quotes from Rakhshanda Jalil on the Ramleela performances, and the quote from Ufuq's play, are sourced from her article 'The Ballad of Ram-e-Hind: Revisiting the Urdu versions of Ramayana that once lit up the stage', *Indian Express* (24 September 2017), https://indianexpress.com/article/lifestyle/art-and-culture/the-ballad-of-ram-e-hind-revisiting-the-urdu-versions-of-ramayana-that-once-lit-up-the-stage-4858217/. The couplet from Ghalib is from 'Hazaaron Khwahishen Aisi'; the translation is my own.

The Uttar Pradesh government's back-pedalling on the Anti-Romeo campaign is noted in 'Pro-Juliet? Yogi govt to rebrand Anti-Romeo Squads as Nari Suraksha Bal', *Hindustan Times* (21 May 2017), https://www.hindustantimes.com/india-news/pro-juliet-yogi-government-to-rebrand-anti-romeo-squads-as-nari-suraksha-bal/story-gSL3Di30S82eU1nAf3tUiI.html. For more information on the concept of shunyata in Buddhist philosophy, see T. R. V. Murti, *The Central Philosophy of Buddhism: A Study of the Madhyamika System* (New Delhi: Munshiram Manoharlal Publishers, 2003). A more general view of the self in Indian philosophical traditions can be found in *Self, No Self? Perspectives from Analytical, Phenomenological, and Indian Traditions,* eds. Mark Siderits, Evan Thompson and Dan Zahavi (Oxford: Oxford University Press, 2011). My speculations about the links between Andalusian Sufi poetry and *Romeo and Juliet* derive from two sources: Abdullah Al-Dabbagh's *Shakespeare, the Orient, and the Critics* (New York: Peter Lang, 2010); and Ranjit Hoskote and Ilija Trojanow, *Confluences: Forgotten Histories from East and West* (New Delhi: Yoda Press, 2012). The quote from Ibn Al-Arabi is from 'Poem 11' of his 'Tarjuman al-Ashwaq', translated by Michael A. Sells. Sarmad's poem about the nothingness of identity is from the seventeenth-century text the *Dabistan*; it appears in M. G. Gupta, *Sarmad the Saint: Life and Works* (Agra: M. G. Publishers, 1991), though Gupta attributes the couplet to Sarmad's lover Abhai Chand. For a reading of how love compulsively courts death in *Romeo and Juliet,* see Julia Kristeva's 'Love-Hatred in the Couple', from *Tales of Love,* trans. Leon S. Roudiez (New York: Columbia University Press, 1987), pp. 209–33. The Marathi website in which Romeo and Juliet are invoked for romantic pickup lines is http://mindurmarathi.com/basic-words-and-phrases/romantic-lines-in-marathi/. The myth of love jihad is widespread across India; it has been particularly prevalent in Uttar Pradesh and Kerala. See G. Anatakrishnan, '"Love Jihad" racket: VHP, Christian groups find common cause', *Times of India* (13 October 2009), https://m.timesofindia.com/india/Love-Jihad-racket-VHP-Christian-groups-find-common-cause/articleshow/5117548.cms; and Saif Khalid, 'The Hadiya case and the myth of "Love Jihad" in India', *Al Jazeera* (24 August 2017), https://www.aljazeera.com/indepth/featues/2017/08/hadiya-case-myth-love-jihad-india-170823181612279.html. On Yogi Adityanath's reference to love jihad from 2014 to the present, see

Rajiv Srivastava, 'Yogi Adityanath: "Love jihad" will be a bypoll issue in UP,' *Times of India* (29 August 2014), https://m.timesofindia. com/india/Yogi-Adityanath-Love-jihad-will-be-a-bypoll-issue-in-UP/ articlshow/41164779.cms; PTI, 'Kairana "Exodus", love jihad key issues for BJP: Yogi Adityanath', *Indian Express* (4 February 2017), https:// indianexpress.com/article/india/kairana-exodus-love-jihad-key-issues-for-bjp-yogi-adityanath/. The overlap of the 'love jihad' myth and the 'anti-Romeo' squad's mission is discussed in 'Yogi Adityanath promised to form an Anti-Romeo squad to stop "Love Jihad"', *Free Press Journal* (8 February 2017), http://www.freepressjournal.in/headlines/up-polls-yogi-adityanath-promised-to-form-an-anti-romeo-squad-to-stop-love-jihad. The incident involving the beating of Sanjay Leela Bhansali by members of the Karni Sena, and the rumour that the film included love scenes between Alauddin Khilji and Padmavati, is reported by Dishank Purohit, 'Sanjay Leela Bhansali roughed up by Rajput Karni Sena in Jaipur', *Times of India* (28 January 2017), https://www.google.co.uk/ amp/s/m.timesofindia.com/city/jaipur/sanjay-leela-bhansali-roughed-up-by-rajput-karni-sena-in-jaipur/amp_articleshow/56818707.cms .The quote from Sanjay Leela Bhansali is taken from an interview with *Hindustan Times* titled 'I am Uncomfortable around People: Sanjay Leela Bhansali' (22 November 2015), https://www.hindustantimes.com/ bollywood/i-am-uncomfortable-around-people-sanjay-leela-bhansali/ story-8z0hZrEE22rkVhmDZ18qRJ.html. On the tendency to equate Indian Muslims with Pakistanis and Bangladeshis, see Ariel Sophia Bardi, 'India's Hindu Nationalists Still Feed Off Partition's Wounds', *Foreign Policy* (14 August 2018), https://foreignpolicy.com/2018/08/14/indias-hindu-nationalists-still-feed-off-partitions-wounds/.

Act Three: Naataks

Karen Newman's essay, 'Renaissance Family Politics and Shakespeare's *The Taming of the Shrew*', *English Literary Renaissance* 16 (1986), pp. 86–100, explores the framing story of the play and how it interacts with Elizabethan social anxiety about gender and power.

My comments about the Mahabharata's use of the frame story device owe much to conversations with Alex Watson. I have also consulted James Whitby Earl, *Beginning the Mahabharata: A Reader's Guide to the Frame Stories* (Woodlands Hills, CA: South Asian Studies Association, 2011). I was guided in some parts of my discussion of the history of

The Taming of the Shrew in India by two essays from *India's Shakespeare* (cited above): Sisir Kumar Das, 'Shakespeare in Indian Languages', pp. 42–64 and Vijaya Guttal, 'Translation and Performance of Shakespeare in Kannada', pp. 95–108. Conversations with Chandan Gowda helped me understand some of the complexities of Kannada language and culture in relation to Shakespeare; Goutam Piduri did the same for the Telugu adaptations. For those who are interested in the legalese of the anti-zamindari legislation, I consulted *The Madras Estates (Abolition and Conversion Into Ryotwari) Act, 1948 (Madras Act XXVI of 1948) and the Rules Made Thereunder (as Modified Up to the 10th August 1951)* (New Delhi: Government Press, 1951).

Sooraj Barjatya's remark about Vidhi Kasliwal is quoted in 'Carrying forth the Barjatya baton', *Times of India* (*Bangalore Times* Section, 10 November 2010), http://epaper.timesofindia.com/Repository/getFiles. asp?Style=OliveXLib:LowLevelEntityToPrint_TOI&Type=text/ html&Locale=english-skin-custom&Path=TOIBG/2010/11/10&ID =Ar03202. Thomas Dekker made his comments about costumes in *The Gull's Horn Book* (London, 1609), pp. 28–29. I have discussed the links between the early modern English playhouses and the rise of consumerism in *Sick Economies: Drama, Mercantilism and Disease in Shakespeare's England* (Philadelphia: University of Pennsylvania Press, 2004), chapter 7. On the performativity of gender in Shakespeare's theatre, see Laura Levine, *Men in Women's Clothing: Antitheatricality and Effeminization, 1579–1642* (Cambridge: Cambridge University Press, 1994). The quote from Chimamanda Ngozi Adichie is from her TED talk, 'The Danger of a Single Story', at TEDGlobal, July 2009.

My discussions of Mohini and the gender fluidity in nautanki and therukkuttu owe much to conversations with Justin McCarthy, as well as Madhavi Menon's *Infinite Variety: A History of Desire in India* (New Delhi: Speaking Tiger Books, 2018). And my understanding of the 'daayraa' of the performance space is inspired by a brilliant unpublished presentation given by Ali Khan Mahmudabad at the first meeting of the Ashoka University Urdu Society in 2017.

Parvati's response to her husband Dr Kishen Chand Seth is in Vikram Seth, *A Suitable Boy* (New Delhi: Penguin Books India, 1993), p. 1034. John Manningham's 'mingled comedy' remark is quoted from John Leslie Hotson's *The First Night of Twelfth Night* (London: Hart-Davis, 1954), p. 202. My discussion of *Twelfth Night* is partly informed by the large body of work on carnival, rituals of inversion, and Shakespeare's festive comedy: see Mikhail Bakhtin, *Rabelais and His World*, trans. Hélène Iswolsky (Bloomington: Indiana University Press, 1984), Peter Stallybrass and Allon White, *The Politics and Poetics of Transgression* (London: Methuen, 1986), and C. L. Barber, *Shakespeare's Festive Comedy: A Study of Dramatic Form and its Relation to Social Custom* (Princeton: Princeton University Press, 1959). For readings of *Twelfth Night* and its various unorthodox sexual possibilities, see Valerie Traub, *Desire and Anxiety: Circulations of Sexuality in Shakespearean Drama* (London and New York: Routledge, 1992), and Madhavi Menon, *Wanton Words: Rhetoric and Sexuality in English Renaissance Drama* (Toronto: University of Toronto Press, 2003).

The incident of the cross-dressed actor who played Viola in the Bombay production of *Twelfth Night* is glimpsed in C. J. Sisson's (tragically forgotten) *Shakespeare in India: Popular Adaptations on the Bombay Stage* (Oxford: Oxford University Press, 1926). On Bal Gandharva and the tradition of cross-dressing from Parsi and Marathi theatre that crossed over into early Hindi film, see Vikram Phukan, 'Bal Gandharva played a woman in more than 25 films', *The Hindu* (9 December 2017), https:// www.thehindu.com/entertainment/movies/bal-gandharva-played-a-woman-in-more-than-25-films/article21300920.ece. *Uran Khatola* was brought to my attention by Rajiva Verma in his article, 'Shakespeare in Hindi Cinema', in *India's Shakespeare* (cited above). Indian cinema's engagement of gender fluidity and same-sex attraction is discussed by Shohini Ghosh in 'The Closet is Ajar', *Outlook* (30 May 2005), https:// www.outlookindia.com/magazine/story/the-closet-is-ajar/227507. For a fascinating discussion of the relations between *Twelfth Night* and *Dil Bole Hadippa!*, see R. S. White, *Shakespeare's Cinema of Love: A Study in Genre and Influence* (Oxford: Oxford University Press, 2015).

Act Four: Dardnak Kahaanis

All quotes from Vishal Bhardwaj's poetry are from *Nude: Poems*, trans. Sukrita Paul Kumar (New Delhi: Harper Collins India, 2018). I am grateful to Rachna Singh for inviting me to discuss Vishal's book with him at the Chennai Lit for Life festival in January 2018. Those who want to see our discussion can watch a recording at https://www. youtube.com/watch?v=VwiilgN_0ac. All Hindi references to Bhardwaj's films are to the official screenplays of Bhardwaj's *Maqbool*, *Omkara* and *Haider* (New Delhi: HarperCollins India, 2014). I have sometimes used the English translations included in these screenplays, but I have usually supplied my own translations in order to better access the literal meanings of the Hindi (and Khariboli) dialogues. For more information on the possible connections between the Hiranyakashipu story and *Macbeth*, see 'Is Shakespeare's Macbeth Based on a Holi Legend?' in *Times of India* (18 March 2011), https://timesofindia.indiatimes.com/Is-Shakespeares-Macbeth-based-on-a-Holi-legend/articleshow/7734376. cms. The dominant interpretation of *Macbeth* when I studied the play at school was A. C. Bradley, *Shakespearean Tragedy: Lectures on Hamlet, Othello, King Lear and Macbeth* (Harmondsworth: Penguin, 1991 [1904]). Terry Eagleton's 'The Witches are the Heroines of the Piece' from his *William Shakespeare* (Oxford: Blackwell, 1986), is a brilliantly concise exposition of the witches' doubleness and their disruption of a stable order. I have written on the untimely smell of gunpowder in 'The Smell of *Macbeth*', *Shakespeare Quarterly* 58 (2007), pp. 465–86. For more on the murder of rationalists, see Pankaj P. Khelkar, 'Who killed Narendra Dabholkar? 4 years after rationalist's murder, his children await justice', *India Today*, (20 August 2017).More information on Bengali adaptations of *Macbeth* can be found in *Performing Shakespeare in India,* eds. Shormishtha Panja and Babli Moitra Saraf (Delhi: Sage: 2016). Utpal Dutt's adaptation of *Macbeth* is discussed in Naina Dey's chapter in the collection, 'Utpal Dutt and *Macbeth* Translated'. Ratan Thiyam's comments on his Manipuri version of Macbeth can be found in 'Macbeth & Thiyam's vision', *The Telegraph* (23 March 2014), https://www.telegraphindia.com/1140323/jsp/calcutta/story_18105968.jsp. The quote about the Kerala chathans is from T. Ramavaran, 'Black magic is big bucks for Kerala village', *Times of India* (8 September 2013), https://timesofindia.indiatimes.com/india/Black-magic-is-big-bucks-for-Kerala-village/articleshow/22408872.cms. Suddhaseel Sen's 'Indigenizing *Macbeth*: Vishal Bhardwaj's *Maqbool*', from *Asian Shakespeares on Screen: Two Films in Perspective* (Special Issue, edited by Alexa Huang, *Borrowers and Lenders* 4.2 [Spring/Summer 2009]), explores *Maqbool* as a trans-cultural (rather than straightforwardly postcolonial) adaptation of *Macbeth*.

The quote from the Siddur Sim Shalom is an adaptation of Louis Ginzburg's prayer for America; it appears in the official version of the text issued by the Rabbinical Assembly of the American Conservative Jewish congregation (1985), p. 149. The quote from Subcomandante Marcos is from a pamphlet entitled 'The Majority Disguised as the Resented Minority', EZLN Press Release (31 May 1994). My references to Moraes Zogoiby and his spice mogul family are from Salman Rushdie,

The Moor's Last Sigh (London: Penguin Random House, 1995), p. 5. Yogi Adityanath and Amit Shah's visit to Kerala to discuss 'love jihad' (Shah cut short his visit after one day) was reported in Mohamed Nazeer, 'Love jihad a reality in Kerala: Yogi Adityanath', *The Hindu* (5 October 2017), https://www.thehindu.com/news/national/kerala/love-jihad-a-fact-in-kerala-yogi-adityanath/article19800559.ece/amp/.

Information about the annual number of caste-related honour killings can be found at http://ncrb.gov.in/StatPublications/CII/CII2016/pdfs/Crime%20Statistics%20-%202016.pdf. The huge increase in the number of killings is noted in '792% spike in honour killing cases, UP tops the list: Govt in Parliament', *Hindustan Times* (7 December 2016), https://www.hindustantimes.com/india-news/792-spike-in-honour-killing-cases-up-tops-the-list-govt-in-parliament/story-x0IfcFpfAljYi15yQtP0YP.html. Sagar's article on Pradeep and Seema's case is 'In Rohtak's Amrit Colony, There Is No Sympathy For A Dalit Woman Allegedly Killed By Her Family For Marrying A Brahmin', *The Caravan* (6 March 2017), http://www.caravanmagazine.in/vantage/rohtak-dalit-woman-killed-family-marrying-brahmin. I found the remarks by Karan Johar about how *Dhadak* will deviate from *Sairat* in 'Jhanvi Kapoor's *Sairat* may not take off', *The Asian Age* (29 October 2017), http://www.asianage.com/entertainment/bollywood/291017/jhanvi-kapoors-sairat-may-not-take-off.html.

For more on the ways in which *Othello* plays upon racial and cultural difference, see Ania Loomba's 'Othello and the Racial Question', in *Shakespeare, Race, and Colonialism* (Oxford: Oxford University Press, 2002), pp. 91–112. The description of *Hrid Majharey* is from the film's IMDb page, https://www.imdb.com/title/tt3867556/. More readings of Othello in Indian cinema can be found in Trisha Mitra's chapter in *Performing Shakespeare in India: Exploring Indianness, Literatures and Cultures* (cited above): 'The Othello-figure in Three Indian Films: *Kaliyattam, Omkara,* and *Saptapadi*', pp. 95–108. Jayaraj's quote on *Kaliyattam* and the film's theyyam setting is from the interview: 'An epiphany forged across the ages—Meet director Jayaraj' in *Full Picture* (17 February 2017), http://fullpicture.in/interview-detail/97/an-epiphany-forged-a.html.

Quotes from the *Manusmriti* are from *Manu's Code of Law: A Critical Edition and Translation of the Manava-Dharmasastra* (Oxford: Oxford University Press, 2010). For a discussion of the Portuguese etymology of caste, see Marcus Banks, *Visual Methods in Social Research* (New Delhi: Sage, 2001), pp. 28–9. The *Othello* quote from 2.1.180–2 differs slightly from the Norton edition. There 'calmness' has been rendered 'calms'; this is what appears in the Quarto edition, which differs quite significantly from the later Folio edition used by most editors. One of the differences is the replacement of 'calmness' by 'calms'. It has been surmised that the Folio edition includes additions and corrections by Shakespeare himself, and there is something about the extra syllable of 'calmness' that certainly reverberates with the uncertainty of Othello the character. The quotes from Ambedkar are from *Annihilation of Caste: The Annotated Critical Edition*, ed. S. Anand (New Delhi: Navayana Publishing, 2014).

Karan Johar's comments on his remake of *Agneepath* can be found in an interview titled 'Agneepath broke my father's heart!', *Times of India* (26 January 2012), http://timesofindia.indiatimes. com/articleshow/11628129.cms?utm_source=contentofinterest&utm_ medium=text&utm_campaign=cppst.

The quote from the study on Prabhakaran is sourced from Major General Raj Mehta's *Lost Victory: The Rise & Fall of LTTE Supremo, V. Prabhakaran* (New Delhi: Pentagon Press, 2010), p. 318; the quote on India's security policy is from 'National Security: A Critique', by P. R. Kumaraswamy, pp. 11–33, in *Security Beyond Survival: Essays for K. Subrahmanyam*, ed. P. R. Kumaraswamy (New Delhi: Sage India, 2004), p.13; the report that condemns India's inefficiency is by R. Barman Chandra, and can be found in *New Economic Policies for a New India*, ed. Surjit S. Bhalla (New Delhi: Har-Anand Publications Pvt Ltd, 2000); Nayantara Sahgal's remarks on Nehru and Hamlet are from *Jawaharlal Nehru: Civilizing a Savage World* (New Delhi: Penguin Books India, 2010), p. 125. Subhuti Anand Waight's adaptation of *Hamlet* is *When Shakespeare Lost the Plot: The Bard Stands on His Head, Hamlet Flies to India and Western Philosophy is Destroyed* (London: Austin Macaulay Publishers, 2016).

My reading of *Hamlet* owes a considerable debt to Jacques Derrida's *Specters of Marx* (cited above), and to two other sources: Janet Adelman's 'Man and Wife is One Flesh: *Hamlet* and the Confrontation with the Maternal Body', from *Suffocating Mothers: Fantasies of Maternal Origin in Shakespeare's Plays, Hamlet to the Tempest* (New York: Routledge, 1992), which reads Hamlet's hesitation in conjunction with his disgust at having originated in the body of his mother; and Michael D. Bristol's 'Funeral Bak'd Meats: Carnival and the Carnivalesque in *Hamlet*', in Susanne Wofford (ed.), *William Shakespeare: Hamlet Case Studies in Contemporary Criticism* (London: Palgrave Macmillian, 1994), pp. 348–68, which thinks about the populist, carnivalesque dimensions of the play.

For a superb discussion of Parsi Theatre *Hamlets*, see Rajiva Verma, 'Shakespeare in Indian Cinema: Appropriation, Assimilation and Engagement', *Shakespearean Yearbook* 12 (2012). On Sam Kerawala's memories of *Hamlet No Omelette*, see 'A time for Natak', *Indian Express* (24 April 2016), https://indianexpress.com/article/lifestyle/art-and-culture/a-time-for-natak-2767246/. Poonam Trivedi interprets the Zauq couplet as a version of 'readiness is all' in 'Hamlets of India', *Indian Express* (4 October 2014), https://indianexpress.com/article/opinion/columns/hamlets-of-india/. For the full implications of the Sanskrit 'neti neti' in relation to *Hamlet*, see Anjum Hasan, *Neti, Neti* (New Delhi: Roli Books, 2009). The Mizo adaptation of *Hamlet* was captured on film in *When Hamlet Came to Mizoram* (dir. Pankaj Butalia, 1989). A huge hole in my knowledge of Goan theatre and its Shakespeare engagements was filled when I read André Rafael Fernandes, *When The Curtains Rise... Understanding Goa's Vibrant Konkani Theatre* (Pananji: Tiatr Academy of Goa, 2010).

Basharat Peer's memoir on Kashmir is *Curfewed Night* (Noida: Penguin Random House India, 2010). A reading of *Haider* that also explores its interest in spectrality, but with slightly different conclusions, is Tarini Mookherjee's 'Absence and Repetition in Vishal Bhardwaj's *Haider*', *Cogent Arts and Humanities* (2016). A useful mainstream discussion of how *Haider* engages Indian and Kashmiri politics is Namrata Joshi's 'Haider, Not Thither', *Outlook* (20 October 2014), https://www.outlookindia.com/magazine/story/haider-not-thither/292204. For more on the legend of Habba Khatoon, see S. N. Wakhlu, *Habba Khatoon: The Nightingale of Kashmir* (Delhi: South Asia Publications, 1994); readers may also be interested in the fictionalized Bollywood-themed tale about Habba Khatoon by Selina Sen, *Zoon* (Delhi: Westland, 2017).

Act Five: Toofaans

Intizar Hussain's session at the 2015 Jashn-e-Rekhta festival, including his nani-amma's story of the zamindar, is on Youtube at https://www.youtube.com/watch?v=Dj9kDJOGjiw; see 22:06. Amitav Ghosh's remarks on climate change are from *The Great Derangement: Climate Change and the Unthinkable* (Gurgaon: Penguin Books India, 2016), p. 43. Walter Benjamin's vision of the Angel of History and the storm of progress can be found in 'Theses on the Philosophy of History', from *Illuminations*, trans. Harry Zohn (New York: Random House Inc, 1955).

My reading of *King Lear* is greatly influenced by Paul Delaney, '*King Lear* and the Decline of Feudalism', *PMLA* 92 (1977), pp. 429–40. I have written on *The Tempest* and its relationship to the past in my short book, *Marvellous Repossessions: The Tempest, Globalization and the Waking Dream of Paradise* (Vancouver: Ronsdale Press, 2013); some of the ideas in that book get reworked here.

The mixing of *King Lear* and *The Tempest* in the South Asian context is a remarkable phenomenon that needs more investigation. I did not have the space here to discuss Mauritian playwright Dev Virahsawmy's Creole-language play, *Toufann* (1991), a riff on *The Tempest* that also features characters from *King Lear*. Purvai Aranya's brilliant graphic novel, *The Return*, remains unpublished; it deserves a wider audience, but it was featured in the international 2016 conference in New Delhi on 'Shakespeare's Ashes' organized by the British Council and the Shakespeare Society of India. Samyuktha P. C.'s description of water in Chennai life is from the event summary for Crea-Shakthi's Tamil adaptation of *The Tempest*; a version can be found in 'A Shakespearean Classic Unfolds on Stage', *Times of India* (1 August 2016), https://timesofindia.indiatimes. com/entertainment/kannada/theatre/A-Shakespearean-classic-unfolds- on-stage/articleshow/53485803.cms. Kusumagraj, the pen name of the Marathi poet-playwright Vishnu Vaman Shirwadkar, wrote *Natsamrat* in 1970; his third and most successful adaptation of Shakespeare after reworkings of *Macbeth* in 1954 (*Rajmukut*, or *The Royal Crown*) and *Othello* in 1960, it remains in print to this day (Mumbai: Popular Prakashan, 2013). For a useful reading of *The Last Lear* in the context of other Shakesperean reimaginings set in Kolkata, see Paromita Chakravarti, 'Urban Histories and Vernacular Shakespeares in Bengal', in Panja and Saraf (eds.), *Performing Shakespeare in India* (cited above), pp. 41–59. The quotations describing Jeet's nightmare vision of India shining and the detritus of the basti in the storm are from Preti Taneja, *We That Are Young*, (Gurgaon: Penguin Random House India, 2017).

Bornila Chatterjee's praise for VOD is sourced from an interview conducted by Nikita Gadal titled 'In conversation with Bornila Chatterjee on her directorial film The Hungry', *The Moviean* (undated), https:// themoviean.com/bornila-chatterjee-interview. Edward Dowden's critique of *Pericles* is from *Shakspere: A Critical Study of His Mind and Art*. (London: Henry S. King and Company, 1875).

INDEX